JOURNAL FOR THE STUDY OF THE NEW TESTAMENT SUPPLEMENT SERIES
130

Executive Editor
Stanley E. Porter

Sheffield Academic Press

Chained in Christ

The Experience and Rhetoric
of Paul's Imprisonments

Craig S. Wansink

Journal for the Study of the New Testament
Supplement Series 130

Copyright © 1996 Sheffield Academic Press

Published by Sheffield Academic Press Ltd
Mansion House
19 Kingfield Road
Sheffield S11 9AS
England

Printed on acid-free paper in Great Britain
by Bookcraft Ltd
Midsomer Norton, Bath

British Library Cataloguing in Publication Data

A catalogue record for this book is available
from the British Library

ISBN 1-85075-605-8

CONTENTS

PREFACE

In *The Passing of Peregrinus* 12–13, Lucian mocks the intensity with which early Christians served their imprisoned brothers and sisters. When I encountered this work for the first time, Lucian's enthusiasm and incredulity raised a variety of questions for me: Could visitors actually enter prisons in the Roman world? What did the imprisoned eat? Was ministering to the imprisoned distinctively Christian? This work seeks not only to enter into Roman prisons and begin to answer those questions, but also—and primarily—to see how imprisonment shaped Paul's letters to the Philippians and to Philemon. The epilogue, then, briefly examines how Paul's imprisonment shaped early Christianity.

I am grateful to L.L. Welborn, formerly of McCormick Theological Seminary, who not only introduced me to the writings of Lucian, but also showed me how exciting the New Testament can be. At Yale University, the influence of Wayne A. Meeks—my dissertation advisor—and Abraham J. Malherbe shaped how I see the New Testament world and showed me how to begin to answer those questions which are important to me. The dissertation form of this monograph was also strengthened by comments and suggestions from Susan R. Garrett and Ramsay MacMullen, and from fellow graduate students Fred Weidmann, Ken Cukrowski, Allen Hilton, Allen Hunt, Jay Smith and Greg Snyder.

Others have helped me in a variety of way. Students from my seminar on 'Persecution and Martyrdom in Earliest Christianity', both at Yale and at Virginia Wesleyan College, have shaped many of the discussions here. During the years of writing, the Charlotte Newcombe Foundation, the Claude Lambe Foundation, and Virginia Wesleyan College have supported me financially. And Robert Jewett, Stanley Porter, Eric Christianson and an unnamed reviewer have offered much helpful advice and many illuminating comments.

Few persons have been blessed with the support, understanding and happiness which my parents, John and Naomi Wansink, and my brother, Brian, have given me. To them, and to my wife, Susan, who reminds me of the most important things in life, whose love and laughter empower me and whose friendship strengthens me in so many ways, this book is dedicated.

ABBREVIATIONS

AB	Anchor Bible
ANRW	*Aufstieg und Niedergang der römischen Welt*
ATR	*Anglican Theological Review*
BAGD	W. Bauer, W.F. Arndt, F.W. Gingrich and F.W. Danker,
	Greek–English Lexicon of the New Testament
BeO	*Bibbia e oriente*
Bib	*Biblica*
BibRev	*Bible Review*
BJRL	*Bulletin of the John Rylands Library*
CBQ	*Catholic Biblical Quarterly*
EKKNT	Evangelisch-Katholischer Kommentar zum Neuen Testament
ExpTim	*Expository Times*
EvQ	*Evangelical Quarterly*
FN	*Filología Neotestamentaria*
HBT	*Horizons in Biblical Theology*
HTR	*Harvard Theological Review*
Int	*Interpretation*
JBL	*Journal of Biblical Literature*
JHS	*Journal of Hellenic Studies*
JRS	*Journal of Roman Studies*
JSNT	*Journal for the Study of the New Testament*
JSNTSup	*Journal for the Study of the New Testament*, Supplement Series
LEC	Library of Early Christianity
LSJ	Liddell–Scott–Jones, *Greek–English Lexicon*
NCB	New Century Bible
NovT	*Novum Testamentum*
NTM	New Testament Message
NTS	*New Testament Studies*
PG	J. Migne (ed.), *Patrologia graeca*
RevExp	*Review and Expositor*
SBL	Society of Biblical Literature
SBLDS	SBL Dissertation Series
SBLMS	SBL Monograph Series
SBLSBS	SBL Sources for Biblical Study
SecCent	*Second Century*
SNTSMS	Society for New Testament Studies Monograph Series
StudBib	*Studia Biblica*

TDNT	G. Kittel and G. Friedrich (eds.), *Theological Dictionary of the New Testament*
THKNT	Theologischer Handkommentar zum Neuen Testament
TynBul	*Tyndale Bulletin*
TZ	*Theologische Zeitschrift*
USQR	*Union Seminary Quarterly Review*
VC	*Vigiliae Christianae*
WBC	Word Biblical Commentary
WEC	Wycliffe Exegetical Commentary
ZNW	*Zeitschrift für die neutestamentliche Wissenschaft*

INTRODUCTION

There followed other episodes in this
prison, some of them insidiously contrived,
and others of mere chance, and not of
sufficient importance to merit my notice.
—Philostratus, *VA* 7.28*

1. *The Problem*

In the midst of a narrative describing Apollonius of Tyana's experiences
in prison, Philostratus' aside to his readers presents just one of the difficulties facing anyone interested in knowing more about prisons in
antiquity. Ancient authors often did not relate situations with which their
readerships were familiar; some things were just 'not of sufficient
importance' to merit their notice.

This is but one frustration facing any modern reader of Paul's epistles.
What was obvious to Paul and his readers in the first century—whether
it be how the first Christians worshipped, or what was involved in
'greeting the brethren with a holy kiss'—was that which Paul either left
unsaid or expressed only cursorily. He knew to what he was referring;
he knew or assumed that his readers knew to what he was referring; and
so short-hand references sufficed in making his point. But just as a wink
shared between friends might have no meaning to an outsider unfamiliar
with the broader context in which that wink has its meaning,[1] so short-
hand references shared between Paul and his churches often leave the
modern reader of Paul's letters unaware. Such is the case with Paul's
references to imprisonment.

* The translations of Greek and Latin authors in the Loeb Classical Library
have been used when available. Biblical texts follow the translation of the Revised
Standard Version (RSV). Translations of other early Christian texts were also taken
from the ANF and H. Musurillo, trans., *The Acts of the Christian Martyrs* (Oxford:
Clarendon Press, 1972).
1. G. Ryle, 'The Thinking of Thoughts', in *Collected Papers*. II. *Collected
Essays 1929–1968* (New York: Barnes & Noble, 1971), pp. 480-81.

Although 'imprisonment' was frequently used as a metaphor in antiquity,[2] and although Paul had no aversion to employing metaphors— referring to himself in terms of his 'enslavement',[3] referring to others as his 'fellow soldiers'[4]—he does not employ 'imprisonment' merely as a metaphor in these letters. His incarceration is discussed as an empirical reality: Phil. 1.19 and Philemon 22, for instance, each share Paul's hope for his release from prison. Such references in themselves, however, tell us little explicit about either what Paul was undergoing or how others perceived his situation.

The letters to the Philippians and Philemon provide a window of vision into how Paul's imprisonment influenced the way in which he communicated with his churches. It is difficult to know what Paul was experiencing when he wrote these letters. It is also difficult to know how these churches perceived his imprisonment. In the final analysis, the only evidence we have to understand such situations is to be found in these epistles themselves. At the same time, however, the 'winks' in Paul's letters—the short-hand references he makes—can be understood better by examining the broader context or setting in which they had their fundamental meaning. The various meanings of these 'short-hand references' often are elusive if they themselves are not seen within their broader context.

Proverbial folk wisdom speaks of persons 'not being able to see the forest for the trees'. Social science, although generally employing more abstractions and models, also emphasizes the dangers of the same—the dangers of not placing events in their broader contexts: 'Social science has almost what amounts to a horror of the event. And not without some justification, for the short time span is the most capricious and the

---

2.   See the section in Chapter 1 entitled '"Prison" as Metaphor'. Note also remarks like those found in Seneca the Elder and in Dio Chrysostom. In the midst of a trial of a husband who caught his wife with an adulterer and then killed her, Musa— speaking for the defence—says 'Different people find different things intolerable. For me adultery is a prison' (Seneca, *Controv.* 9.1.1). The figure Charidemus (in Dio Chrysostom, *Or.* 30) sees all of human life as taking place in one large prison.

3.   Rom. 1.1; 1 Cor. 7.22; etc. See D.B. Martin, *Slavery as Salvation: The Metaphor of Slavery in Pauline Christianity* (New Haven: Yale University Press, 1990), esp. pp. 132-35.

4.   Phil. 2.23; Phlm. 2. For an examination of how martial language was used metaphorically in the first century, see A.J. Malherbe, 'Antisthenes and Odysseus, and Paul at War', in *HTR* 76 (1983), pp. 143-73.

most delusive of all.'[5] By looking at the broader context, by looking at the nature and perception of Roman prisons in antiquity, readers can begin to see the concrete social situations which gave birth to Paul's letters. To put Paul's imprisonment in context, knowing what persons said and heard about prisons in the Roman empire is very important. Looking at such factors as the role of the prison in antiquity, the conditions of prisons, the daily life of prisoners, and the way in which persons (both within and outside prison) discussed and perceived imprisonment are all significant.

A variety of questions need to be posed: What were prisons like? What did prisoners do there? What did they feel or experience? What sort of punishments did they undergo? How were women prisoners treated differently from men? Could visitors freely enter and leave? What characterized prison guards? What would people in the Roman empire have known about prison?

2. *Ancient Prisons and the Modern Scholarly World*

In seeking access to those passages in the 'prison epistles' which deal with Paul's incarceration, most New Testament scholars have employed theological and modern literary criteria as their primary exegetical instruments.[6] Even those scholars whose book titles (e.g. *Paul's Letters from Prison*) imply concern for the social dimensions of Paul's imprisonment have essentially chosen their titles for what they see as superficial reasons.[7] Houlden's reflection can be seen as representative of numerous commentaries:

5. F. Braudel, 'History and the Social Sciences: The *Longue Durée*', in *idem*, *On History* (trans. Sarah Matthews; Chicago: The University of Chicago Press, 1980), p. 28.

6. Although B.M. Rapske is not concerned primarily with Paul's epistles, two of his works take seriously a knowledge of prisons in antiquity: 'The Importance of Helpers to the Imprisoned Paul in the Book of Acts', *TynBul* 42 (1991), pp. 3-30; and *The Book of Acts and Paul in Roman Custody* (Grand Rapids, MI: Eerdmans, 1994).

7. For example, E. Haupt, *Die Gefangenschaftsbriefe* (Göttingen: Vandenhoeck und Ruprecht, 1897); J.L. Houlden, *Paul's Letters from Prison* (Baltimore: Penguin Books, 1970); and G.B. Caird, *Paul's Letters from Prison* (Oxford: Oxford University Press, 1976).

> These letters have been traditionally grouped together because all come as
> from Paul the prisoner. There, it may be, the resemblance stops...In any
> case, the fact that they were, supposedly at least, written in prison is not
> among the more significant features of any of them.[8]

Although 'imprisonment' sometimes is used as a rubric by which to
group epistles together, Paul's actual imprisonment is rarely seen as
having had any concrete effect on these letters.[9] As a result, a perspective based on what might be called 'the social world of ancient prisons'
has been conspicuously absent from much of the secondary work which
has dealt with Paul's prison epistles.

The Provenance of the Epistles

When New Testament scholars *have* posed questions about Paul's
imprisonment, they have tended to focus less on 'prisons' *per se*
and more on the provenance of the prison epistles,[10] debating whether
these letters were written from a Roman, Ephesian or Caesarean
imprisonment.[11] Traditional interpretation has assumed that the letters to
the Philippians and to Philemon were each written from an imprisonment in Rome.[12] Research within the last century, however, has looked

---

8.   *Paul's Letters from Prison*, pp. 23-24.

9.   Houlden, for instance, sees the 'usefulness' of these letters in primarily
existential terms: 'The strangeness of Paul's idiom cannot disguise the fact that he is
dealing with permanent questions of man's existence in the world in a way which is
not only original but also profound' (*Paul's Letters from Prison*, p. 25).

10.   In this section, I am not interested in summarizing or analyzing the data in
favor of the various proposals. Part of this, as I mention later, is because I am not
convinced by the limited evidence and, as a result, I remain agnostic about the provenance of the epistles. The footnotes in this section, however, will point the reader to
the key primary and secondary sources in the discussion. For a quick survey of the
evidence, G.B. Caird, *Paul's Letters from Prison*, pp. 2-6, is quite helpful. For a
much more thorough examination, see G.S. Duncan, the giant on whose shoulders
most other scholars in this area have stood. See, in particular, chs. 5–12 of his *St
Paul's Ephesian Ministry: A Reconstruction* (London: Hodder and Stoughton, 1929).

11.   Corinth has also been mentioned as a possible location. See A. Moda, 'La
Lettera a Filippesi e gli ultimi anni di Paolo prigioniero', *BeO* 27 (1985), pp. 17-30.

12.See C.H. Dodd, *New Testament Studies* (Manchester: Manchester University
Press, 1953), pp. 83-128. The claim for a Roman imprisonment is, in part, based on
external attestation: the Vulgate ('Marcionite') Prologues claim that the epistles to
Philemon, to the Philippians and to the Ephesians were written from Rome (with the
one to the Colossians having been written from Ephesus). It must be noted, however,
that such 'external attestation' may simply have resulted from inferences from the

much more seriously at the possibility that Paul was writing from an imprisonment either in Ephesus[13] or in Caesarea.[14]

Different factors are at stake when determining the provenance of the letters. The debate on where individual epistles were written from can be linked to concerns about when they were written, about whom they were written to oppose,[15] and about what theological or historical issues they were seeking to engage.[16]

For instance, starting with the assumption that Onesimus was a runaway slave, Eduard Lohse claims that Paul could not have written either from Rome or from Caesarea. Both cities, he says, 'are such a considerable distance from Colossae that it is difficult to imagine how a runaway slave could have travelled so far without being detected'.[17] Such a statement begs at least two questions: it assumes 1) that Onesimus was a

texts. Cf. N.A. Dahl, 'The Origin of the Earliest Prologues to the Pauline Letters', *Semeia* 12 (1978), pp. 233-77.

13. The classic argument for this position is in G.S. Duncan, *St. Paul's Ephesian Ministry: A Reconstruction*, esp. chs. 5–12. Also see A.E. Wilhelm-Hooijbergh, 'In 2 Tim. 1.17 the Greek and Latin Texts May Have a Different Meaning', *StudBib* 3 (1978), pp. 435-38; G.S. Duncan, 'Important Hypotheses Reconsidered: VI. Were Paul's Imprisonment Epistles Written from Ephesus?' *ExpTim* 67 (1955), pp. 163-66; A. Deissmann, 'Zur ephesinischen Gefangenschaft des Apostels Paulus', in W.H. Buckler and W.M. Calder (eds.), *Anatolian Studies Presented to Sir W.M. Ramsay* (Manchester: Manchester University Press, 1923), pp. 121-27; and D.T. Rowlingson, 'Paul's Ephesian Imprisonment: An Evaluation of the Evidence', *ATR* 32 (1950), pp. 1-7. Helmut Koester argues, with respect to Philippians and Philemon, that 'there is clearly a preponderance (of data) in favor of their composition during an Ephesian imprisonment', *History and Literature of Early Christianity* (Philadelphia: Fortress Press, 1983), p. 131.

14. E. Lohmeyer, *Die Briefe an die Philipper, an die Kolosser und an Philemon* (Göttingen: Vandenhoeck & Ruprecht, 1930); and J.J. Gunther, *Paul: Messenger and Exile* (Valley Forge, PA: Judson, 1972), ch. 4.

15. In J.-F. Collange, *The Epistle of Saint Paul to the Philippians* (trans. A.W. Heathcote; London: Epworth Press, 1979), pp. 18-19, for example, the author establishes a link between the argument for Ephesus and the opponents of Paul (Collange believes that 2 Cor. and Phil. 3 refer to the same opponents).

16. A.D. Nock, *St Paul* (New York: Oxford University Press, 1953), pp. 221-22, recognizes, for instance, that the confirmation of the Ephesian hypothesis would necessarily result in changes in his 'general view of the evolution of ideas'. Note, as Nock implies here, that an Ephesian imprisonment generally implies an earlier dating for the appropriate epistles.

17. *Colossians and Philemon* (trans. W.R. Poehlmann and R.J. Karris; Philadelphia: Fortress Press, 1971), p. 188.

runaway (as opposed to his having been sent to serve Paul), and 2) that
travel took an inordinate amount of time. Similarly, numerous scholars
have pointed to the geographical distance between Rome and Philippi,
and the number of communications which apparently took place between
the imprisoned Paul and the Philippians, and have assumed that Rome
was simply too far away to permit such a scenario. Thus, they also have
posited an Ephesian provenance for the epistle to the Philippians.[18]
Other historical conclusions are also at stake. D.T. Rowlingson claims
that Paul was imprisoned in Ephesus. This, he says, means that 'every
one of Paul's letters which we possess emerged from the Aegean
ministry covered by Acts 15.40–20.38', and thus, 'the Aegean ministry
is the most significant in which Paul was engaged'.[19]

The only explicit tradition which refers to Paul as imprisoned in
Ephesus is found in *The Acts of Paul* 6. Regardless, many scholars have
come to believe that Paul wrote to the Philippians and to Philemon while
in Ephesus. In some respects, then, it is ironic that another site for Paul's
imprisonment—in the city of Philippi—is generally omitted in scholarly
discussion. Few scholars deny that Paul was likely imprisoned in Philippi
(Acts 16.19-40). However, they tacitly dismiss the possibility that Paul
wrote epistles from this or any other Philippian imprisonment. Philippi is
dismissed even though early Christian tradition does hold that Paul wrote
at least one letter, *3 Corinthians*, from a Philippian imprisonment.[20]

Granted, few if any scholars would claim that *3 Corinthians* was
penned by Paul; it simply appears to be a product of a later time.[21]
However, the fact that some tradition did hold that Paul wrote during a
Philippian imprisonment must make scholars cautious about their own
ability to pin down the locations from where specific letters were written.
Rome, Ephesus, Caesarea and Philippi are only four of numerous possible
locations. From Paul's claim in 2 Cor. 11.23 (where he says he has
experienced 'far more imprisonments' than other 'servants of Christ'),[22]
to the statement in *1 Clem.* 5.6 (which could imply that Paul was

18. Duncan, *St Paul's Ephesian Ministry: A Reconstruction*, pp. 80-82.
19. Rowlingson, 'Paul's Ephesian Imprisonment', p. 7. Rowlingson's argument
is weak, but it does point to one possible significance of knowing the epistles'
provenance.
20. See *The Acts of Paul* 8.
21. For a brief summary of the arguments against Pauline authorship of
3 Corinthians, see M. Prior, *Paul the Letter-Writer and the Second Letter to Timothy*
(JSNTSup, 23; Sheffield: Sheffield Academic Press, 1990), p. 21.
22. Cf. 2 Cor. 6.5.

imprisoned in as many as seven different locations),[23] students of early Christianity are left only with the knowledge that Paul had been imprisoned often.

Although scholars such as George S. Duncan have done masterful work in seeking to determine the city from which Paul wrote these epistles, his conclusions still are short of compelling.[24] In the final analysis we just do not know. Speculating about where Paul may have been imprisoned when he wrote Philippians and Philemon, although enjoyable and intriguing, leaves us with little more than enjoyable and intriguing speculation. Moisés Silva offers a healthy agnostic perspective on the question of the epistles' provenance. Although Silva opts for a Roman origin of Philippians, he does so with refreshing humility, writing that 'It remains little more than a theory, and any exegetical conclusions that lean heavily on it must be regarded as methodologically weak or even invalid.'[25]

Roman Law and Roman Prisons
As with New Testament scholars, most classicists have had only an indirect interest in ancient incarceration, with their focus generally centered on those references to prison found in Roman legal texts. Such is the case with one work which New Testament scholarship often has accepted uncritically as a description of Roman prison life: Theodore Mommsen's classic *Römisches Strafrecht*.[26] Mommsen, although he has

---

23. Against V.P. Furnish, *II Corinthians* (AB, 32A; Garden City: Doubleday, 1984), p. 354, I find little reason to believe that Clement's statement 'may be hyperbole, or it may be a way of indicating that various members of Paul's company have suffered incarceration'. J.D. Quinn, '"Seven Times he Wore Chains" (I Clem. 5.6)', *JBL* 97 (1978), pp. 574-76, proposes that the author of *1 Clement* here is referring not to actual imprisonments, but, rather, to 'the number of documents which were at his disposal in the Roman church that referred to Paul as imprisoned'. However, even aside from Clement's mentioning nothing about a *bibliotheca sacra*, the immediate literary context of his description would argue against a reading such as Quinn's: just as Clement says that Peter faced *repeated* trials, so he describes Paul as having faced *repeated* imprisonments. Paul's imprisonments are held up as an example of how Paul 'showed the way to the prize of endurance'.

24. As M. Silva, *Philippians* (WEC; Chicago: Moody Press, 1988), p. 7, writes, 'The Ephesian theory, in any case, labors under two serious disadvantages: we have no positive evidence either for an imprisonment of Paul in Ephesus or for the presence of a praetorian guard in a senatorial province.'

25. *Philippians*, p. 8.

26. T. Mommsen, *Römisches Strafrecht* (Leipzig: Verlag von Duncker & Humbolt, 1899).

been interpreted otherwise, makes few claims or pretensions to having sketched out anything like a definitive work on ancient prisons. A lawyer-turned-historian, his focus is on Roman law, and this focus is reflected in the sources he employs. Since law is concerned inevitably with crime and punishment, Mommsen finds occasion to look at prisons or, more specifically, at discussions of imprisonment as reflected in ancient legal codes.

By granting Mommsen's statements final say in discussions of ancient imprisonment, many commentaries and resource materials tacitly employ legal material in making social and historical observations.[27] Thus, the definition of 'prison' in *The Oxford Classical Dictionary*, although it does begin with the disclaimer 'Roman criminal law did not recognize...', still describes 'prisons' exclusively through the eyes of Roman law.[28] This in itself is potentially problematic: a legal code for the state of Iowa would not necessarily communicate much about what actually happens in Iowa prisons.

In addition to drawing dubious social-historical conclusions from premises which come from the legal realm, scholars also need to be careful lest they attribute too strong a causation between laws and their enforcement. Many modern states have laws against jaywalking, speeding, etc. Historians of the future, however, might make inappropriate conclusions about actual practices unless they pause to consider that these laws are not always enforced. Sometimes laws are prescriptive and only point to ideals. Sometimes they remain in legal codes long after they have been dismissed as irrelevant by enforcement agencies. Sometimes they actually apply only to particular segments of the population. Sometimes they serve to mask subtler realities of the law. Jane F. Gardner writes,

> Law...is about what people may or may not do, not what they actually do. Law is created for a number of purposes, but, in general, it is meant to serve what a given society conceives as its interests, by proscribing or prescribing particular actions.[29]

Because of the difficulties in using Roman legal codes, because they are late, and because they often skew the reality of prison life, it is

27. This will be discussed in the actual descriptions of prisons. See, below in Chapter 1, 'The Role of Ancient Roman Prisons'.

28. A. Berger, 'Prison', in N.G.L. Hammond and H.H. Scullard (eds.), *The Oxford Classical Dictionary* (Oxford: Clarendon Press, 2nd edn, 1970), p. 879.

29. J.F. Gardner, *Women in Roman Law and Society* (Bloomington: Indiana University Press, 1986), p. 3.

important to use such material only in conjunction with a variety of other sources.

3. *Methodological Considerations*

There is at least one concrete reason why scholars have not employed comparative materials in their analysis either of texts about prison or of texts written from prison: those sources concerned with life in prison are scattered and varied. In addition, the best sources are often the latest: for example, Justinian's *Digest*, Philostratus' *Life of Apollonius*, and Libanius, *Or.* 45 ('Concerning the Prisoners').[30] There is no single ancient source to which one might turn so as to understand better what prisons were like and how they were perceived. As a result, our knowledge of prisons in antiquity is similar to a patch-work quilt.[31]

Two attempts to sew such a 'quilt' together can be found in F.A.K. Krauss's *Im Kerker vor und nach Christus* [32] and in B.M. Rapske's *The Book of Acts and Paul in Roman Custody*. The former brings together a wide variety of material from imprisonment around the world, but is concerned less with prison life as with the legal and social function of imprisonment within particular societies. The work is particularly interesting in its discussion of the evidence relating to prisons in specific locales. The latter, by collecting evidence on ancient trials and imprisonment, seeks to better understand Paul's incarceration and the legal trials in the book of Acts. Rapske's focus, then, is on the portrayal of Paul's imprisonment specifically in Acts.[33]

---

30. Although these resources are late, these are nonetheless valuable both in corroborating other data and in illuminating concepts described only briefly in earlier literature.

31. The following articles all point to illuminating primary resources: F.A.K. Krass, 'Die Gefangenen und die Verbrecher unter dem Einflusse des Christenthums', *Blätter für Gefängnisskunde* 25 (1989–90), pp. 1-95; S. Arbandt-W. Macheiner, 'Gefangenschaft', in T. Klauser (ed.), *Reallexikon für Antike und Christentum*, IX (Stuttgart: Anton Hiersemann, 1976), pp. 318-45; Mommsen, *Römisches Strafrecht*, pp. 300-318, 928-31 and 960-63; H. Hitzig, 'Carcer', in G. Wissowa (ed.), *Pauly's Realencyclopädie der classischen Altertumswissenschaft*, III.2 (Stuttgart: J.B. Metzlersche Verlagsbuchhandlung, 1899), pp. 1576-81; and A.H.J. Greenidge, *The Legal Procedure of Cicero's Time* (Oxford: Clarendon Press, 1901). These articles and entries are characterized by a positivist approach to the data: very little attention is given to any sort of systematic analysis.

32. Tübingen: Mohr, 1895.

33. Rapske's discussions are illuminating and his emphasis on the legal aspects

Any study of prisons in the Roman Empire needs to collect and ana-
lyze a wide variety of data; data found in sources as diverse as novels,
martyrologies, moral tractates, historical treatises, personal epistles, law
codes, dream interpretations and magical papyri. Since such material can
be dated from the second century BCE through the fourth century CE,
any analysis also needs to avoid anachronistic comparisons. Thus, there
are at least three points of method which need to concern readers of
those texts which describe ancient prisons: 1) the tendentiousness of
the sources needs to be factored into consideration; 2) the texts cannot
be collapsed together or harmonized as if there were an 'ideal' prison
type; and 3) the approach needs to remain a historical one, not a
phenomenological one.

In examining data from such a variety of sources, the reader has to be
cautious so as to recognize the limitations and tendencies of the various
types of evidence. In Stoic moral treatises, for instance, one would not
be entirely surprised if imprisonment were not seen as a particularly bad
fate. Imprisonment, after all, often falls into lists of the sorts of theoretical
hardships which should not and do not affect true philosophers.[34]
Conversely, one should not be shocked if early Christian martyrologies
point to the horrors of imprisonment and to the sacrifices which faithful
souls underwent for the sake of a higher calling. As Robin Lane Fox
writes, 'Christian stories of martyrdom linked obscene violence with
natural serenity'.[35] The more violent the backdrop, the more brilliant the
Christians' endurance sparkled.[36]

of imprisonment are excellent. In the discussion of imprisonment in Chapter 1 of this
monograph, the focus, however, is less on legal evidence and more on what may be
seen as the popular perception of ancient imprisonment. A variety of evidence from
ancient astrological codes, dream interpretation manuals and magical papyri, for
instance, is brought together with other popular sources. This work is concerned
primarily with ancient *perceptions* of prison and imprisonment.

34. The discussion on 'Eating' in Chapter 1 presents a typical example of how
such hardship catalogues were employed. Also see J.T. Fitzgerald, *Cracks in an
Earthen Vessel: An Examination of the Catalogues of Hardships in the Corinthian
Correspondence* (SBLDS, 99; Atlanta: Scholars Press, 1988), esp. pp. 47-116.

35. R.L. Fox, *Pagans and Christians* (San Francisco: Harper & Row, 1986),
p. 439.

36. S.P. Brock and S.A. Harvey, *Holy Women of the Syrian Orient* (Berkeley:
University of California Press, 1987), p. 15, write, 'Christian literature has painted the
experience of martyrdom and persecution as far more extreme than generally
happened—perhaps not so surprising in terms of the romantic appeal of religious
propaganda, but an important feature even so.'

Each source, whether it exists for legal, literary, entertainment or inspirational reasons, has its own particular tendency. Thus, all evidence needs to be carefully scrutinized. The texts preserved very well may reflect either an author's own concerns or his or her interest in the bizarre or unique.

Anyone interested in Roman imprisonment during the first centuries of the first millennium also needs to refrain from engaging in an attempt to create a description of a 'typical Roman prison'. Any attempt to reconstruct a picture of a typical prison is foiled by a host of difficulties. There were different types of prisons in the ancient world. Furthermore, what one would have experienced as a prisoner would have depended on a wide variety of factors: the social status of the prisoner;[37] the province in which one was imprisoned; the decade during which one was imprisoned; the emperor or governor under whom one was imprisoned;[38] the jailer or prisonkeeper watching over one's imprisonment.[39]

Because chapters two through five of this monograph will focus on Paul's rhetoric, ideally his language would be compared to the sorts of language which other prisoners would have employed during this same time period. Unfortunately, there are extremely few first-person accounts of life in prison. There are obvious reasons why. Those persons who could write may well have been wealthy enough to have avoided imprisonment in the first place. Those persons who found themselves imprisoned may not have been able to write, or they may not have had access to a scribe, an amanuensis or a literate friend. Furthermore, of those prisoners who could write, many would have been discouraged from doing so, if they had no way to ensure the delivery of the letter or

37. See 'The Status of Prisoners and Differential Treatment' in Chapter 1.

38. As in the American West, there were 'hanging judges' throughout the Roman empire. Juvenal refers to the danger of holding Rutilus forth as an example, since he 'delights in the sound of a cruel flogging...never happy until he has summoned a torturer, and he can brand some one with a hot iron for stealing a couple of towels...revelling in the clanking of a chain, and taking wondrous pleasure in branded slaves, in prisons...' (*Sat.* 14.24). In a later period, Libanius refers to the governors of the provinces, in general, as 'murderers' (*Or.* 45.3).

39In Lucian, *Tox.* 29, the Egyptian prisonkeeper watching over Antiphilus was superstitious and thought that he could 'gratify and avenge his god' through harsh treatment of Antiphilus (who was accused of being a temple-robber). In Josephus, *Ant.* 2.61-62, the keeper of the prison, favoring Joseph, 'gave him some relief from his chains and rendered his cruel fate lighter and more tolerable, allowing him moreover rations superior to prisoners' fare'.

account. Another difficulty we face is that the first-person accounts of imprisonment which do exist are later than Paul's: Apollonius' experiences were written down and preserved;[40] Perpetua kept a diary in prison;[41] the imprisoned Montanus and Lucius wrote to the church at Carthage.[42]

Because the texts and sources used in this monograph span a number of centuries, the method here consciously seeks to avoid the conflation or harmonization of texts which, on the basis of chronological differences, are incompatible. In some respects, this is one of the primary reasons for being cautious in the use of such often-employed legal codes as Justinian's *Digest*.[43] At the same time, such caution should not result in a total refusal to examine later sources. Unfamiliar with Roman torture, we may find that a later source such as *The Letter of Phileas*[44] goes a long way towards illuminating concepts which are nothing less than alien to those of us in the twentieth century.

4. *Caveats and Goals*

A number of issues involving Paul's imprisonment will not be addressed or will be addressed only indirectly: Paul's crime or the reason why he was imprisoned; the location of Paul's imprisonment; information on private prisons;[45] and 'house arrests' in antiquity.[46] Some of these issues

40. Philostratus, *VA* 7.

41. *The Martyrdom of Perpetua and Felicitas*.

42. *The Martyrdom of Saints Montanus and Lucius*.

43. The *Digest* was compiled, starting in the year 530 CE, and is basically a collection of works, by classical jurists, from the second through the fourth centuries. Although the *Digest* does summarize more than it innovates, and although it does reflect laws from an earlier era, one cannot simply project all of these laws back onto prison life in the first century.

44. The letter from this fourth century bishop is found in Eusebius, *Hist. eccl.* 8.10.

45. A study of the institution of private prisons is both inapplicable and beyond the scope of this work. From the time of Hadrian, imprisonment in private prisons was legally forbidden (*Hist. Aug. Hadr.* 18.10; cf. Pliny the Elder, *HN* 18.36). R. Taubenschlag, *The Law of Greco-Roman Egypt in the Light of the Papyri 332 BC–640 AD.* (New York: Herald Press, 1944), p. 412, notes that 'the papyri show that the officials used to comply with them (the injunction to imprison) in spite of the Tebt. decree forbidding imprisonment for private delicts'. For persons interested in private prisons, I would encourage them to look at the sources presented in R. MacMullen, *Corruption and the Decline of Rome* (New Haven: Yale University Press, 1988),

would lead us too far astray from the central focus of this work; some could not be discussed intelligently without more evidence.

A number of questions, however, can be answered. Chapter 1 is concerned with bringing together that which was said about Roman prisons in antiquity. Just as most moderns have not been to prison, but still have their own impressions of what is involved in imprisonment,[47] so many ancients had never been incarcerated—perhaps they had never even

p. 248 n.93; J. Shelton, *As the Romans Did: A Source Book in Roman Social History* (Oxford: Oxford University Press, 1988), pp. 73, 172, and 178, and B. Levick, *The Government of the Roman Empire: A Sourcebook* (Totowa, New Jersey: Barnes & Noble Books, 1985), pp. 174-81. Also see Aulus Gellius, Book 20.1.44-46, which describes how owners of private prisons punished imprisoned creditors.

46. If one assumes that Philippians and Philemon were written from Rome (in particular, during the captivity discussed in Acts 28.30-31), he or she might be disappointed not to see a more detailed discussion of 'house arrests' in this work. As I have argued above, however, attempts to claim that Paul's prison epistles were written from Rome, let alone from a 'house arrest', are far from conclusive. Ramsay MacMullen has shown me that those figures described as being under house arrest in antiquity (see below) are persons who had either high status or great connections. Regardless of whether or not Paul actually had been under house arrest (*contra The Acts of Paul* 11), the author of Acts 28 would have had good reason to want to portray the apostle as the sort of person who would have experienced a house arrest. Even if, however, these epistles were written from a house arrest in Rome, many of the descriptions of imprisonment in Chapter 1 still can be seen as applicable in understanding what such prisoners experienced.

There is not a great deal of material on what scholars have called 'house arrests'. Such imprisonments were rare. However, those interested in learning more about house arrests might begin by looking at the following texts. In Pausanius, *Elis*, Book 6, an athlete, Astylus of Crotona, is described as having proclaimed that he was a Syracusan in order to win favor with Hiero, the son of Deinomenes. The people of Crotona, angry at this measure, condemned his house to be a prison (*Elis* 2.13.1). Around 220 BCE, a certain Cleomenes, who was apparently going to initiate a revolt against the king, was put into custody. As Polybius, 5.38.6-7, describes, 'A huge house was put at his disposal in which he resided under watch and ward, differing from ordinary prisoners only that he had a bigger jail to live in'.

Similarly, in 213 BCE, Altinius, a prisoner of war, was placed in custody in Cales. Here 'he was free to go about by day followed by guards, at night confined and watched by them' (Livy, 24.45.10). Cf. Josephus, *Ant.* 18.235, which refers to Herod Agrippa's house arrest after the death of Tiberius.

47. Television and movies have supplied many of the images which we have of prisons: helicopter escapes from prison courtyards; prisoners lifting weights or watching television; metal files hidden in birthday cakes; *Andy Griffith*'s Barney Fife delivering Aunt Bea's home cooking to Otis; etc.

seen a prison—but they still had ideas and opinions about prisons. Whether or not these impressions were correct is another matter. Regardless, just as persons communicate not a generic message, but a message based also on the relationship with the audience and on a (limited) knowledge of the audience's perceptions, so anyone writing from prison would have to do the same. By triangulating a wide variety of data from antiquity—data which refer to what happened in prison or to what was said about prison—we may then know the sorts of things with which persons in antiquity were familiar. From this, we can begin to understand better what Paul and his churches might have experienced and felt during his imprisonment.

The next four chapters will then focus on Paul's letters to the Philippians and to Philemon. The letters were undoubtedly intended to communicate certain kinds of knowledge, perceptions and expectations, many of which are unknown to us. Our understanding of these will always remain imperfect. However, we can begin to acquire some of this knowledge and to understand more of what Paul's audiences must have felt by examining how imprisonment was viewed and perceived in the literature of the time. Thus, Chapters 2–5 each build both on Chapter 1 and on epistolary traditions in antiquity (especially those of Cicero and Ignatius). Whereas the first chapter is concerned with a general knowledge of prisons in antiquity, the other four are primarily exegetical, seeking to interpret Paul's epistles in light of his incarceration.

The second and third chapters focus on Paul's letter to the Philippians. In this letter, the apostle justifies his imprisonment, he reconciles it with the gospel, and he uses his incarceration to bring the Philippians to reconsider their relationship with him and with each other.

Chapter 2 focuses on an odd expression in Phil. 1.18b-26. When Paul writes—concerning life and death—'which I shall choose I cannot tell' (Phil. 1.22b), does he really mean that this choice lies before him? To choose either life or death? By looking both at suicide in prison and at the willing, passive sacrifice of many Christians, by examining Cicero's rhetoric of suicide, and by looking at the rhetorical context in which Phil. 1.18b-26 fits, we can better understand both what Paul is implying by this rhetoric and what he expects of his readers.

The Philippians sent Paul a gift in prison. In responding to them, however, Paul did not explicitly acknowledge this support until the end of his letter, in Phil. 4.10-20. By looking at another example of 'delayed thanks' (Cicero, *QFr.* 1.3), by examining why the imprisoned were often deserted or abandoned, and by looking at the importance of the 'gospel' in Paul's letter to the Philippians, Chapter 3 argues that the discussion of the Philippians' gift fits into the rhetoric of the epistle as a whole. Imprisonment changed relations between people. By postponing the discussion of the gift, Paul wants the Philippians to realize that—despite whatever changes may have resulted from his imprisonment—their 'partnership in the gospel' has not changed.

Chapters 4 and 5 focus on Paul's letter to Philemon. Because Philemon presumably knew of Paul's incarceration, because Paul does not dwell on mundane aspects of his imprisonment, knowledge of both ancient metaphors and prison visitation helps to illuminate the message of this brief epistle.

Paul does not see himself as a prisoner of the Roman state: in Philemon 1 and 9, he sees himself as a 'prisoner of Christ Jesus'. Chapter 4 argues that Paul employs this expression within a context of martial imagery with which his readers would have been familiar. Paul's imprisonment to Christ Jesus points to his dedication to the gospel. Like Socrates, the famous imprisoned philosopher, the apostle Paul refused to desert his post, regardless if it would lead to imprisonment or death.

Finally, Chapter 5 is interested in the figure of Onesimus, the slave who was with Paul in prison. By looking at the role of messengers in antiquity, by examining the need for attendants to the imprisoned, and by focusing on one of the earliest references to Paul's letter to Philemon, this chapter argues that Onesimus was no runaway but, rather, was sent by his owner to aid the imprisoned Paul.

An epilogue of a literary work frequently includes a discussion of the future of the characters who have been described within that work. Similarly, the epilogue to this monograph examines how the image of 'the imprisoned apostle' came to be used in later Christian writings. Some scholars claim that Paul only wrote two epistles from prison: Philippians and Philemon. Regardless, Paul was remembered as an imprisoned apostle long after his imprisonment and death. The epilogue demonstrates some of the ways in which he was remembered.

Much scholarship on Philippians and Philemon has been concerned with theology and with the history of ideas. As such, it has considered Paul's imprisonment only secondarily, isolating the epistles from their social context. If Paul, however, spent as much time in prison as most scholars believe, for these scholars not to recognize the ways in which this would have affected Paul's thought and writing is simply irresponsible.

Although Paul is often described as 'the apostle to the Gentiles' or as a traveling missionary, it is important to remember that this apostle's concerns, rhetoric and theology often were shaped during those times when chains constrained him from traveling.

Chapter 1

PRISONS IN THE ANCIENT ROMAN WORLD

The days we passed there and the nights we endured cannot be expressed
in human words. The torments we suffered in prison go beyond anything
we could describe.

—The Martyrdom of Saints Montanus and Lucius 3

1. *Introduction*

Late Roman legal codes, like the *Digest,* are responsible for many of the
opinions and impressions which moderns have about imprisonment in
the Roman Empire. Scholars who have focused on this evidence often
have seen prescriptive statements as descriptive ones, have imposed late
evidence on situations from earlier centuries, and have accepted legal
material as if the laws described were both significant and enforced. This
chapter, by gathering and analyzing data not only from legal codes, but
also from such sources as moral tractates, personal epistles, historical
treatises, dream interpretations and magical papyri, seeks to draw a
more accurate picture both of what prisons[1] were like and, perhaps even
more significantly, of how they would have been perceived.

    1.   In modern English usage, the words 'jail' and 'prison' have fairly different
connotations. 'Prisons' are often thought of as being larger, harsher and more imper-
sonal than 'jails'; they are often seen as places where persons face longer periods of
confinement than in jails. Such a distinction, however, was not made in the ancient
Roman world. In Greek and Latin, there were no words to preserve the distinction
between 'prison' and 'jail', largely because there was no need for such words. A
variety of terms, used similarly and having similar connotations, described imprisonment in the Greco-Roman world: *carcer, publica vincula,* δεσμωτήριον, φρουρά,
εἰρκτή, φυλακή. In reading ancient literature, one also needs to be aware of less
commonly used words for 'prison'. In particular, there are a variety of euphemisms
and circumlocutions: οἴκημα (in Plutarch, *Sol.* 15.3, this word is said to have been
used by the Athenians, 'to cover up the ugliness of things'); δημόσιον (Thucydides,
5.18); νομοφυλάκιον (Pollux, *Onomasticon* 8.102); etc.

In setting the stage for the exegetical chapters which follow, this chapter is not trying to sketch a social world or symbolic universe into which some sort of passive actor (e.g. Paul, the Philippians, Philemon) was dropped. Paul's thoughts, actions and words were not products of a predictable world order. However, this chapter does seek to bring together and make sense of that data which better illuminate both what occurred in prison, and the sorts of reactions which imprisonment elicited.

In the absence of explicit evidence of what Paul underwent in prison, this approach offers the best insight into what Paul might have experienced. There are alternative models of understanding what Paul's imprisonment may have been like, but such tacit models are often anachronistic: Paul was not in an eighteenth-century British debtor prison; he was not in the cell of a monastary; he was not in a scene from *Quo Vadis, Spartacus* or *Ben Hur*.[2] At the very least, this monograph seeks to bring to bear the historical realities of Roman prison life on our analysis of Paul. The alternative, too often, is to grant each reader's fantasy free rein.

2. *The Role of Ancient Roman Prisons*

Much scholarship assumes that there was no such thing as long-term incarceration in the ancient world. This position is generally supported by reference to what has become a classic text in the discussion: *Carcer enim ad continendos homines non ad puniendos haberi debet* ('Prison indeed ought to be employed for confining men, not for punishing them', *Dig.* 48.18.9).[3] Primarily on the basis of this text, scholars have claimed that prisons were used as 'holding tanks' in antiquity. Thus, we get the sort of definition of 'prison' which we see in *The Oxford Classical Dictionary*:

> Roman criminal law did not recognize the imprisonment of free persons as a form of punishment. The public prison (*carcer, publica vincula*) served only for a short incarceration applied as a coercive measure (*coercitio, q.v.*)

2.   Similarly, this monograph will not examine prisons in light of models posed by modern studies such as M. Foucault, *Discipline & Punishment: The Birth of the Prison* (trans. A. Sheridan; New York: Vintage Books, 1979). Foucault is concerned with a different time period; one with very different perspectives on incarceration.

3.   Cf. *Dig.* 48.3.5. Translations of Justinian's *Digest* come from T. Mommsen *et al.* (eds.), *The Digest of Justinian*, I–IV (Philadelphia: University of Pennsylvania Press, 1985). Here Venuleius Saturninus notes that 'Should the accused confess, he shall be thrown into a public prison until sentence is passed on him.'

by magistrates for disobedience or recalcitrance to their orders. During
inquiry in a criminal trial the accused person could be detained (*custodia
reorum*) so as to be at the disposal of the authorities...[4]

Prisons were used as 'holding tanks' for a wide variety of reasons: in
The Acts of Paul 3.17, the governor commanded that Paul 'be bound
and led off to prison until he should find leisure to give him a more
attentive hearing'; in *The Acts of Thomas* 21–24, Thomas was imprisoned
while the king both investigated Thomas' case and pondered 'by what
manner of death' this prisoner should die; Christians in Lyons were
'locked up in prison to await the arrival of the governor' (*The Martyrs
of Lyons* 8); because wild animals did not attack her during gladiatorial
combat, Blandina was locked again in prison to await her next ordeal
(*The Martyrs of Lyons* 42); five women were put in prison 'for a while',
because they were too young to execute (*The Martyrdom of Saints
Agapê, Irenê and Chionê* 4.4); Apollonius was given three days in
prison, by the proconsul Perennis, to consider whether he would desert
his faith (*The Martyrdom of Apollonius* 10).

Certainly prisons did serve to hold the imprisoned until they obeyed
the magistrate, were tried in court or were executed.[5] The prolific philo-
logist Varro describes well the most basic function of the prison when he
notes that the word '*carcer*' ('prison') comes from the word '*coercere*'
('to confine'), 'because those who are in it are prevented from going
out' (*Ling.* 5.151).

The claim that prisons were primarily 'holding tanks' is helpful in some
respects, because it does point to at least one basic difference between
modern and ancient imprisonment: in general, ancient imprisonment
showed little or no concern with 'fixed sentences' or with the reform or
penitence of the prisoner.[6] However, it is not entirely true that 'the

4.   A. Berger, 'Prison', in N.G.L. Hammond and H.H. Scullard (eds.), *The
Oxford Classical Dictionary* (Oxford: Clarendon Press, 2nd edn, 1970), p. 879. This
sort of definition has filtered down into numerous descriptions of ancient prisons:
e.g., D.E. Aune, 'Revelation', in J.L. Mays (ed.), *Harper's Bible Commentary* (San
Francisco: Harper & Row, 1988), p. 1306.

5.   Also see such texts as Livy, 8.20.7 and Diodorus Siculus, 15.8.5. Cicero describes a man who was put into prison 'until they could get ready the sack into which
he was to be placed before being thrown into the river' (*Inv. Rhet.* 2.49.149).

6.   Philo, *Jos.* 85–87 does state that when Joseph was running the prison, it was
less a prison and more of a house of reform. Reform or penitence of the prisoner,
although perhaps a side-effect of imprisonment, does not seem to lie behind any ancient
philosophy of imprisonment nor does it appear to have been a goal of imprisonment.

public prison...served only for a short incarceration'. Furthermore, what is most problematic is that a vision of prisons as 'holding tanks' frequently leaves readers with the impression that imprisonment was fairly benign; similar to the sort of overnight incubation which town drunks might face today in small rural communities.

Prisons did serve as 'holding tanks' for those awaiting trial, but they were no simple 'waiting rooms'.[7] In addition, prisoners were often 'held' for a long, long time. As the *Digest* itself acknowledges, 'Governors are in the habit of condemning men to be kept in prison or in chains, but they ought not to do this; for punishments of this type are forbidden' (48.19.9). They may have been forbidden, but they were not unusual. In seeking to mete out appropriate punishment to a group which threatened the stability of the state, Caesar emphasized the exemplary nature of life-time imprisonment:

> Caesar feels that death has been ordained by the immortal gods not as a means of punishment but as a necessity of nature or a relief from all our toil and woe. That is why philosophers have never been reluctant to face it and brave men have often faced it even gladly. Confinement, however, and for life at that, is an exemplary punishment indeed for a heinous crime. (Cicero, *Cat.* 4.7)[8]

Cicero goes on to say that life imprisonment removes hope, the only consolation that the prisoners might have, and that by confiscating the imprisoned's property—which Caesar proposed to do—criminals would be left only with their lives and with mental and physical suffering. Cicero also goes on to say that his ancestors would have seen such punishment as befitting only 'the next world' because, without fear of such punishment, 'death by itself was nothing very frightening' (*Cat.* 4.8-9).

Such punishment, however, was not just a theoretical proposal. Prisoners often were left in prison for years and years.[9] When Ptolemy

---

7. See the ground-breaking article by W. Eisenhut, 'Die römische Gefängnisstrafe', *ANRW* I.2, pp. 268-82.

8. A version of this speech is also found in Plutarch, *Cic.* 21–22. Here Silanus refers to 'imprisonment' as the 'extremest punishment' (21.3). Sallust, *Cat.* 51 also presents a version of Caesar's speech. Here, Caesar's words against the death penalty are more direct: 'Amid grief and wretchedness death is a relief from woes, not a punishment; that it puts an end to all mortal ills and leaves no room either for joy or for sorrow.' Also see Josephus, *War* 2.179-80, 6.434. In addition to incarceration for life, persons were often incarcerated until they either made payment of a debt or died (cf. Mt. 18.30, 34; Plutarch, *Cim.* 3; *Dem.* 26.1-2; *P. Oxy.* 3104).

9. See the discussion on extended incarceration in B. Rapske, *The Book of Acts*

Philadelphus married his sister, Sotades made a joke at his expense and 'rotted in prison for many years' (Ps.-Plutarch, *Mor.* 11A). Jonathan, the Macabbean high priest, was sentenced to 'perpetual imprisonment' (Josephus, *War* 6.434). After Agrippa openly prayed that Tiberius might die, the emperor threw him into prison and treated him violently until the emperor himself died (Josephus, *War* 2.179-80). These are just a few examples of those who spent an inordinate amount of time in prison.[10]

The temporary nature of imprisonment was not that which was most salient in the minds of the ancients. Prison was a threat and it was to be feared. Seneca does not describe imprisonment as a temporary state, but, rather, he lists it within a catalogue of ascending punishments:

> To every form of punishment will I resort, but only as a remedy. If you are lingering as yet in the first stage of error and are lapsing, not seriously, but often, I shall try to correct you by chiding, first in private, then in public. If you have already advanced so far that words can no longer bring you to your senses, then you shall be held in check by public disgrace. Should it be necessary to brand you in more drastic fashion, with a punishment you can feel, you shall be sent into exile, banished to an unknown region. Should your wickedness have become deep-rooted, demanding harsher remedies to meet your case, to chains and the state-prison we shall have resort. (*De Ira* 1.16.2-3)

Imprisonment, as Caesar is reported as saying, was indeed 'an exemplary punishment'. The threat of imprisonment was used to influence persons' behavior,[11] with it often being referred to as a fate worse than death.[12] In a speech in Sallust, *Iug.* 14.15, we are told that 'Of those taken by Jugurtha some have been crucified, others thrown to wild beasts; a few, whose lives were spared, in gloomy dungeons amid sorrow and lamentation drag out an existence worse than death.'

The psychological torment of such an imprisonment obviously had a great effect. It is said that rather than execute Gallus, Tiberius had him under guard for several years 'to make the prisoner suffer as long as

and Paul in Roman Custody (Grand Rapids, MI: Eerdmans, 1994), pp. 315-23.

10. Also see Josephus, *Ant.* 18.179; Diodorus Siculus, 17.80.2; Acts 24.27; *The Martyrdom of Saints Ptolemaeus and Lucius* 11; and *P. Oxy.* 777 (a petition of a prisoner who claims to have produced sureties, but remained imprisoned regardless).

11. E.g., Suetonius, *Tib.* 57.

12. The notion here is not primarily metaphorical or rhetorical. It does seem to reflect a reality. Josephus, in *War* 7.373-74, declares that 'most miserable of all must be reckoned those still alive, who have often prayed for death and are denied the boon'.

possible both from the loss of his civic rights and from terror'. Gallus
was guarded 'not to prevent his escape, but to prevent his death':

> He had no companion or servant with him, spoke to no one, and saw no
> one, except when he was compelled to take food. And the food was of
> such quality and amount as neither to afford him any satisfaction or
> strength nor yet to allow him to die. This was, in fact, the most terrible part
> of his punishment. (Dio, 58.3.5-6)

In this same section, Dio reports that Tiberius imprisoned one of his
companions and then, 'when there was talk about executing him, he
said: "I have not yet made my peace with him"'.[13] Suetonius reports a
very similar story, saying that 'when he [Tiberius] was inspecting the
prisons and a man begged for a speedy death, he replied: "I have not
yet become your friend"' (*Tib.* 61.5).[14]

If one had been buried in prison for many years, and then was somehow released, the change would have been stunning. In Plutarch, *Luc.*
18.1, when Lucullus captured Cabira, he found a number of prisons 'in
which many Greeks and many kinsfolk of the king were confined. As
they had long been given up for dead, it was not so much a rescue as it
was a resurrection and a sort of second birth, for which they were
indebted to the favour of Lucullus.' Similarly, when Gaius succeeded
Tiberius, he freed those who had been imprisoned for *maiestas* and
similar charges, among them being a certain Quintus Pomponius, who
had been kept in prison and maltreated for over a period of seven
years.[15] Prison was no simple holding tank.

---

13. It should be noted, however, that if it were believed that a later ruler might
release the prisoners, or if it were thought that the prisoners' families might avenge
them, it was often expedient—rather than letting the prisoners die slowly and
painfully—simply to kill them. See, for instance, Josephus, *War* 4.143-46, where
eleven persons 'entered the gaol with drawn swords and butchered the prisoners'.

14. Cf. Josephus, *Ant.* 18.178. Tiberius, it is said here, procrastinated in hearing
the cases of prisoners, because (as he himself explained it), 'an immediate hearing
would alleviate the present miseries of those condemned to death, whereas they did
not deserve to meet with such luck. When, however, they were kept waiting, the weight
of their misfortune was rendered more severe by the vexation which was laid upon
them.'

Tiberius engaged in large-scale convictions of life imprisonment. He con-
signed to life imprisonment (*in perpetua vincula*) the Decurions and many of the
citizens of Pollentia, when they went against his orders (Suetonius, *Tib.* 37.3).

15. Dio, 59.6.2-3; 60.4.2.

3. *The Physical Conditions of Prison*

> I was terrified, as I had never before been in such a dark hole. What a
> difficult time it was! With the crowd the heat was stifling; then there was
> the extortion of the soldiers; and to crown all, I was tortured with worry for
> my baby there.
>
> —*The Martyrdom of Perpetua and Felicitas* 3

Perhaps one of the most interesting descriptions of the horrors of
prison can be seen in a letter which Nemesianus, Dativus, Felix and
Victor wrote to the bishop Cyprian. Cyprian had written a letter of
support to imprisoned Christians and, as a result of this letter, he was
thanked by Nemesianus and the others. They wrote to him, saying,

> you have refreshed their suffering breasts; have healed their limbs
> wounded with clubs; have loosened their feet bound with fetters; have
> smoothed the hair of their half-shorn head; have illuminated the darkness
> of the dungeon; have brought down the mountains of the mine to a smooth
> surface; have even placed fragrant flowers to their nostrils, and have shut
> out the foul odour of the smoke. (*Ep.* 77.3)

The praises heaped upon Cyprian, by Nemesianus and the others, show
well what many prisoners must have experienced: suffering, beatings,
chains, darkness and squalor. Furthermore, prisoners knew that imprisonment might lead to death: either execution by the authorities or
death resulting from disease, torture or the psychological trauma of
imprisonment itself.

Aside from the other types of darkness which hung over imprisonment, actual darkness was a persistent part of daily life in these underground prisons. Darkness is mentioned so frequently that it cannot be
discounted as a passing description of poor illumination.[16] In some cases,
the darkness is mentioned with little comment. In *The Acts of Thomas*
119, when Mygdonia is surprised to see Judas Thomas out of prison,
one of the first things she asks is 'Who is he who brought thee out of
the prison to behold the sun?' In Philostratus, *VA* 7.31, we are told that
when day came, Apollonius 'offered his prayers to the Sun, as best he
could in prison'.[17] Cicero notes that Gavius of Consa, having escaped

---

16. Conditions were so poor that *C. Th.* 9.3.1 legislated that prisoners were to be
allowed light and air, lest they die. Sallust, *Cat.* 55.3-4 comments on the darkness of
the Tullianum in particular; saying that it is hideous to behold. Cf. Lucan, 2.79-80.

17. Cf. *T. Jos.* 9.1.

from prison, 'had come forth from the awful shadow of death, revived and strengthened by the light of freedom and the fresh air of justice' (*Verr.* 2.5.61).[18] In *The Testament of Joseph* 9.1, the seductress tells the imprisoned Joseph, 'Acquiesce in fulfilling my desire, and I will release you from the fetters and liberate you from the darkness'.

Deprivation of the sun and of light must have had a tremendous psychological effect on the imprisoned. Cicero, in trying to assess the trauma of Apollonius' imprisonment, emphasizes the horrors brought through the darkness:

> There is the darkness—the chains—the prison—the tortures of being shut up, of being shut off from the sight of parent and child, nay, from drawing free breath and looking upon the common light of day: from such evils escape may well be bought with life itself—I cannot assess them in terms of money (*Verr.* 2.5.9).

The negative effects which darkness generally had on the imprisoned are emphasized even more when they are denied. In a rhetorical flourish in *The Martyrdom of Saints Marian and James* 6.1, the author says to the readers, 'Well, now, pagans, do you still believe that Christians, for whom awaits the joy of eternal light, feel the torments of prison or shrink from the dungeons of this world?'[19] Not only could the future illuminate the darkness of imprisonment, but the Spirit—as described in *The Martyrdom of Saints Montanus and Lucius* 4.2—was seen as having a similar effect: 'The dismal prison soon began to shine with the light of the Spirit, and the ardour of our faith clothed us with the brilliance of day to protect us against the ugly shadows and the pitch-black veil of night.'[20]

Comparing imprisonment with burial or with Hades seemed natural to the ancients. In Artemidorus's second-century book, *The Interpretation of Dreams*, it is said that 'to dream one is buried alive signifies benefits for no one, since it generally signifies prison and fetters' (2.50). Similarly, Artemidorus claims that 'If a man dreams that he has descended into Hades and is prevented from returning to the Upperworld, it signifies that he will be forcibly restrained by certain people and thrown into prison' (2.55). Prisons served as a prototype for Hades; what was undergone in prison was a foretaste of what one might expect

---

18. Cf. Cicero, *Cat.* 4.10.
19. Cf. *The Martyrdom of Saints Marian and James* 8.2.
20. Cf. Cyprian, *Ep.* 15.2 and Tertullian, *Ad Mart.* 2.

in Hades.[21] Thus, in Lucian, *Luct.*, the description of the common people's understanding of Hades sounds remarkably similar to descriptions of prisons. Hades is a place under the earth, murky and sunless (2), where persons are racked, burned, turned upon a wheel, etc. (8). Josephus, similarly, notes that both the Essenes and the Greeks think of Hades in terms of prison. Josephus says that these groups 'relegate base souls to a murky and tempestuous dungeon, big with never-ending punishments' (*War* 2.155).[22] Lucretius denies that Tartarus exists, but he acknowledges that

> in this life there is fear of punishment for evil deeds, fear as notorious as the deeds are notorious, and atonement for crime, prison, and the horrible casting down from the Rock, stripes, tortureres, condemned cell, pitch, red-hot plates, firebrands: and even if these are absent, yet the guilty conscience, terrifed before aught can come to pass, applies the goad and scorces itself with whips, and meanwhile sees not where can be the end to its miseries or the final limit to its punishment, and fear at the same time that all this may become heavier after death (*De Rerum Natura* 3.1012-1023).

Dark, crowded prisons created a variety of problems. Perpetua mentioned that 'with the crowd the heat was stifling'. Prisons were generally hot and not ventilated. Thus, prisoners frequently had difficulties breathing.[23] Diodorus Siculus, describing the prison at Alba Fucens, says of the prisoners that 'since their food and everything pertaining to their other needs was all foully commingled, a stench so terrible assailed anyone who drew near that it could scarcely be endured' (31.9.2). In making an analogy with imprisonment, Philo (*Ebr.* 101) writes that when the mind 'is cooped up in the city of the body and mortal life, it is

---

21. Cf. *1 En.* 10.13. Bert Harrill has pointed me to Sophocles' *Antigone*, for another interesting link between prison and Hades. When Kreon punished Antigone for attending to the corpse of Polyneikes, she was not stoned to death (see 36; this is the prescribed punishment for such an offence), but, rather, she was imprisoned underground in rock in a deserted place. This punishment, R. Seaford, 'The Imprisonment of Women in Greek Tragedy', *JHS* 110 (1990), p. 76, argues, was particularly appropriate for Antigone. Kreon himself remarks how ironic it is that in an underground prison 'she can ask Hades to save her from death, Hades who is the only god she reveres'.

22. Also, in *Apol.* 11.11, Tertullian refers his readers to 'Tartarus, which you, when you so please, affirm to be the prison of infernal punishment'.

23. Cf. Cicero, *Verr.* 2.61; Tertullian, *Ad Mart.* 2; *The Martyrdom of Perpetua and Felicitas* 3; Sallust, *Cat.* 55.3-4.

cabined and cribbed and like a prisoner in the gaol declares roundly that it cannot even draw a breath of free air'.

The stench of the prison, the numbers of prisoners, and the lack of ventilation meant that many prisons were filled with illness.[24] Thucydides' description of prisoners' experiences in the stone-quarries reflects typical prison conditions: the days were crowded and hot, the nights cold, illness was common, the dead were heaped upon one another, and the prisoners were both hungry and thirsty (7.87.1-3). In *The Martyrdom of Saints Montanus and Lucius* 6.5, we are told that 'there were very many ill, suffering from the prison fare and the cold water'. Diodorus Siculus tells of the wonder-worker and king Eunus, who was 'put in prison, where his body was ravaged and eaten away by lice' (34.2.22-23).

These prison conditions are described well in Lucian, *Tox.* 29. Here, Antiphilus was sick and ill, he slept on the ground, at night his legs were confined in stocks, and during the day he had to wear a collar around his neck and a manacle on one hand:

> Moreover, the stench of the room and its stifling air (since many were confined in the same place, cramped for room, and scarcely able to draw breath), the clash of iron, the scanty sleep—all these conditions were difficult and intolerable for such a man, unwonted to them and unschooled to a life so rigorous.

Lucian continues by writing that after Demetrius—Antiphilus' friend—secured entrance to the prison,

> he made a long search for Antiphilus, who had become unrecognisable through his miseries. He went about examining each of the prisoners just as people do who seek out their own dead among the altered bodies on battle-fields. Indeed, had he not called his name aloud, 'Antiphilus, son of Deinomenes', he would not for a long time have known which was he, so greatly had he been changed by his dire straits.

In prison, then, persons' looks gradually began to change; they became filthy and disheveled. When Joseph was taken out of prison (in Philo, *Jos.* 105), 'first they had him shaven and shorn, for in his confinement the hair had grown long and thick on his head and chin. Then they put on him a bright and clean raiment instead of his filthy

---

24. Arthur Shippee has pointed me to a quotation of John Chrysostom, which reflects this well. If one wanted to study horrible or unique diseases, Chrysostom notes, one should visit prison ('On the Incomprehensible Nature of God' 5.7, in *PG* 47, p. 490). Cf. *The Martyrdom of Perpetua and Felicitas* 3; Plutarch, *Per.* 31.5.; Cyprian, *Ep.* 15.3, 25.7.

prison clothes.' Joseph and Antiphilus' situations were not unusual. In Petronius' *Satyricon*, we are told of a situation on board a ship, where two persons' hair was cut. Lichas, in charge of the ship, thought it bad luck to cut hair 'on board ship, unless winds and waves are raging' (104-105). Eumolpus defended the action, saying 'It was because these ruffians had long, dirty hair. I did not want to turn the ship into a prison, so I ordered the filth to be cleared off the brutes' (105).[25] Prisons were filthy; persons in antiquity knew this.[26]

Not all prisons were filthy, poorly ventilated, and buried underground, but those characteristics are part of the standard *portrayal* of prisons. In addition, prisons are frequently described as having 'outer' and 'inner' rooms; with the inner room being darker, more terrible, and more secure.[27] Prisoners were placed in the inner part of the prison for security and for punishment. After the Philippian jailer was ordered to watch over Paul and Silas, we are told that he 'put them into the inner prison and fastened their feet in the stocks' (Acts 16.23-24). In *The Martyrdom of Pionius* 11.4, when the jailers received no bribes from the prisoners, they put them in the inner part of the prison. Similarly, when the *legatus* was not able to take the Christian writings away from the bishop Felix, Felix also was 'put into the lowest part of the prison' (*The Martyrdom of St Felix the Bishop* 26).

Although some prisons may have been divided into two parts, prisons in the ancient Roman world do not seem to have had individual cells: prisoners were generally crowded together and chained together. There is little data available on how many persons would be in a prison at any time; this, of course, depended on the size of the prison. In Philostratus, *VA* 7.26, we are told of a prison that contained around fifty persons. In *The Acts of Andrew and Matthias* 21, we are told of a prison escape which resulted in the release of 248 men and 49 women. Although it is

25. The *Mishnah*, *M. Qat.* 3.1, lists those persons who may cut their hair on the intermediate days of a festival, and includes those persons who come out of prison. *M. Qat.* 3.2, similarly, includes those who have left prison among those who are permitted to 'wash their clothes on the intermediate days of a festival'.

26. In *The Martyrdom of Saints Montanus and Lucius*, when Flavian approached the prison, the prison gates were 'slower in opening and more difficult than usual...it seemed as though...Flavian...was unworthy to be soiled by the filth of a prison' (17.1).

27. In *The Martyrdom of Perpetua and Felicitas* 3.7, the deacons Tertius and Pomponius are described as having bribed the guards of the prison, so that the Christians might go to 'a better part of the prison' to refresh themselves for a while.

difficult to postulate how large an 'average prison' may have been, the sources do agree on one fact: prisons were very crowded (e.g. Lucian, *Tox.* 29). The prison at Alba Fucens is described by Diodorus Siculus as 'a deep under-ground dungeon, no larger than a nine-couch room, dark, and noisome from the large numbers committed to the place' (31.9.1-2). In *Or.* 45.8, Libanius emphasizes that the prisons of his day were packed with bodies: 'No one comes out—or precious few, at least—though many go in.' Elsewhere, Libanius emphasizes that many prisoners had died from close confinement (*Or.* 33.41 and 45.11) and that they had even trampled each other to death (*Or.* 45.31).

As a result of the crowded conditions, a large number of prisoners would be in the same room while awaiting trial. In any given room, you might have a number of Joshuas or Matthews. As a result, individuals in prison were sometimes confused with other persons of the same name.[28] Suetonius reports that 'when a different man than he [Caligula] had intended had been killed, through a mistake in the names, he said that the victim too had deserved the same fate' (*Calig.* 30.1).[29]

Prisons may have generally been described as dark, filthy, disease-filled and crowded, but there were exceptions. Not all prisons in the Roman world could be described with those attributes.[30] Discussions of Paul's imprisonment in the book of Acts alone point to a wide variety of types of incarceration. Furthermore, as D.G. Reid notes, 'an official prison was not necessarily the norm; parts of buildings largely devoted to other uses could serve as prisons'.[31]

Archaeological evidence of ancient prisons is scarce and that which

28. At least on one level, this would support P. Winter's conjecture, in *On the Trial of Jesus* (New York: de Gruyter, 1974), pp. 142-43, that there might have been confusion during Jesus' trial between 'Jesus of Nazareth' and a certain 'Jesus Barabbas' (see the textual variants for Mt. 27.16).

29. A similar incident, this time involving Tiberius, is reported in Dio, 58.7. One way to prevent such confusion between prisoners can be seen in the fantastic writing known as *The Acts of Andrew and Matthias*. Here, in the Casanatensis 1104 manuscript, the prisoners are said to have had some type of identification tickets tied to their hands.

30. For extended discussions of specific prisons in the ancient Roman world, see the classic discussion in Krauss, *Im Kerker vor und nach Christus*, pp. 55-80. Cf. Rapske, *The Book of Acts and Paul in Roman Custody*, pp. 20-32.

31. D.G. Reid, 'Prison, Prisoner', in G.F. Hawthorne and R.P. Martin (eds.), *Dictionary of Paul and his Letters* (Downers Grove, IL: Inter-Varsity Press, 1993), p. 752.

has become available adds little to the evidence offered by literary sources.[32] One difficulty faced by archaeologists is determining whether an ancient site actually was a prison. For instance, although a cistern in Philippi and a fortification of a wall in Ephesus each came to be referred to as prisons where Paul had spent time, these claims were established fairly late and there is little evidence to argue for the validity of them.[33]

Furthermore, some archaeologists have pointed to the ruins of a building in Athens and have claimed that these ruins may well represent what was once a state prison. This building is near the Agora, at the southwest corner. It is large (40 by 17 meters). And thirteen little clay medicine bottles have been found at this site. Some have seen these bottles as having been used for hemlock. Did this building function as a prison? J.M. Camp writes that 'it probably served a public function'.[34] In describing the building, Camp notes

> a long corridor leads back to a large courtyard; five square rooms open off one side of the corridor, and three off the other. At the entrance there is a complex of four rooms, built on a different orientation but apparently contemporary.[35]

Camp mentions that the arrangement would work well as a prison, with the larger rooms serving as cells, the courtyard for multiple arrests, and the other four rooms for the guards. However, there is no clear evidence that these ruins were a prison. Rather, it needs to be noted that the building was not below ground (which one would expect), and it had individual rooms (which would have been odd for a prison). Furthermore, as Camp notes, 'set in an industrial area, the structure has

32. Because Josephus describes large numbers of prisoners in Jerusalem alone (e.g., the Idumaeans are said on one occasion to have freed some two thousand prisoners, *War* 4.353), it seems somewhat unusual that more archaeological evidence of ancient prisons is not available.

33. For a detailed discusion, see E. Dassmann, 'Archaeological Traces of Early Christian Veneration of Paul', in W.S. Babcock (ed.), *Paul and the Legacies of Paul* (Dallas: Southern Methodist University Press, 1990), esp. pp. 288-92. Unidentifiable sites near a city's forum are sometimes described as prisons. Cf. J. Finegan, *The Archaeology of the New Testament* (Boulder, CO: Westview Press, 1981), p. 105, writes that 'The location of the crypt as the possible place of imprisonment of Paul and Silas fits with a statement by Vitruvius…to the effect that prisons were ususally beside or near the forum of a city' (*On Architecture*, v. 2, 1).

34. J.M. Camp, *The Athenian Agora: Excavations in the Heart of Classical Athens* (New Aspects of Antiquity; London: Thames and Hudson, 1986), p. 113.

35. Camp, *The Athenian Agora*, pp. 113-16.

a plan suitable for a market building or *xenon* [hostel]'.[36]

One archaeological site known to tourists is the state prison of Rome; one of the oldest prisons. Juvenal looks longingly back to a time when this prison was the only one needed: 'Happy the days of old which under Kings and Tribunes beheld Rome satisfied with a single gaol' (*Sat.* 4.313-15). Livy also alludes to it, when he writes that 'Ancus Martius, to overawe the growing lawlessness, built a prison in the heart of the city overlooking the Forum'(Livy, 1.33.8). Two cells of this prison remain. M. Grant writes,

> The upper cell, which was originally one of a number, possesses a rounded vault of the tunnel or barrel variety, constructed with the help of concrete. The far end of the chamber is walled in by the rock of the Capitoline Hill, and at the side runs a transverse wall cutting into the vault.[37]

The lower cell, the most renowned execution-cell in Roman history, is known as the *Tullianum*. Sallust says of the Tullianum, that it is

> about twelve feet below the surface of the ground. It is enclosed on all sides by walls, and above it is a chamber with a vaulted roof of stone. Neglect, darkness, and stench make it hideous and fearsome to behold. (*Cat.* 55.3-4)

The *Tullianum* had the shape of a beehive, it originally had a wooden roof, and it probably served at one time as a reservoir for water.[38] It is not surprising that once individuals believed that the *Tullianum* was the place where Peter died, traditions would then build up around it. Today, for instance, at the top of the stairs leading down into the *Tullianum*, there is an inscription, by a large indenture in the wall, which claims, 'On this stone, Saint Peter's head was dashed by the guards and the marvel remains'.[39] Although the *Tullianum* offers some sense of what may have characterized incarceration, archaeological evidence in general has added little to our knowledge of ancient imprisonment.

---

36. Camp, *The Athenian Agora*, p. 116.

37. M. Grant, *The Roman Forum* (London: Weidenfeld and Nicolson, 1970), p. 127.

38. Cf. the description and illustrations of the *Tullianum* in C. Huelsen, *Das Forum Romanum: seine Geschichte und seine Denkmäler* (Rom: Verlag von Loescher & Co., 1905), pp. 112-16.

39. C. Berkeley, *Some Roman Monuments in the Light of History* (Banbury: F. Gough, 1931), p. 14.

4. *Prisoners' Status and Differential Treatment*

What determined whether individuals were imprisoned or how they were treated while in prison? Persons facing imprisonment generally were treated differently on the basis of their status. Although moderns generally take the concept 'equal before the law' for granted, just the opposite was assumed in Roman society: under the law, all persons were not equal. Marcus Cato, as quoted by Aulus Gellius, 11.18.18, writes, 'Those who commit private theft pass their lives in confinement and fetters; plunderers of the public, in purple and gold.' Ramsay MacMullen writes similarly that 'The higher your rank, the less severity to which you might be subjected. Two broad terms in law, *humiliores* and *honestiores*, eventually divided society formally for appropriate treatments by the judge.'[40] Those of the higher rank (*honestiores*) were not punished as severely as those of the lower rank (*humiliores*). Although legislation towards the end of the second century CE made these differences in punishment into legal fixtures, previous to such formal distinctions there was still a *de facto* recognition that status played a large role in determining how one was to be treated under the law:[41]

> Among Romans, everything depended on status. Several large distinctions received recognition in the courts: between those who were citizens, and aliens (most often called provincials, in the period of empire), or between those who were free, and slaves. Additionally, judges recognized the status of senators, town councillors (decurions or *curiales*), their kin and descendants, and looser categories both social and moral.[42]

Thus, sometimes the *honestiores* did not even find themselves with the option of being imprisoned; they might have been deported or sent into exile. J.P.V.D. Balsdon writes that

40. 'Personal Power in the Roman Empire', in *idem*, *Changes in the Roman Empire: Essays in the Ordinary* (Princeton: Princeton University Press, 1990), p. 192.

41. See J.M. Kelly, 'Improper Influences in Roman Litigation', *Roman Litigation* (Oxford: Oxford University Press, 1966), pp. 31-68. Also see P. Garnsey, *Social Status and Legal Privilege in the Roman Empire* (Oxford: Oxford University Press, 1970), pp. 207-209. For a listing of concrete examples of the differences in punishment, see W.A. Hunter, *Roman Law* (London: William Maxwell & Son, 2nd edn, 1885), pp. 1064-68.

42. MacMullen, 'Judicial Savagery in the Roman Empire', in *idem*, *Changes in the Roman Empire*, p. 204.

It was better to rid Rome of the physical presence of such convicted men or women than to take their life by execution. For, though there was nothing to offend anybody in the sight of slaves or members of the lower class dying in the torment of crucifixion or being thrown to make a meal for wild animals in the arena, the notion of execution of members of the upper class, however criminal, was offensive to the members of that class, who constituted the government.[43]

It is not surprising that Appius referred to the prison as 'the home of the Roman plebs' (Livy, 3.17.4).[44] As Dio Chrysostom wrote, people 'would never imagine that a beggar or a prisoner or man without repute was once king' (*Or*. 14.22).

At other times, status per se did not have as much to do with how one was treated. One's ability and opportunity to bribe the judge, the jailer, or others could become the significant factor in shaping how one would be treated.[45] During the administration of Albinus (who followed Festus), we are told that he accepted ransom from the relatives of those 'who had been imprisoned for robbery by the local councils or by former procurators; and the only persons left in gaol as malefactors were those who failed to pay the price'.[46] As will be seen later, bribes determined even whether or not the executioner would use a sharpened blade during a beheading. At times, however, status or even the ability to bribe had no influence on how one would be treated.[47]

Those who were financially liquid might avoid the horrors of prison

43. J.P.V.D. Balsdon, *Romans and Aliens* (London: Gerald Duckworth, 1979), p. 106.

44. Cf. *Dig*. 26.10.4: 'I do not think that those who have been placed in some position of rank ought to be confined in the state prison'. Also see *Dig*. 48.8.3.5-6.

45. See 'Visitors and Bribery', below, for a more detailed discussion of how bribes made a prisoner's lot much easier. During a later period, Libanius emphasized that 'the weaker, penniless masses' were treated particularly poorly (*Or*. 45.4).

46. Josephus, *War* 2.273. Cf. Achilles Tatius, *Clit. and Leuc*. 7.3.8.

47. Livy seems to highlight the fact that status had no influence, for instance, in the imprisonment of Lucius Scipio:

> But, of course, what cannot be obtained from his property the foes of Lucius Scipio will seek from his body and from his back, by means of persecution and insults, so that this most distinguished man may be shut up in prison among thieves of the night and brigands and may die in the darkness of a cell and then be cast out naked before the prison (38.59.10, cf. 38.58.4).

Livy's emphasis seems to be on the unusual nature of this treatment (also see Livy, 38.60).

not only through bribery, but also through posting of bail or sureties.[48] Under Antoninus Pius, accused persons who could put up bail were not to be imprisoned unless the charges were particularly grave.[49] Dionysius of Halicarnassus, *Ant. Rom.* 11.46.3, for instance, tells us that Appius was not allowed to post bail.[50]

Whether one was a Roman citizen was also supposed to determine how one was treated. Thus, Paul became indignant after he and Silas, uncondemned Roman citizens, were beaten publicly and thrown into prison (Acts 16.37). Verres, similarly, 'began to talk indignantly to people in Messena of how he, a Roman citizen, had been thrown into prison' (Cicero, *Verr.* 2.5.61).[51] Roman citizens were also supposed to face less violent deaths than aliens. In *The Martyrs of Lyons* 47, we are told that the governor beheaded all whom he thought to possess Roman citizenship, and the rest he condemned to the animals.[52] Roman citizenship was supposed to offer some protection, but such a status sometimes made little difference. Suetonius reports that Galba mocked a prisoner who said that he was a Roman citizen and, thus, should not be crucified. To insult this man even further, Galba 'honored' him by making his cross higher than the others and by painting it white (*Gal.* 9).

The figure of death, in prison, did not discriminate. As Libanius (*Or.* 45.11) wrote of those who had died in prison, 'Among them slaves and free die alike, some guilty of no offence at all, others of offences that do not deserve death.'

48. Ulpian notes that 'The proconsul normally determines the custody of accused persons, whether someone is to be lodged in prison, handed over to the military, entrusted to sureties, or even on his own recognizances. He normally does this by reference to the nature of the charge brought, the honorable status, or the great wealth, or the harmlessness, or the rank of the accused' (*Duties of Proconsul*, book 2, in *Dig.* 48.3.1). Cf. the discussion of bail in R. Taubenschlag, *The Law of Greco–Roman Egypt in the Light of the Papyri 332 BC–640 AD* (New York: Herald Press, 1944), pp. 412-13.

49. *Dig.* 48.3.3. Also see Achilles Tatius, *Clit. and Leuc.* 7.16.2; Livy, 3.13.5-13; 25.4.8-9, 25.4.11 (note here that eventually sureties made little difference in some situations). *P. Oxy.* 259 is an interesting example of a note which describes the bail posted for a particular prisoner named Sarapion.

50. Antiphon, *De caed. Her.* 17–18.

51. Cicero discusses the cry 'I am a Roman citizen' at more length in *Verr.* 2.5.65-67. As Cicero writes in 2.5.66, 'To bind a Roman citizen is a crime, to flog him is an abomination, to slay him is almost an act of murder: to crucify him is— what?'

52. Eusebius, *Hist. eccl.* 5.1.47. Cf. *The Acts of Paul* 11.3.

5. *Daily Life in Prison*

What sorts of activities, situations and events would have been familiar to those who had heard about imprisonment? Execution and torture would have stood out. However, most persons also would have had a basic knowledge of mundane affairs, of how prisoners kept active, of how they coped with incarceration, of how they were visited and treated.

Executions

Aside from prisoners dying as a result of the physical conditions of the prison itself, criminals also were executed, with strangulation, beheading, and hanging as the most common means employed by the Roman state.[53] When most people heard of prisons, the execution of criminals is one image which certainly must have come to mind: Cicero describes the *carcer* as the place 'where following the ordinances of our ancestors, we exact the penalty for heinous crimes when they have been exposed' (*Cat.* 2.27).

Execution in prison was common and to be expected, but records and reports also allow us glimpses into executions which stood beyond the pale of prison life. Dio, 18.1.3, describes the death of a certain Sabinus who was imprisoned in 28 CE, killed without trial, and whose body was then thrown into the river. Dio goes on to relate an incident which is so strange that it must reflect reality:

> This affair was tragic enough in itself in the eyes of all; but it was rendered still more tragic by the behaviour of a dog belonging to Sabinus that went with him to prison, remained beside him at his death, and finally leaped into the river with his body.[54]

53. E.g., Cicero, *Cat.* 4.13; *Vat.* 11; Livy 29.19.5-6; Plutarch, *Cic.* 22.2; *Phoc.* 36.2-4; Dio, 60.16.1; Pliny, *Ep.* 2.11.8; Tacitus, *Ann.* 3.51; *The Martyrs of Lyons* 27. J.S. Pobee, *Persecution and Martyrdom in the Theology of Paul* (JSNTSup, 6; Sheffield: JSOT Press, 1985), pp. 1-6, discusses this at more length, pointing to a number of primary sources which discuss executions by the Roman government. Note, however, that a wide variety of methods of execution were employed. For instance, Cicero mentions that Clodius, unable to extort money from an ambassador named Plator, threw him into prison. After Clodius called his own physician, he had him 'brutally' open Plator's veins (*Har. Resp.* 16). Others died after drinking poison (e.g., Josephus, *War* 1.639-40). Furthermore, rather than execute prisoners, some officials had a *de facto* policy which encouraged suicide. See 'Suicide' below.

54. Pliny the Elder, *HN* 8.61.145 also refers to this incident, writing that after Sabinus was killed and after his body was thrown outside, the dog was 'uttering

Dio also reports that Tiberius tortured one man very harshly and then, after realizing that the man had been falsely accused, he had him killed immediately 'declaring that he had been too terribly outraged to live with honour' (Dio, 58.3.7).[55]

Such wicked executions often were used as an exhibition of the magistrate's power. Gaius Caligula employed such power regularly. He was so conscious of the fear that his power radiated, that he published the names of those whom he had condemned, lest people not learn of the fate and condemnation of such persons (Dio, 59.18.2). Elsewhere, 'on signing the list of prisoners who were to be put to death later, he said that he was clearing his accounts' (Suetonius, *Calig.* 29.2).[56] When he saw a crowd of prisoners, he gave orders that they should be killed 'from baldhead to baldhead' (Dio, 59.22.3).[57] Furthermore, when putting prisoners to death, Caligula demanded that they die from numerous slight wounds. This soon became a well-known saying: 'Strike so that he may feel that he is dying' (Suetonius, *Calig.* 30.1).[58] Dio also describes one incident when Gaius had a certain praetor by the name of Junius Priscus accused with various charges, even though his death was due to Gaius' belief that he was wealthy: 'In this case Gaius, on learning that the man had possessed nothing to make his death worthwhile, made the remarkable statement: "He fooled me and perished needlessly, when he might just as well have lived"'. (Dio, 59.18.5)[59]

sorrowful howls to the vast concourse of the Roman public around, and when one of them threw it food it carried it to the mouth of its dead master; also when his corpse had been thrown into the Tiber it swam to it and tried to keep it afloat'. Dio, 61.35.4, notes that it was standard practice for the public executioners 'to drag the bodies of those executed in the prison to the Forum with large hooks, and from there [to haul] them to the river'. Cf. Suetonius, *Tib.* 61.

55. Suetonius also discusses this incident in *Tib.* 62.1.

56. Cicero also discusses a prison record kept under the reign of Verres. This record had the dates on which prisoners were received and the day on which they had died (*Verr.* 2.5.57 and 2.5.63).

57. Cf. Suetonius, *Gal.* 27.1-2.

58. Gaius' predecessor, Tiberius, also had the reputation for making executions drawn out and grisly. Cf. Suetonius, *Tib.* 63.2-3. In *Hist. eccl.* 8.9.4, Eusebius discusses an incident in which there were so many executions that 'the murderous axe was dulled and, worn out, was broken in pieces'.

59. This appears to be typical behavior for Caligula. Later in Dio 59.22.3-4, we are told that 'At another time he was playing at dice, and finding that he had no money, he called for the census lists of the Gauls and ordered the wealthiest of them to be put to death; then, returning to his fellow-gamesters, he said: "Here you are

Under Gaius' reign—actually under any emperor or governor's reign—death came upon prisoners in a variety of unpredictable ways. A Cornelius Celsus reports that certain Ptolemies in Egypt allowed physicians the opportunity to perform vivisections on persons taken from the prison:

> It becomes necessary to lay open the bodies of the dead and to scrutinize their viscera and intestines. They hold that Herophilus and Erasistratus did this in the best way by far, when they laid open men whilst alive—criminals received out of prison from the kings—and whilst these were still breathing, observed parts which beforehand nature had concealed... Nor is it, as most people say, cruel that in the execution of criminals, and but a few of them, we should seek remedies for innocent people of all future ages. (Cornelius Celsus, *Medicina* 1, *prooemium* 23–24, 26)

Other prisoners were subjected to drug testing. Galen reports that some kings who were interested in toxic substances experimented with antidotes on criminals under sentence (*De antidotis* 1.1).[60]

Torture
For the imprisoned, however, death was not the only fear. Terror and torture came in many forms:

> And yet what is to keep us from denying that even prisoners under sentence of death are punished until their necks are severed...if we account as punishment only the final moment of punishment and ignore the intervening sufferings, terrors, forebodings...?[61]

In addition to mental torture, bondage and physical torture were part of everyday life. Imprisonment so frequently involved being placed in chains that *synecdoche* was employed in texts, with the Greek and Latin words for 'chains' often interchangably used with the words for 'prison'.[62] Thus, Blandus talks about people making a reproach of his

playing for a few denarii, while I have taken in a good hundred and fifty million."'

60. See Herophilus, *The Art of Medicine in Early Alexandria* (ed., trans., and essays by H. Von Staden; New York: Cambridge University Press, 1989), p. 147. Cleopatra is said to have tested deadly poisons on prisoners condemned to death (Plutarch, *Ant.* 71.4; Dio 51.11.2).

61. Plutarch, *Mor.* 554E.

62. This reflects common usage. Legally, however, a distinction was preserved. Ulpian notes that 'It is right to suppose that someone who is shut up in prison is neither "bound" nor "in chains" unless chains are actually applied to his body' (*Dig.* 50.16.216). For a thorough discussion of the variety of chains employed, see Krauss, *Im Kerker vor und nach Christus*, p. 50.

chains (Seneca the Elder, *Controv.* 9.1.7), Paul refers to the Philippians as 'partakers of his bonds' (Phil. 1.7)[63], the author of Colossians exhorts his readers to 'remember my fetters' (Col. 4.18), and Ignatius says that he was learning in 'bonds to give up all desires' (*Rom.* 43).[64]

Prisons created a demand for chains. Yearning for days gone by, the days when Rome needed just one prison, Juvenal bemoans the crime and terror, and all the effort which necessarily went into curtailing them:

> What furnaces, what anvils are not groaning with the forging of chains? That is how our iron is mostly used; and you may well fear that ere long none will be left for plough-shares, none for hoes and mattocks. (*Sat.* 3.309-11)

Prisoners appear to have been chained almost all the time[65] and at night they were often put in stocks or some other type of intensified restraint.[66] Limbs were stretched in the stocks: *The Acts of Phileas* 1 (The Bodmer Papyrus) discusses rackings which went beyond the fourth peg; *The Martyrs of Lyons* 27 refers to 'the stretching of limbs in the stocks to the fifth notch'. Prisoners sometimes shared chains or irons;[67] sometimes their hands were tied behind them;[68] sometimes they were chained to guards.[69] Suetonius even notes an incident in 65 CE in which a number of conspirators 'made their defence in triple sets of fetters' (*Nero* 36.2).

It is difficult for us to imagine how painful such chains could have been, but Plutarch describes it well, when he describes the blessing of sleep:

63. Cf. Phil. 1.13, 14, 17; Phlm. 10, 13.

64. Ignatius repeatedly sees his identity in terms of the chains he wears and in terms of his being bound: *Eph.* 1.2, 11.2, 21.2; *Magn.* 1.2; *Trall.* 1.1, 5.2, 12.2; *Rom.* 1.1, 4.3; *Phld.* 5.1, 7.2; *Smyrn.* 10.2.

65. There were also prisons 'where the captives were not bound' (Philostratus, *VA* 7.22 and 7.40; note, however, that Apollonius is fettered in 7.28). Slaves legally had to be kept in chains until the conclusion of their trial (*Dig.* 48.16.16).

66. See Plutarch, *Mor.* 598B and Lucian, *Tox.* 29. In the latter passage, Lucian notes that Antiphilus, by day, wore a collar and manacles on one hand, but 'for the night he had to be fully secured by his bonds'. Livy (32.36.18) describes how magistrates in Rome, fearing an escape, increased the guard and made sure that the prisoners were 'loaded with chains of not less than ten pounds' weight'. Cf. Aullus Gellius, 20.1.45-46.

67. E.g., Lucian, *Tox.* 32; Josephus, *Ant.* 2.63.

68. *The Acts of Andrew and Matthias* 26.

69. Acts 12.6 describes Peter as 'sleeping between two soldiers, bound with two chains'. Cf. Josephus, *Ant.* 18.196 and 18.203; Seneca, *Ep.* 5.7.

> Sleep makes light the chains of prisoners, and the inflammations surround-
> ing wounds, the savage gnawing of ulcers in the flesh, and tormenting
> pains are removed from those who are fallen asleep. (*Mor.* 165E)[70]

An excellent example of the pain caused by chains can be seen in
Philostratus, *VA* 7.36. In this passage, a spy—sent into the prison by the
emperor Domitian—asks Apollonius,

> 'How can your leg endure the weight of the fetters?' 'I don't know', said
> Apollonius, 'for my mind is intent upon other matters'. 'And yet the
> mind', said the other, 'must attend to what causes pain'. 'Not necessarily',
> said Apollonius, 'for if you are a man like myself, your mind will either
> not feel the pain or will order it to cease.' 'And what is it that occupies
> your mind?' 'The necessity', answered Apollonius, 'of not noticing such
> things.'

Chains signified, among other things, shame and humiliation.[71] A
particularly interesting use of the symbolism of chains can be seen
among the Chatti, a Germanic tribe known for its *Blitzkrieg* approach to
battle. Tacitus notes that, among the soldiers of the Chatti, the bravest
'wear a ring of iron—the badge of shame on other occasions among this
people—in token of chains, until each man frees himself by the slaughter
of an enemy' (*Ger.* 31).

Chains signalled humiliation and shame. Thus, when a person had
been unjustly placed in irons, a symbolic removal of chains served to
also represent a removal of the disgrace which accompanied the chains.
Thus, in Josephus, *War* 4.628, Titus says to Vespasian, 'Justice demands,
father, that Josephus should lose his disgrace along with his fetters. If
instead of loosing, we sever his chains, he will be as though he had never
been in bonds at all'. We are told that an attendant then severed
Josephus' chain with an axe. Josephus relates that Gaius engaged in a

---

70. My thanks to L.L. Welborn for pointing me to this text. In Lucan, 2.73,
similarly, we are told of an old man's flesh which 'was corroded by iron fetters and
the squalor of long captivity'.

71. Numerous texts see chains as serving to humiliate the imprisoned (with chains
sometimes being used to lead prisoners in triumphal processions): e.g. Josephus, *Ant.*
18.119, 18.189-93, 18.195, 18.200, 18.232, 19.295, 20.114, 20.131; *Life* 13; *War*
2.229, 2.246, 2.457, 7.36, 7.154, 7.449; Plutarch, *Mar.* 12.2-3; Dio, 36.4, 41.3,
43.10.1-2, 58.3, 58.11.1, 63.3.4; Tacitus, *Ann.* 1.58, 4.28, 11.1; Pliny, *Ep.* 10.57;
Achilles Tatius, *Clit. and Leuc.* 8.8.4, 8.8.9-10; Cyprian, *Ep.* 76.2; *The Acts of
Thomas* 106; Livy, 26.13.15, 29.9.8, 29.19.5; Ovid, *Con. Liv.* 271-76; Diodorus
Siculus, 13.103.2; Dionysius of Halicarnassus, *Ant. Rom.* 20.16.1.

different sort of symbolic action when, after freeing Agrippa, 'in exchange for his iron chain, he gave him a golden one of equal weight' (*Ant.* 18.237 and 19.294).

Those who remained in chains often referred to them in a symbolic manner, seeing them as signs of power and prestige. In a description in *The Martyrs of Lyons* 35, for instance, we are told that the martyrs' 'chains were worn on them like some lovely ornament, as for a bride adorned with golden embroidered tassels'. In *The Martyrdom of Saints Montanus and Lucius* 6.2-4, the author seems to revel in being chained: 'The glory of being in bonds! The chains that were the object of all our prayers! Iron more noble and precious to us than the finest gold! Ah, the clanking of the chains as they were drawn over one another!' Furthermore, in *The Martydom of Pionius* 2–3, the presbyter Pionius 'took three sets of woven chains and placed them around his own neck and the necks of Sabina and Asclepiades'. Although they were not arrested for another full day, by wearing chains they had sought to make clear that they were ready to be led to prison rather than compromise their faith. Their willing acceptance of the chains took the sting and shame away from them.

Tales of more active physical torture are discussed in a wide variety of literature. Persons familiar with prisons, persons who would have heard about prisons, would have known of the types of torture which occurred there:[72] a description of such torture can be seen even in a child's bilingual school-book from this period:

---

72. Although torture—as mentioned below—often served as entertainment for the public, the imprisoned would anticipate the possibility of torture not only in the courtroom and the amphitheater, but also within the prison itself. For more detailed descriptions of methods of torture, see Antonio Gallonio, *De sanctorum martyrum cruciatibus* (Paris, 1660; English edition, *Tortures and Torments of the Christian Martyrs* [trans. A.R. Allinson; Paris, 1903]; republished Los Angeles: Feral House, 1989). That torture was a large part of prison can be seen in numerous texts. Philo's description of his visit to Gaius focuses on the role of torture in prison: 'Such was this combination of a theatre and a prison in place of a tribunal, theatre-like in the cackling of their hisses, their mockery and unbounded jeering, prison-like in the strokes inflicted on our flesh, the torture, the racking of the whole soul through the blasphemies against God and menaces launched upon us by this mighty despot' (*Leg. Gai.* 368). The brief discussion of torture in this monograph is representative of the primary sources, but is by no means exhaustive.

> The defendant, a bandit, stands. He is interrogated according to his deserts.
> He is tortured: the torturer beats him, his chest is constricted, he is hung
> up, racked, beaten with clubs, he goes through the whole gamut of tortures
> and still he denies. He is to be punished…he is led to the sword.[73]

Often the torture started even before one entered the prison.[74] King
Misdaeus, for instance, is said to have had the apostle Thomas scourged
with 128 lashes before he was chained in prison (*The Acts of Thomas*
106). Phileas describes prisoners who, after being tortured harshly, were
dragged naked to prison, 'and there with their limbs locked in the stocks
they were cast down on their backs, torn with fresh wounds, on ground
strewn with pieces of potsherd' (*The Letter of Phileas* 7–8).[75] In *The
Martyrs of Lyons* 28, we are told about young people who 'had not
suffered bodily torture before' and 'could not support the burden of
imprisonment and died in gaol'.

Torture was intended to break a prisoner down from the start. Seneca
refers to imprisonment and the various tortures which could accompany
it, in his emphasizing how fear, or the anticipation of possible torture,
could crush a prisoner's spirit. Seneca writes that if one imagined a huge
parade, one involving all the various types of torture, this itself would be
enough to break a person down:

> Surrounding it [the huge parade] is a retinue of swords and fire and chains
> and a mob of beasts to be let loose upon the disembowelled entrails of
> men. Picture to yourself under this head the prison, the cross, the rack, the
> hook, and the stake which they drive straight through a man until it pro-
> trudes from his throat. Think of human limbs torn apart by chariots driven
> in opposite directions, of the terrible shirt smeared and interwoven with
> inflammable materials, and of all the other contrivances devised by cruelty,
> in addition to those which I have mentioned!…the torturer accomplishes
> more in proportion to the number of instruments which he displays—
> indeed, the spectacle overcomes those who would have patiently withstood
> the suffering. (*Ep.* 15.4-6)

73. A.C. Dionisotti, 'From Ausonius' Schooldays? A Schoolbook and its
Relatives', *JRS* 72 (1982), p. 105.

74. Paul and Silas were also beaten with rods before being thrown into the prison
at Philippi (Acts 16.22-23). Also note that a certain Pothinus, who was over 90 years
old and quite ill, was beaten and then thrown into prison where he died two days later
(*The Martyrs of Lyons* 29–31). Cf. Josephus, *War* 2.269; 5.526. Cf. *The Martyrdom
of Pionius* 18.10-12.

75. *The Letter of Phileas* 9 discusses persons who were tortured, then, while
semi-conscious, thrown into prison where they would die a few days later.

Torture involved a variety of methods, mechanisms and machines: claws, whips, racks and metal plates were but four devices employed by soldiers and guards in Roman prisons.[76]

The ripping of claws is easy to imagine. A certain Papylus, it is said, 'was hung up and scraped and endured three pairs (of torturers)' (*The Martyrdom of Saints Carpus, Papylus, and Agathonicê* 35). Although Tertullian describes how the pampered prisoner Pristinus was so drunk with drugged wine that he thought the claws were a form of tickling (*De Ieiun.* 12), it is clear that that device reflected a horrible form of torture. One of the most thorough descriptions of what 'scraping' actually involved can be found in *The Letter of Phileas* 5 (the Latin version of Rufinus):

> Indeed, to be scraped with claws was considered an ancient and easy penalty. And if this type of torture happened to be used on anyone, they did not merely lay open their sides (as in the case of robbers and murderers), but also the belly, thighs, and legs, the claws coming even to the soles of their feet, so that even their faces and foreheads were not free of torment. And to crown all, after these human bodies were mangled without any humanity, they were exposed to public view: stripped not only of their clothing but even of their skin, they thus became a grim spectacle to all passers-by.

The Babylonian rabbis write that this was also the torture which faced Rabbi Akiba, after his imprisonment and before his death. As described in *b. Ber.* 61b, 'as the soldiers began to tear the living flesh off his bones with hooks of iron, he began to recite the Shema'.[77] Tertullian, in *De Ieiun.* 12, describes the importance of imprisoned Christians not paying undue attention to their physical condition in prison. When a Christian does not overindulge, as Tertullian writes, 'the tortures may not even have material to work on, since he is cuirassed in a mere dry skin, and cased in horn to meet the claws'.

Other prisoners, we are told, were 'chastised with whips. They were scourged until their flesh was torn to shreds, and their blood reddened the ground'.[78] Prisoners were sometimes beaten with cudgels, with rods,

---

76. See Eusebius, *Hist. eccl.* 8.10.3-10.

77. Cited in D.R. Cartlidge and D.L. Dungan, *Documents for the Study of the Gospels* (Philadelphia: Fortress Press, 1980), pp. 184-85.

78. *The Martyrdom of the Saints Justin, Chariton, Charito, Evelpistus, Hierax, Paeon, and Valerian* 5.

with scourges, with thongs, with whips of rope.[79] When Nero found out that he had been declared a public enemy by the senate and that the senate was planning on punishing him in the ancient fashion (*mos maiorum*), he learned that this meant that he would be 'stripped, fastened by the neck in a fork, and then beaten to death with rods' (Suetonius, *Nero* 49.3).

Some prisoners faced the rack. Racking in antiquity is associated often with Procrustes, the wily innkeeper who stretched those who did not fit into his bed. Those who did not fit into Roman society encountered a similar fate. Some were attached to wooden horses with pulleys, by which the prisoners' limbs were pulled apart:

> Others were fastened by one hand and hauled up from the portico, and no pain could have been more intense than the stretching of their joints and limbs. Others were tied to columns facing inwards with their feet off the ground, the weight of the body forcing the bonds to tighten.[80]

A martyr named Marian was put on the rack with the thongs which bore the weight put on the joints of his thumbs instead of about his hands; unequal weights then were put on each of his legs.[81] Apelles, we are told, 'was thrown by Gaius into chains of iron and tortured by the rack and the wheel in turns like people suffering from recurring fevers'.[82]

Metal plates were also used in torture. Cicero describes how Verres bound and flogged a Roman citizen, and then continued to torture him with 'fire and hot metal plates and the like'.[83] Similarly, in *The Martyrs of Lyons* 20ff., Sanctus is described as having been tortured with red-hot bronze plates being placed against the tenderest parts of his body, so that 'his body bore witness to his suffering, being all one bruise, and one wound, stretched and distorted out of any recognizably human shape'. Potamiaena faced her death in prison through an extended form of torture, where 'boiling pitch was slowly poured drop by drop over different parts of her body, from her toes to the top of her head'.[84]

---

79. *The Letter of Phileas* 5 (the Greek text of Eusebius).
80. *The Letter of Phileas* 5 (the Greek text of Eusebius).
81. *The Martyrdom of Marian and James* 5.5-7.
82. Philo, *Leg. Gai.* 30.206. Apuleius discusses a slave who also underwent the wheel and the rack (Apuleius, *Met.* 10.10), and we read descriptions of a barber in Athens who was fastened to the wheel and was racked for a long time (Plutarch, *Nic.* 30). Cf. Demosthenes, *Aphobus* 3.40.
83. *Verr.* 2.5.63. Cf. Ovid, *Met.* 3.695-700.
84. *The Martyrdom of Potamiaena and Basilides* 4.

Where torture was ineffective in exacting the sort of response a magistrate desired, other options were available. *The Martyrdom of Saint Conon* 5 refers to a prefect who became angry with Conon and who, in the process, lists a catalogue of horrors which hanged above the heads of those who were imprisoned:

> You may not obey me, but the tortures will teach you to cower. And if you despise the tortures, I shall kill you by throwing you to a most fierce lion, or else I shall give you as food to the beasts of the sea, or I shall have you put to death by hanging on a cross, or I shall throw you into a cauldron heated by a blazing fire and so melt away your flesh unless you sacrifice to the invincible and eternal gods.[85]

The arena and the amphitheater hosted all sorts of brutal punishments ranging from torture to execution and from fighting with wild beasts to battling with gladiators.[86] By making torture and execution into a public spectacle, private patrons and the Roman government were able not only to punish the imprisoned[87] and not only to provide an effective means of discouraging others from committing similar crimes, but also to find a means to entertain the citizenry.[88] Josephus refers to Jewish prisoners who, 'half-devoured by wild beasts, have been preserved alive to provide them with a second repast, after affording merriment and sport for their foes' (*War* 7.373-74). A better description of what was involved in such 'merriment' can be found in Philo's description of Flaccus' persecution of the Jews. Philo writes that Flaccus crucified a number of them

85. Much of the terror involved in any form of imprisonment involved expectations. Josephus notes that Jewish prisoners of the Zealots were terrified because of the unexpected fury of their captors. These 'tortured wretches in the prisons pronounced even the unburied happy in comparison with themselves' (*War* 4.384).

86. See Ammianus Marcellinus, *Constantius et Gallus* 14.2.1; Tacitus, *Ann.* 15.44; Suetonius, *Calig.* 18; Philostratus, *VA* 4.22; Josephus, *Apion* 1.43; 2.53-54; and Josephus, *Ant.* 19.7.5. Cf. MacMullen, 'Judicial Savagery in the Roman Empire', in *idem, Changes in the Roman Empire*, pp. 206-207 and p. 358.

87. Generally those who had committed the most serious crimes were the ones who were forced into the amphitheater. E.g., Callistratus, *Dig.* 48.28; Paulus, *Sent.* 6.7.3.1; Quintillian, *De Cognit.* 6.9, 21. Furthermore, it should be noted that Roman citizens generally were exempt from this sort of punishment. See above, 'The Status of Prisoners and Differential Treatment'.

88. Not all citizens, however, were entertained. Seneca, *Ep.* 7, spoke out against these events, emphasizing that they brought out the worst traits of the spectators.

after maltreating them with the lash in the middle of the theatre and torturing them with fire and the sword. The show had been arranged in parts. The first spectacle lasting from dawn till the third or fourth hour consisted of Jews being scourged, hung up, bound to the wheel, brutally mauled and haled for their death march through the middle of the orchestra. After this splendid exhibition came dancers and mimes and flute players and all the other amusements of theatrical competitions. (*In. Flacc.* 84–85)

Some prisoners played a key role in the amphitheater show, even though they did not make it as far as the arena. It is reported that Gaius Caligula , when cattle became too costly to feed to the wild beasts which he had provided for a gladiator show, randomly removed persons from the prison and let the beasts devour them.[89]

We are also told of convicted criminals who were forced to dress up as particular characters and, in the course of acting in tragedies, were killed as part of the show. Tertullian says 'We have seen at one time or other Atys, that god from Pessinus, being castrated; and a man, who was being burned alive, had been rigged out as Hercules'.[90] Claudius, keen on exhibiting a naval battle on the Fucine Lake, built a huge wooden wall around the lake, erected stands, placed one hundred boats in the lake (fifty for each side), and then used condemned criminals to take part in this sea-fight: 'one party being styled "Rhodians" and the other "Sicilians"' (Dio, 61.33.3).

Aside from torture's use in 'public entertainment', the most perverse or brutal magistrates may have used torture also as after-dinner entertainment. In the *Controversies* of Seneca the Elder we are presented with a case where the proconsul Flamininus was asked by a prostitute with whom he was dining, whether she might be able to see a man's head cut off. So as to entertain his guest, Flamininus complied. A random condemned criminal was taken from prison and 'the victim of sadism was slaughtered', but, as a result, the proconsul did have to face legal charges (*Controv.* 9.2). Another dinnertime execution might be more familiar to readers of the Gospels. When Herodias' daughter

89. Suetonius, *Calig.* 29. To place this action in its broader context, see G. Jennison, *Animals for Show and Pleasure in Ancient Rome* (Manchester: Manchester University Press, 1937), pp. 28-98 and pp. 137-82; and O.F. Robinson, *Ancient Rome: City Planning and Administration* (New York: Routledge & Kegan Paul, 1992), pp. 168-69.

90. Tertullian, *Apol.* 15.5. See 15.4-7, along with *De Spect.* 7, where Domitian is described as having staged a play where one of the characters, played by a condemned prisoner, was actually crucified on stage.

requested the head of the imprisoned John on a platter, the king sent a soldier of the guard to accomplish the task (Mk 6.17-29; Mt. 14.3-12).

Women's Prison Experience

Women in antiquity, whom the state condemned of crimes, were punished in a variety of manners. Although men were judged by the state, women often were turned over to relatives and judged by their own family.[91] Thus, in 154 BCE, after the wives of two consulars were convicted of poisoning their husbands, their relatives condemned these women and executed them through strangulation. Conversely, although the Senate found Pomponia Graecina accused of 'foreign superstition', her husband acquitted her. The patriarchal system in Rome made the family, or more specifically the patriarch, responsible if someone in his family broke the law.[92]

If not judged by their family, women who committed a crime faced a variety of fates. Sometimes they were put into brothels.[93] Often,

91. For a full discussion of this, see J.F. Gardner, *Women in Roman Law and Society* (Bloomington: Indiana University Press, 1986), pp. 5-30 (also note her qualifications on p. 26 n.6). Cf. Livy, 39.18.6. Here Livy writes—with respect to the Bacchanalia controversy—'Convicted women were turned over to their relatives or to those who had authority over them, that they might be punished in private: if there was no suitable person to exact it, the penalty was inflicted by the state.' D.L. Balch, *Let Wives Be Submissive: The Domestic Code in I Peter* (SBLDS, 26; Atlanta: Scholars Press, 1981) also provides much illuminating material on how household codes functioned, and on how society controlled the roles of women.

92. Gardner, *Women in Roman Law and Society*, p. 7, describes this well when she writes, 'The *paterfamilias* was legally liable for the actions of his children, both male and female, as well as his slaves, and if one of these committed a delict, the *pater* must either make himself responsible in court for the damages, or surrender the guilty person'. The responsibility of the patriarch for his family is also seen in such early Christian documents as 1 Timothy, Titus and *The Shepherd of Hermas*, where church officers must have their own house in order before they assume office. Plutarch, in *Mor.* 70C and 144C, emphasizes that those who wish to be involved in public life need to show a home life characterized by concord. Unlike twentieth century politics, where debates often rage over whether public and private life should be seen in light of each other, the system of patriarchy in the ancient world did not afford the *paterfamilias* the luxury of asking that such distinctions be made: 'public' and 'private life' were intertwined.

93. In *The Martyrdom of Pionius* 7.6, it is said that 'Women who refuse to sacrifice are put into a brothel'. In *The Martyrdom of Agapê, Irenê, and Chionê* 5.8, Irenê was sentenced to be placed naked in the public brothel. Tertullian refers to a similar incident in *Apol.* 50.12, writing, 'Lately, when you condemned a Christian girl

preceding their sentencing, they were placed in prison with men.[94]

Of course women faced situations in prison peculiar to their gender. Perpetua appealed and received permission that her young, nursing baby might stay with her in prison (*The Martyrdom of Perpetua and Felicitas* 3.9). Similarly, Dion's wife was imprisoned while pregnant, and gave birth to a boy. The women in the prison then had to receive permission from the guards to raise the child (Plutarch, *Dion* 57.5). Raising a child in prison appears to have been a somewhat rare practice, although there are numerous accounts of women giving birth while there. Births in prison resulted, at least in part, from an Egyptian law which the Greeks and Romans adopted. This law stipulated that a pregnant woman under sentence of death would be allowed to remain alive in prison until the child was born.[95] This law is said to have distressed Felicitas:

> She feared that her martyrdom would be postponed because of her pregnancy...Thus she might have to shed her holy, innocent blood afterwards along with others who were common criminals. (*The Martyrdom of Perpetua and Felicitas* 15)

Some women, it appears, may even have gotten pregnant while in prison. In the *Babylonian Talmud*, in *b. ʿAbod., Zar.* 22b, we are told that 'A woman who had been imprisoned by heathens in connection with money matters, is permissible to her husband, but if on a capital charge, she is forbidden to her husband.' In *b. Sanh.* 37b, we are told that Assir (meaning 'imprisoned') received his name because his mother conceived him in prison.[96]

Women faced other horrors in prison. In the name of piety, prison

to the pander rather than the panther, you admitted that we count an injury to our chastity more awful than any penalty, than any death.'

94. Cf. *The Martyrdom of Pionius* 11.2-3, *The Martyrdom of Perpetua and Felicitas*, and Dio 60.16.1. Since we have no prosopographies of ancient prisons, it is difficult to tell how many women were imprisoned and what the ratio of women to men was. Because of the role of the family, women were very likely in the minority in prison.

95. Cf. *Dig.* 48.19.3; Plutarch, *Mor.* 552D; Aelian, *VH* 5.18; Philo, *Virt.* 139; *The Martyrdom of Agapê, Irenê, and Chionê* 3.7; and Clement, *Strom.* 2.18.93. A pregnant woman was also 'not to be interrogated under torture so long as she is pregnant' (*Dig.* 48.19.4).

96. Cf. *b. Hullin* 11b. The *Babylonian Talmud* goes so far as to describe when a child is to be circumcised, if both the mother and the father are imprisoned (*b. Yeb.* 71b).

guards raped condemned virgins: 'Since ancient usage made it impious to strangle maidens, young girls were first violated by the executioner and then strangled'.[97] A young girl who herself had done no wrong, but was the daughter of a Senator who had committed a crime, was thrown into prison, 'having been first outraged by the public executioner on the principle that it was unlawful for a virgin to be put to death in the prison' (Dio, 58.3.5). Plutarch also tells us of an instance where two maidens, rather than being raped and executed, were allowed to take their own lives.[98]

Aside from all of these horrors, brave women who underwent torture faced not only racks and claws, but also male egos. A number of examples stand out. After Nero, for instance, ordered Epicharis to be racked, 'neither the lash nor fire, nor yet the anger of the torturers, who redoubled their efforts rather than be braved by a woman, broke down her denial of the allegations'.[99] In his *Metamorphoses*, Apuleius refers to a particularly perverse execution: a woman was sentenced to have sex with a mule in the arena and, during their intercourse, the woman and mule were to be slaughtered by wild animals.[100] Finally, Eusebius notes that Christian women were tortured in a manner that even insulted their chastity:

97. Suetonius, *Tib.* 61.5. Cf. Tacitus, *Ann.* 6.5.9. This also appears to be the subject of conversation in *The Martyrdom of Potamiaena and Basilides* when the judge threatens to hand Potamiaena 'over to his gladiators to assault her physically'. Thecla, in *The Acts of Paul* 3.27, somehow avoided this fate by asking 'of the governor that she might remain pure until she was to fight with the beasts'. Although rape was a capital charge (see Gardner, *Women in Roman Law and Society*, pp. 118-21), the violation of condemned women appears to have been beyond the law. It does not take a great deal of imagination to assume that jailers and guards did not violate merely condemned women. In Plutarch, *Mor.* 598, we are specifically told that 'not a few women' prisoners, now set free, trod and spat on the corpse of a particular jailer, whom the women's rescuers had run through with a cavalry lance.

98. Plutarch, *Mor.* 253C-E. Here, Megisto, along with a group of other women, curbs the violence of the crowd by claiming that a people who claims to be democratic cannot engage in 'recklessness and wanton violence like despots'. Eusebius also describes a woman and her daughters who took their own lives rather than face sexual abuse (*Hist. eccl.* 8.12.3-4, cf. *Hist. eccl.* 8.14.14).

99. Tacitus, *Ann.* 15.57. *The Martyrs of Lyons* 18 emphasizes that Blandina underwent horrid punishment, but that she 'was filled with such power that even those who were taking turns to torture her in every way from dawn to dusk were weary and exhausted'.

100. *Met.* 11.23, 28-29, and 34.

> Women were fastened by one foot and swung aloft through the air, head-downwards, to a height by certain machines, their bodies completely naked with not even a covering; and thus they presented this most disgraceful, cruel and inhuman of all spectacles to the whole company of onlookers. (*Hist. eccl.* 8.9.1)

Suicide and Shame

With all the tales of torture in antiquity, with the fear of insult during trial, it is not surprising to read about the frequency of suicide in Roman prisons. Often the magistrates and guards needed to ensure that prisoners did not take their own lives.[101] The Senate of Rome, for instance, warned the Areands to keep especially close guard over Minius Cerrinius, 'not only to prevent his escape but also to allow him no opportunity to commit suicide' (Livy, 39.19.2). As mentioned earlier, Gallus—during the reign of Tiberius—was imprisoned and guarded 'not to prevent his escape, but to prevent his death' (Dio, 58.3.5). Furthermore, Habrocomes, in Xenophon's *An Ephesian Tale*, desired to commit suicide, but he had no opportunity because of all the guards.[102] Other prisoners sought to take their own life, but were prevented from doing so by friends: for example, Sejanus 'opened his veins with a penknife, but allowed himself to be bandaged and restored...because of the entreaties of his friends' (Suetonius, *Vit.* 2.3).

At least four different—but often complementary—reasons lie behind the imprisoned wanting to take their own lives. Some did so out of despair. Some persons took their own lives to avoid 'insult and outrage' in their conviction. Some did so apparently to avoid a fate worse than death. Some did so in order that their property might not be taken by the government and denied to their children.

Philostratus offers what seems to be a typical picture of the emotions of prisoners in his *VA* 7.26. He writes that of those imprisoned with Apollonius, 'some of them were sick, some of them had given way to dejection, some of them expected death with certainty and with resignation, some of them bewailed and called upon their children and their parents and their wives'. Such despair led numerous prisoners to take their own lives. If one had been falsely accused, if freedom seemed like an unrealistic dream, or if one felt totally abandoned, depression natu-

---

101. The *Digest* 48.3.14.3-6 discusses legal actions, from Herennius Modestinus, which were to be followed if a prisoner died during a particular guard's watch.

102. See below.

rally set in. When Habrocomes was 'fettered and cast into prison, dark despair seized upon him, and especially when he saw no Anthia. He tried many methods of inducing death, but could find none, for those who guarded him were many' (Xenophon of Ephesus, *An Ephesian Tale* 7.1). The prisoner Antiphilus, who was not used to a life as severe as that which prison dealt and who found the conditions of the prison intolerable for him, was 'giving up the struggle and refusing even to take food' when his friend Demetrius found him and helped give him the strength to continue.[103]

Imprisonment was also a shame for many.[104] We are told that Herod's brother Phasael, not wanting to bear the shame of imprisonment by the Parthians and 'considering death with honour better than life at any cost, died by his own hand' (Josephus, *Ant.* 15.12-13). Not wanting to die at the hands of a foe, he 'dashed his head against a rock' (Josephus, *Ant.* 14.367-69). Similar motivations seem to be reflected in two deaths which Seneca relates in *Ep.* 70. In the first instance, we are told of a German prisoner at a wild-beast gladiator training school. After going to relieve himself (the only thing which he was allowed to do in private and without a guard), he grabbed the stick of wood and sponge, which was used for cleaning the anus, and stuffed it down his throat, clogging his windpipe and choking himself to death (70.20). In another instance, a prisoner, who was being taken in a wagon to fight in the gladiator games, let his head fall until it became caught in the spokes; 'then he kept his body in position long enough to break his neck by the revolution of the wheel' (70.23).

The shame one experienced in prison must have had long-term effects. The term δεσμῶτα, which is used in Achilles Tatius, *Clit. and*

103. Lucian, *Tox.* 29–30. A few centuries later, Libanius expressed this sentiment well: 'It is a much easier matter for the prisoners to give up the ghost than to see their bones sticking out through their hides' (*Or.* 33.41). Cf. Achilles Tatius, *Clit. and Leuc.* 7.6.

104. Dio, 58.15.2. Also see the rash of suicides which broke out during the reign of Tiberius (e.g. Dio, 58.27.3-5; Tacitus, *Ann.* 6.40). A.J.L. van Hooff, *From Autothanasia to Suicide: Self-Killing in Classical Antiquity* (New York: Routledge & Kegan Paul, 1990), p. 15, writes that 'during the Late Republic and the Early Empire committing suicide becomes something of a moral duty for the nobleman who loses face or the favour of the emperor'. Note that in Quintillian, *Inst.* 7.4.39, there is a discussion of cases where 'a senator sets forth to the senate the reasons which determine him to commit suicide'. Perhaps shame is what drove Aristonicus to end his life in prison (Strabo, *Geography* 14.1.38).

Leuc. 8.1.3, is clearly used in a pejorative sense.[105] Diogenes Laertius mentions that Anaxagoras, even after he was freed from prison, felt that he had suffered such indignity that he took his own life (2.13). Solon, so many years earlier, argued that thieves must not only restore what they stole but, in addition, should also be imprisoned: 'they must pay double; they must be imprisoned as well as fined, and so live in disgrace for the rest of their lives' (Demosthenes, *In Timocr.* 115).

Others were imprisoned, we are told, as a way of humbling and humiliating them. Camillus was said to have been so hated by the civil tribunes, that they desired that this man who had won the most famous wars might incur disgrace by being hauled to prison by the tribunes (Dionysius of Halicarnassus, *Ant. Rom.* 13.5.1). Livy, 3.18.1-2, notes that Gaius Claudius went about the Forum (ca. 449 BCE), entreating persons so that the Claudian race would not be branded 'with the shame of being held to merit imprisonment and chains'. Disgrace and shame accompanied imprisonment, and they led the imprisoned frequently to take their own lives.

Other prisoners killed themselves rather than encounter a worse fate.[106] After Epicharis had undergone torture for an entire day, she was dragged back in a chair for more. Rather than undergo this,

> she fastened the breast-band (which she had stripped from her bosom) in a sort of noose to the canopy of the chair, thrust her neck into it, and, throwing the weight of her body into the effort, squeezed out such feeble breath as remained to her. (Tacitus, *Ann.* 15.57)

Similarly, Plutarch tells us of the two young maidens (mentioned above) who chose suicide rather than face rape and execution (*Mor.* 253C-E).

Some of the imprisoned committed suicide because of fiscal reasons. It was said that if the imprisoned killed themselves, the government would not impound their property and, thus, their children could legally inherit it.[107] In *Ann.* 6.29.1, Tacitus describes how this 'legal loophole' worked and, as a result, why some took their own lives:

> This kind of death was often put into people's minds by fear of the executioner, and also because, if convicted, a man's property was confiscated and his burial forbidden, whereas those who settled their own fates had

105. Cf. *The Acts of Thomas* 145.
106. E.g., Dio, 59.18.3; Tacitus, *Ann.* 11.2.
107. E.g., Dio, 58.15.4. Cf. Livy, 29.19.5-6; *Dig.* 48.21.3; 49.14.45.1-2. Cf. R.S. Rogers, *Criminal Trials and Criminal Legislation Under Tiberius* (Middletown, CT: American Philological Association, 1935), p. 50.

their bodies buried and their wills respected—a bonus for getting it over quickly.

Such a policy was advantageous to the imprisoned and their children (or it was more advantageous than some scenarios), but this policy also created a margin of safety for Tiberius who, by encouraging persons to become their own murderers, tried to avoid the reputation of having killed for political reasons.[108]

Sleeping and Dreaming

It is difficult to say how persons managed to sleep in prison. Plutarch tells us that sleep was a welcome comfort, that it 'makes light the chains of prisoners' (*Mor*. 165E), but numerous sources say that the imprisoned did not sleep well. Plutarch mentions that Philopoemen could not sleep, being 'overwhelmed with trouble and grief' (*Phil*. 20.2). That reaction was typical. In a dangerous, hot, crowded environment, where torture and the fear of death were everpresent, prisoners did not sleep well.[109] Persons outside the prison even bribed the guards, so that they might stay with their imprisoned friends and gave them the opportunity to sleep.[110]

In any case, there is very little extant evidence which mentions 'prisoners' sleeping quarters'. Prisoners likely slept where they were chained. Apollonius, it is said, slept on a cot (Philostratus, *VA* 7.30), Agrippa slept on a make-shift bed which his friends made out of garments (Josephus, *Ant*. 18.204), Philopoemen was lying down wrapped in his soldier's cloak (Plutarch, *Phil*. 20.2), some prisoners slept on pallets and others slept in the stocks (Plutarch, *Mor*. 598B). Although Antiphilus slept on the ground, this might be a reflection of the particularly harsh treatment which he experienced (Lucian, *Tox*. 29).

When the imprisoned slept, they often had intense dreams.[111] From as

108. In Diodorus Siculus, 31.9.3, we are told that Perseus was even encouraged to kill himself: 'A sword with which to kill himself was thrown down to him, and a noose for hanging, with full freedom to use them as he might wish.'

109. E.g., Philostratus, *VA* 7.30; Lucian, *Tox*. 29 and 32; *Peregr*. 12. When Perseus offended his guards, he 'was prevented from sleeping until he died of it' (Diodorus Siculus, 31.9.7).

110. See Chapter 5 for a more detailed discussion of how visitors to prison refreshed the incarcerated.

111. A belief in the ability of dreams to communicate messages (generally about the future) was prevalent in classical antiquity to a degree wholly unknown among moderns. Therefore, it is not surprising that the ancients would have seen the dreams

far back as the book of Genesis, we are told that the imprisoned Joseph
had the opportunity to interpret the dreams of two fellow prisoners: the
chief butler and the chief baker of the king.[112] Some would say that the
trauma of confinement lent itself well to inspirational dreams and visions.
Robin Lane Fox claims that the physical conditions of prison, linked
with the psychological trauma which accompanied imprisonment, likely
would have resulted in some fantastic visual experiences:

> Every inmate was awaiting trial and sentence in a setting which was hot,
> cramped, and dark. These 'sensory deprivations' are fast breeders of
> visions, seen with remarkable rapidity by subjects placed 'in a dark room'.
> It is not, then, so surprising that the promises in the Gospels were freely
> realized. Visions abounded, and like the prisoners in Solzhenitsyn's First
> Circle, the waiting Christians kept up morale by telling each other their
> dreams.[113]

Dreaming was bound to occur in such cramped, hot, uncomfortable
quarters. Plutarch has an extensive discussion on how prisoners (specifically, guilty prisoners) have dreams—'agonies of terror'—which torment
them and remind them of the evil they have done (*Mor.* 554E–555C).[114]

Dreams were also common, however, among those innocent who
were imprisoned. In Xenophon, *An Ephesian Tale* 8.2, Habrocomes has
a hopeful dream where his father Lycomedes comes to the prison and
releases him. Perpetua—in *The Martyrdom of Perpetua and Felicitas*
4.1—is said to be 'greatly privileged' and to have the ability to ask for

---

of persons in prison as being significant or revelatory. For an interesting discussion
of the differences between ancient and modern dream interpretation, see S.R.F. Price,
'The Future of Dreams: From Freud to Artemidorus', *Past and Present* 113 (1986),
pp. 3-37.

112. Gen. 40. Also see Philo, *Jos.* 17 and Josephus, *Ant.* 2.63-86.

113. Fox, *Pagans and Christians*, pp. 400-401.

114. Although Plutarch is referring initially to the bad dreams which come upon
prisoners, the examples he then offers do *not* explicitly mention imprisonment.
Regardless, they are illustrative. After Apollodorus murdered a boy named Callimeles
and then served the boy's body and blood to his fellow-conspirators (see Polyaenus
6.7.2), he dreamt that he saw himself flayed and then boiled by Scythians (555B). He
also had a nightmare in which he saw his daughters on fire and running all about him,
possibly a reference to an incident told in Polyaenus 6.7.1 (555B). Plutarch then tells
us that during one night in Byzantium, Pausanias sent for a woman named Cleonicê
so that he might sleep with her. However, as she approached him, Pausanias became
wildly suspicious and killed her. From then on he was tormented by her in his
dreams, with her saying 'come meet thy doom; by pride are men undone' (555C).

visions. Although her dreams (4.2-10; 7.3-8 and 10.1-14) are signs of liberation, they are, at least in modern terms, fairly macabre: she dreams of a vicious dragon; she dreams of her tortured brother, who had 'died horribly of cancer of the face'; she dreams that she becomes a man and has to battle with, and eventually pummel, an Egyptian.[115] Many in antiquity believed that imprisoned persons, on the verge of death, had insights into a different realm.[116] Such a perspective is described in Juvenal, *Sat.* 6.560-64:

> For nowadays no astrologer has credit unless he has been imprisoned in some distant camp, with chains clanking on either arm; none believe in his powers unless he has been condemned and all but put to death, having just contrived to get deported to a Cyclad, or to escape at last from the diminutive Seriphos.

Eating

In *The Acts of Andrew and Matthias* 1–2, we are told that the cannibals who lived in Myrmidonia seized visitors to their city, gouged out their eyes, and forced them to drink a drug, after which these cannibals led the visitors to a prison where, without clothing, the visitors would be forced to fatten up on hay and grass for thirty days.[117] Of course, such an account says little, if anything, about eating in ancient prisons. It is unfortunate that some of the most basic facts concerning life in prison are not reported at greater length. There are few descriptions either of prisoners eating or of what they ate; only isolated instances are known.

One discussion of prison food comes in a document from the late fourth century: Libanius' *45th Oration* ('Concerning the Prisoners'). In ch. 9, Libanius' concerns both for penal reform and for prisoners' relatives (who had to beg to support the imprisoned) lead to a discussion of the diet of prisoners:

115. Christian martyrdoms contain many descriptions of dreams. In *The Martyrdom of Saints Marian and James*, Marian—after experiencing harsh bodily torture—falls into an unusually deep sleep and has an intense dream (6.5). In 7.1 and 11.3 James then dreams, and in 8.1 a man named Aemilian also has a revelatory dream. Cf. *The Martyrdom of Saints Montanus and Lucius* 5.1; 7.1-8; 8.1-7; 11.1-5; *The Acts of Andrew* 8.

116. Cf. Plutarch, *Mor.* 431E–433E. Here Lamprias, speaking apparently for Plutarch, states that all souls are able to prophesy, but this generally occurs in dreams and near the time of death.

117. D.R. MacDonald, *The Acts of Andrew and The Acts of Andrew and Matthias in the City of the Cannibals* (Atlanta: Scholars Press, 1990), pp. 72-73.

Where does the food come from for all these? The soup in their pots, their few greens, and anything else besides, all this, they say, is much below their needs. Their wives, sisters, daughters, who were supported by them before their imprisonment, must needs be the ones to support them now.[118]

Written a little closer to the time period with which we are concerned, Seneca's *Epistle* 18 directs his readers to lead a disciplined regimen, lest they not be prepared when forced to cope with a harsher lifestyle. A regulated diet is central to such a disciplined life. Seneca writes

For though water, barley-meal, and crusts of barley-bread, are not a cheerful diet, yet it is the highest kind of pleasure to be able to derive pleasure from this sort of food, and to have reduced one's needs to that modicum which no unfairness of Fortune can snatch away. Even prison fare is more generous; and those who have been set apart for capital punishment are not so meanly fed by the man who is to execute them. Therefore, what a noble soul must one have, to descend of one's own free will to a diet which even those who have been sentenced to death have not to fear! This is indeed forestalling the spear-thrusts of Fortune. (*Ep.* 18.10-11)

Both Libanius and Seneca are partisan in their writing. Libanius is concerned with prison reform, and so he is more than willing to paint the bleakest picture possible of prison life. Seneca is concerned with showing the rigors which need to be undergone in the life of a true student of philosophy, and so he—on the other hand—is more than willing to use his description of prison as a foil. He believes that persons will experience the highest pleasure by leading a disciplined life; a life even more austere, in some respects, than that of a prisoner.

What did prisoners eat? Libanius mentions soup and greens. Athenaeus' *Deipnosophistae* 4.161C describes prison fare as bread and water. Regardless of what prisoners received, it was generally seen as unappetizing. Dio Chrysostom presents Charidemus as referring to the 'unappetizing and wretched food which is given to prisoners'(*Or.* 30). In *The Martyrdom of Saints Montanus and Lucius* 6.5, we are told that 'there were very many ill, suffering from the prison fare and the cold water' (cf. 12.2).

Furthermore, the quantity of food which each prisoner received was not enough to sustain. *The Martyrdom of Saints Montanus and Lucius*

118. Libanius continues by describing some of the psychological pain which results from this situation: wives, sisters, and daughters, ugly and aged beg, 'while those who have any looks at all endure every kind of outrage'. R.A. Pack, *Studies in Libanius and Antiochene Society under Theodosius* (1935), presents a series of essays on Libanius and this particular oration.

21.12 mentions the 'skimpy prison rations'. *The Martyrdom of Saints Marian and James* 8.2 presents a pagan antagonist confronting a Christian by asking how he was dealing with 'the starvation of prison'. Plutarch, in *Mar.* 12.4, describes the imprisoned Jugurtha as 'struggling with hunger'. Drusus, the son of Germanicus, is said to have been 'so tortured by hunger that he tried to eat the stuffing of his mattress' (Suetonius, *Tib.* 54).[119] And Gallus, imprisoned under Tiberius in 30 CE, found that 'the food was of such quality and amount as neither to afford him any satisfaction or strength nor yet to allow him to die' (Dio, 58.6). Because the rations in prison tended to be so meager, prisoners sometimes fasted, so that others could eat more.[120] Numerous people are said to have died from hunger.[121]

It is to be noted, as Libanius says, that friends and relatives frequently took food to the imprisoned. Whether this was out of necessity or not, the texts leave the impression that it was very important.[122] This practice, however, was not without abuses. Lucian informs us that the meals which Christians took to the imprisoned Peregrinus were quite elaborate (*Peregr.* 12). Tertullian even mocks some Christians' practice of 'furnishing cookshops in the prisons to untrustworthy martyrs, for fear they should miss their accustomed usages, grow weary of life, (and) be stumbled at the novel discipline of abstinence' (*De Ieiun.* 12).

One type of meal eaten by the imprisoned is particularly notable. The 'free banquet' (*cena libera*)[123] was the last meal—the elaborate dinner—

119. Cf. Tacitus, *Ann.* 6.23.

120. E.g., Lucian, *Tox.* 30 mentions that Antiphilus refused to take food. It is also to be noted that in later centuries, imprisoned Christians often fasted, sometimes on specific days (as they would have even if they had not been in prison), sometimes more often (for altruistic reasons). *The Martyrdom of Fructuosus* 3.2 refers to the imprisoned Fructuosus observing the stational fast on Wednesday. The author of *The Martyrdom of Saints Montanus and Lucius* 21.12 mentions that 'when the others took even their meagre fare from the worst sort of skimpy prison rations, Flavian alone abstained from his tiny share, preferring to be worn by frequent and voluntary fasts provided the others could be fed on his food'. *The Martyrdom of Saints Marian and James* 8.1 also refers to Aemilian as fasting in prison (cf. 8.4, which emphasizes 'the satisfying food of God's word').

121. Eusebius, *Hist. eccl.* 8.8.2. Cf. Cyprian, *Ep.* 21.2.

122. For examples of friends and relatives delivering food to the imprisoned, see 'Visitors and Bribery' below and Chapter 5.

123. Cf. Plutarch, *Mor.* 1099B; and Tertullian, *Apol.* 42.5. Tertullian mentions that he does not attend these feasts, feasts which appear to have been open to the public. In *The Martyrdom of Perpetua and Felicitas* 17.1, we are told that the imprisoned

eaten by those prisoners who were forced to engage in gladiatorial battle in the arena. Such extravegence on the part of the Roman government did not stem from generosity. This was no offer of a last request or a final cigarette to the condemned. Rather, such an offer was specifically made to those who were going to be engaging in gladiatorial battle; in other words, to those who were going to serve as entertainment for the Roman masses. A last meal might give the combatants the extra strength which would make for an enjoyable show.[124] After all, the Roman masses would find a weak or emaciated opponent bad entertainment or even pitiful.[125]

Preparing for Trial

To ensure that they would not face the executioner in the future, some prisoners kept busy preparing the defence for their trial. Thus, when Apollonius entered prison, although he wished to chat with the other prisoners so as to simply keep himself busy, his sidekick Damis innocently asked 'Will they not think us babblers and bores, if we interrupt them in the preparation of their defence...?' (Philostratus, *VA* 7.22). Apollonius goes on to say that the imprisoned were just the sorts of persons who wanted someone to talk with them and comfort them. Of course, part of the reason why Apollonius might have assumed that conversation would have been more valuable to these persons than the preparation of their defence is the fact that he himself put little, if any, forethought into his defence. One night before falling asleep, he and Damis discussed his plan:

> 'And how could I prepare myself', said Apollonius, 'when I do not even know what questions he will ask of me?' 'Then you are going to defend your life *extempore*?' said Damis. 'Yes, by Heaven', he replied, 'for it is an *extempore* life that I have always led'.[126]

Christians 'celebrated not a banquet but rather a love feast'.

124. Although I am talking here about functions which the meal may have had (for this, also see *The Martyrdom of Perpetua and Felicitas* 16.4), this explanation does not account for the origin of the meal. On this, see M.Z. Brettler and M. Poliakoff, 'Rabbi Simeon ben Lakish at the Gladiator's Banquet: Rabbinic Observations on the Roman Arena', *HTR* 83 (1990), pp. 93-98. Brettler and Poliakoff argue that this dinner 'is not a last request but a ritual, paralleled by many societies, for making a worthy sacrificial victim: his blood becomes, then, in the rabbis' words, "sweet"' (p. 97).

125. Seneca, *Prov.* 3.4, emphasizes that even gladiators believed it was disgraceful to be matched with an inferior.

126. *VA* 7.30. Apollonius here is modeled after Socrates. When Hermogenes saw

Others, however, put much more thought into their defence: some of these defences were unsuccessful; some, successful; some, of unknown outcome. Plutarch tells readers of one plan which backfired (*Alc.* 21.2-4). While in prison, a certain Timaeus convinced Andocides, a fellow prisoner, to turn state's evidence against himself. Timaeus was convinced that this would result both in Andocides' immunity and in the freedom of others. Although Andocides was indeed then set free, the others—including Timaeus—were put to death.

Other defences, written in prison, appear to have been more successful, even if they did not manage to save the lives of those who wrote them. Cicero refers to the defence of Furius of Heraclia, written against Verres, and claims that 'there is no one in Sicily today who does not possess this speech, and read it, and learn from it, Verres, the tale of your crimes and your cruelty' (*Verr.* 2.5.43).

Other reports of defences leave little or no record of the effectiveness of the efforts. *P. Yale* 34 presents an example of a prisoner's (?) efforts to find a witness who would be of great help in building his case:

> Skythes to Ptolemaios, greeting. Come to Talao immediately, bringing also the shepherd who is to give evidence about the matters of which you spoke to me. If you do this slowly you will harm yourself, for I am not at leisure to remain longer. Farewell.[127]

A similar effort at planning a defence (or in creating the impression that a defence was being planned) can be seen in 2 Tim. 4.9-13. Michael Prior offers a compelling case that these requests at the end of the letter make much more sense if one presumes 'that both the cloak and the parchments were required in connection with the public hearing of Paul's case' (perhaps as proof of his status as a Roman).[128] If Paul did not write 2 Timothy, these admonitions might be seen as emphasizing the abandonment of Paul. If, as Prior argues, Paul did write 2 Timothy,

---

that Socrates was discussing 'any and every subject rather than the trial, he had said: "Socrates, ought you not to be giving some thought to what defence you are going to make?" That Socrates had at first replied, "Why, do I not seem to you to have spent my whole life in preparing to defend myself?"'(Xenophon, *Ap.* 2–3). In *VA* 4.46, the imprisoned Musonius writes to Apollonius, saying, 'Socrates was put to death, because he would not take the trouble to defend himself, but I shall defend myself'.

127. This translation is found in M. Prior, *Paul the Letter-Writer and the Second Letter to Timothy* (JSNTSup, 23; Sheffield: JSOT Press, 1989), p. 231 n.10. Also see Prior's discussion of a similar document, *P. Yale* 42 (p. 231, n.11).

128. Prior, *Paul the Letter-Writer*, pp. 153-54.

these admonitions serve a very practical function. Having been abandoned, Paul now needs witnesses and evidence.

Writing, Working and Talking

In addition to persons working on their defence, they also needed to find other ways to keep active in prison. If they were to be imprisoned for an extended period of time, if they simply did not know when their imprisonment would end (through death, freedom or trial), they had to find ways to use their time and to make sense of their day. Thus, a wide variety of fairly mundane events occurred in prison. Some prisoners played dice or draughts (Plutarch, *Mor.* 554D). Canus, Seneca writes, was playing chess (*ludebat latrunculis*), when he was summoned to his death (*Tranq.* 14.7).[129] Rabbi Akiba, an authority on the calendar, computed three leap years while in prison (*b. Sanh.* 12a). Furthermore, R. Akiba even had Jews address legal questions to him while he was imprisoned.[130] The Mishnah reflects that some persons composed a writ of divorce while imprisoned.[131] And Cicero tells of a man whose friends brought tablets and witnesses to the prison, where they wrote his will (*Inv. Rhet.* 2.49.149).

Christians engaged in a wide variety of activities, not all of which were uniquely Christian. Tertullian reports that the imprisoned Pristinus, in 'free custody', apparently had access to 'all the baths...to all the retreats of voluptuousness...and to all the allurements of this life' (*De Ieiun.* 12). More positive pictures of imprisoned Christians show them reading their sacred books aloud,[132] breaking bread,[133] praying[134] and singing.[135] Later

---

129. Seneca notes that Canus 'counted the pawns and said to his partner: "See that after my death you do not claim falsely that you won"; then nodding to the centurion, he said: "You will bear witness that I am one pawn ahead".'

130. Two examples are found in the *Babylonian Talmud: b. Yeb.* 105b, 108b. Also see *b. Git.* 6.7.

131. *Git.* 6.5 and 6.7.

132. *Peregr.* 12.

133. *The Acts of Paul* 7.

134. Acts 16.25; *The Acts of Thomas* 107–108; and *The Acts of Andrew and Matthias* 3 and 21. In the former, as Thomas prayed, 'all the prisoners looked at him, and besought him to pray for them'. Also see *The Martyrdom of Perpetua and Felicitas* 7.1, 15.4-5; *The Martyrdom of Pionius* 11.7 and 18.12; *The Martyrdom of Saints Marian and James* 5.10, 8.1; *The Martyrdom of Bishop Fructuosus* 12.1.4; *The Martyrdom of Saints Montanus and Lucius* 17.4. It should also be noted that, in *The Testament of Joseph* 8.5 and 9.4, Joseph is described as frequently at prayer in prison.

135. Acts 16.25; *The Acts of Andrew and Matthias* 3. After Jesus appeared to

accounts of imprisoned Christians mention that baptisms took place within prison.[136]

Other prisoners are reported as continuing their work. Ulpian, in *Dig.* 4.6.10, says that prisoners are to be helped, 'if they are shown not to have been able to look after their own business'.[137] It is repeatedly noted that Socrates wrote and presented some of his most memorable discourses in prison.[138] Naevius, similarly, wrote two plays: the *Soothsayer* and the *Leon*.[139] Sextius Paconianus composed verses in prison against the king (Tacitus, *Ann.* 6.39).[140] And Anaxagoras was 'busied with squaring the circle' (Plutarch, *Mor.* 607F).[141]

A variety of horrors and perils also awaited prisoners. Sometimes prisoners exploited each other. When Jugurtha was cast into prison, Plutarch notes, 'some tore his tunic from his body, and others were so eager to snatch away his golden ear-ring that they tore off with it the lobe of his ear' (*Mar.* 12.3). Petronius tells of 'a boy who played the part of a woman in a slaves' prison (*ergatulum*)' (*Sat.* 81). Furthermore, prisoners were sometimes forced to be active on work details,[142] prisoners' lives were subject to the whims and mood swings of jailers or magistrates[143] and prisoners sometimes were killed by fellow prisoners (e.g. Lucan, 2.75-83).

Matthias in prison and promised deliverance to him, Matthias praised him and began to sing. Later, when Andrew came to rescue Matthias (in ch. 19), Matthias was occupied, singing by himself. Cf. Acts 16.25.

136. E.g., *The Martyrdom of Saints Montanus and Lucius* 2; *The Martyrdom of Bishop Fructuosus* 2.1; *The Acts of Paul* 7.

137. Cf. Rapske, *The Book of Acts and Paul in Roman Custody*, p. 325. Rapske notes that this law is concerned primarily with 'legal actions from which an individual might suffer disadvantage or loss related to business or other material interests he or she holds outside the prison'.

138. Cf. Plato, *Phd.* 60D; Epictetus, *Diss.* 2.1.32; 2.6.26-27; and 2.13.24; Diogenes Laertius, 2.24, 42; Plutarch, *Mor.* 607F and 466F; Cicero, *Tusc.* 1.40.96-97; and Seneca, *Ep.* 67.7 (cf. *Ep.* 24.4). Also see Aeschines' *Epistle to Xenophon* 5–6 (trans. S. Stowers), in A.J. Malherbe, *The Cynic Epistles: A Study Edition* (SBLSBS, 12; Missoula, MT: Scholars Press, 1977), pp. 254-57.

139. Aulus Gellius, 3.3.15.

140. It should also be noted, however, that he was subsequently strangled in prison for having composed these verses.

141. Cf. Aeschines' *Epistle to Xenophon* 5–6.

142. Eg., Philostratus, *VA* 5.19; Livy, 13.19.4; Philostratus, *Life of Nero (or The Digging of the Isthmus)* 3.

143. In Philostratus, *VA* 7.34 stands a representative example. Domitian, irritated

The imprisoned also simply talked and had conversations. Referring to prisoners' conversations, Achilles Tatius writes, 'In misfortune man is a creature always inquisitive to hear about another's woes; community of suffering is something of a medicine for one's own troubles' (*Clit. and Leuc.* 7.2.3). Socrates kept busy with philosophy and encouraged those with him to do the same (Plutarch, *Mor.* 607F). Apollonius said 'I lead exactly the same life here (in prison) as I would outside; for I converse about casual topics, and I do not need anything' (Philostratus, *VA* 7.28).

It should be noted, however, that prison officials sometimes refused to allow prisoners the right even to speak in prison. Tiberius denied some in prison from 'not only the consolation of reading, but even the privilege of conversing and talking together' (Suetonius, *Tib.* 62).[144] In *The Martyrdom of Pionius*, the Christians in prison celebrated, 'for they were at liberty to discourse and to pray night and day' (11.7). Even when prisoners had the right to speak, however, often it was prudent for them to curb their tongue, since informers sometimes were sent into prison to spy, to encourage persons to slander the Emperor, or to get information for prosecutors.[145]

With the presumption of guilt often hanging over them,[146] prisoners needed some outlet to cope with incarceration in ways other than simply playing dice. Some people coped through the help of other prisoners, who served as psychagogues and moral counselors. Others coped by turning to philosophical teachings or to God. And others recalled Platonic notions of dualism, so as to put their imprisonment in a broader perspective.

Psychagogues and Moral Counselors

Those individuals who were able to guide and help other prisoners often are held forth, in ancient texts, as exemplary figures. In Philo, *Jos.* 81, it is said concerning Joseph that 'in the prison he displayed such a wealth of virtue that even the vilest of the inmates were astounded and over-

with Apollonius, 'began to insult the sage, by cutting off his beard, and hair, and confining him among the vilest felons'.

144. Also note that during his imprisonment by Tiberius, Gallus did not speak or see anyone (Dio, 58.5).

145. See Philostratus, *VA* 4.44; 7.27; 7.36 and Achilles Tatius, *Clit. and Leuc.* 7.1-2 and 7.4. Cf. Epictetus, *Diss.* 4.13.5.

146. Although Saint Syncletice uses the reference to make a spiritual point, she writes that 'People in the world who commit crime are thrown into prison against their will' (*Apophthegmata Patrum* 7.18, as quoted in O. Chadwick, *Western Asceticism* (Philadelphia: Westminster Press, 1958), p. 87.

awed, and considered that they had found in him a consolation for misfortunes and a defence against future ills'. In sections 85–87, when Joseph is granted the opportunity to watch over the jail, having gained the trust of the prisonkeeper,[147] then

> the place, as they felt, could not rightly be called a prison, but a house of correction [σωφρονιστήριον]. For instead of the tortures and punishments which they used to endure night and day under the lash or in manacles or in every possible affliction, they were rebuked by his wise words and doctrines of philosophy, while the conduct of their teacher effected more than any words. For by setting before them his life or temperance and every virtue, like an original picture of skilled workmanship, he converted even those who seemed to be quite incurable.

Joseph's exodus from the prison is so formative and is seen as such a vindication that righteousness will overcome bondage, that it is remembered in the *Babylonian Talmud* as having taken place on New Year (cf. *Roš. Haš.* 11a).

Similarly, the imprisoned Apollonius took it upon himself to comfort the other prisoners, 'lest their own feelings destroy them before Domitian' could do it. His words are said to have had such an effect on his companions in the prison, that most of them 'wiped away their tears, and walked in hope, believing that they could never come to harm as long as they were in his company' (Philostratus, *VA* 7.26).

This sort of comfort and consolation is repeatedly seen in descriptions of the imprisonment of Christian apostles. *The Passion of Andrew* says that Andrew spoke 'with his fellow inmates, whom he already had strengthened by encouraging them to believe in the Lord...even though imprisoned he was not quiet, but in fact urged on his fellow inmates and extolled in the Lord's power' (28–29). Similarly, *The Acts of Andrew* has Andrew encouraging andexhorting a great crowd of the brethren (15–18).[148]

The most influential psychagogue, however, seems to have been Socrates. Although Socrates served his fellow prisoners, writing paeans during his imprisonment (Epictetus, *Diss.* 2.6.27), Seneca ascribes to him a more significant role for prisoners throughout history. In *Ep.* 24.4-5, Seneca emphasizes that Socrates refused to flee from prison, but he

---

147. Cf. *T. Jos.* 2.3.

148. Similarly, when Judas Thomas was taken out of prison in *The Acts of Thomas* 125, 'all the prisoners were grieved because the apostle was departing from them'. Cf. *The Acts of Paul* 11.3.

stayed, 'in order to free mankind from the fear of two most grievous things, death and imprisonment'.[149]

Psychagogy and Moral Exhortation

One way in which philosophy encouraged persons to work through their imprisonment was to expect it; they were to prepare for the worst. Epictetus emphasizes that when crises call, his students are not to run off to read their compositions, but they must show their ability to undergo hardships, showing confidence and trust in the one who has called them to undergo such hardships. Epictetus writes, 'Let others practise lawsuits, others problems, others syllogisms; do you practise how to die, how to be enchained, how to be racked, how to be exiled' (*Diss*. 2.1.38).[150] In a similar manner, Epictetus encourages his students to prepare for the worst, to assume, for instance, that they would face imprisonment. When evil does befall them, then, 'immediately the thought that it was not unexpected will be the first thing to lighten the burden' (*Diss*. 3.24.103-109).[151]

Much literature in antiquity dealt with imprisoned persons trying to understand their predicament. Often this literature referred to great persons, such as Socrates, who were unjustifiably imprisoned by those who were their inferiors. The 'just man' was often imprisoned, and those in prison reminded themselves of those figures who had gone before them.[152] Thus, Apollonius of Tyana, in an oration to his fellow-prisoners, says,

149. Elsewhere, Seneca notes that Socrates spent thirty days in prison not hoping for freedom or other options, but seeking to 'show himself submissive to the laws and make the last moments of Socrates an edification to his friends' (*Ep*. 70.9).

150. Seneca, similarly, encourages his readers to follow the advice of Epicurus and 'Think on death'. Seneca goes on to write, 'he who has learned to die has unlearned slavery; he is above any external power, or, at any rate, he is beyond it. What terrors have prisons and bonds and bars for him' (*Ep*. 26.10).

151. Cf. *Diss*. 1.4.23-24 where Epictetus refers to the important goal of studying 'how a man may rid his life of sorrows and lamentations, and of such cries as "Woe is me!" and "Wretch that I am!" and of misfortune and failure, and to learn the meaning of death, exile, prison, hemlock; that he may be able to say in prison, "Dear Crito, if so it pleases the gods, so be it", rather than, "Alas, poor me, an old man, it is for this that I have kept my grey hairs!"'

152. See Plato, *Rep*. 361E-362A; and Cicero, *Rep*. 3.17.27 for classic discussions of the suffering which the just man endures. Also see J.T. Fitzgerald, *Cracks in an Earthen Vessel: An Examination of the Catalogues of Hardships in the Corinthian Correspondence* (SBLDS, 99; Atlanta: Scholars Press, 1988) esp. pp. 55-100.

When we think of these things, and reflect on the many wise and blessed men who have been thrown into prison by wanton mobs, or insulted by despots, let us accept our fate with resignation, that we may not be found inferior to those who have accepted the same before us. (Philostratus, *VA* 7.26)

In his defense, the Christian apostle Apollonius employed passages both from the Septuagint and from the canon of philosophy:

For the wicked have no use for the righteous. Wherefore it is written that the ignorant say unjustly, 'Let us imprison the just man, for he is useless to us'.[153] So too one of the Greeks has written for us to hear: 'The just man', he says, 'will be whipped, tortured, bound, his eyes gouged out, and after suffering all sorts of penalties will finally be impaled on the gallows.'[154]

Another way in which Epictetus encouraged persons to accept their hardships was to bring them to realize that divine forces (specifically, Zeus) were using such hardships as tests. Zeus exposes his creatures to poverty, exile and imprisonment neither because he hates them nor because he neglects them, but 'because He is training me, and making use of me as a witness to the rest of men' (*Diss.* 3.24.113-14).[155] If one remembers these things, Epictetus goes on to emphasize, 'you will never need a person to console you, or strengthen you'. Finding one's strength in God or in fate was one way in which prisoners found meaning in their condition.[156] Plutarch argues, similarly, that even Fortune 'compounds

153. Isa. 3.10 (LXX).

154. *The Martyrdom of Apollonius* 38–40. This final quotation is adapted from Plato, *Rep.* 2.5.361E.

155. Similarly, in *Prov.* 4.8, Seneca writes, 'All those who are called to suffer what would make cowards and poltroons weep may say, "God has deemed us worthy instruments of his purpose to discover how much human nature can endure."' Comparably, Tertullian writes, 'We, with the crown eternal in our eye, look upon the prison as our training-ground, that at the goal of final judgment we may be brought forth well disciplined by many a trial; since virtue is built up by hardships, as by voluptuous indulgence it is overthrown' (*Ad Mart.* 3).

156. In *The Acts of John* 103, 'the Lord' is described as being 'at hand even now in prisons for our sakes, and in tombs, in bonds and dungeons,…being the God of those who are imprisoned, bringing us help through his own compassion'. Similarly, in *T. Jos.* 1.6 and 2.3-4, Joseph is presented as saying, 'I was in prison, and the Savior acted graciously on my behalf. I was in bonds and he loosed me…I was jailed, I was whipped, I was sneered at, but the Lord granted me mercy in the sight of the prison-keeper. For the Lord does not abandon those who fear him, neither in darkness, or chains, or tribulation or direst need.'

hemlock, she carries swords...she claps on fetters, and builds prison-enclosures' (*Mor.* 499A). Referring to Rutilius's exile, Regulus's torture, and Socrates' death, Seneca says that Fortune 'seeks out the bravest men to match with her; some she passes by in disdain' (*Prov.* 3.4). Tertullian similarly notes that a Christian in prison should 'suffer there not penalty, but discipline, and not the world's tortures, but his own habitual observances' (*De Ieiun.* 12). In addressing martyrs, he writes, 'You have come within its (the prison's) walls for the very purpose of trampling the wicked one under foot in his chosen abode' (*Ad Mart.* 1).

Prisoners may also have been reminded—as philosophical texts taught—that 'adversity has little or no effect on the calmness and joy of the wise man'.[157] Epictetus captures this well:

> What, then, is the punishment of those who do not accept [their condition]? To be just as they are... 'Throw him into prison.' What sort of prison? Where he now is. For he is there against his will, and where a man is against his will, that for him is a prison. Just as Socrates was not in prison, for he was there willingly. (*Diss.* 1.12.21-23)

Epictetus elsewhere emphasizes that even when 'external things'[158] might look bleak, the sage keeps the situation in perspective:

> When the tyrant threatens and summons me, I answer 'Whom are you threatening?' If he says, 'I will put you in chains', I reply, 'He is threatening my hands and my feet.' If he says, 'I will behead you', I answer, 'He is threatening my neck.' If he says, 'I will throw you into prison', I say, 'He is threatening my whole paltry body.' (*Diss.* 1.29.5)[159]

Finally, philosophical teachings reminded prisoners not to lose hope. Diogenes is presented as saying that all human ills have one consolation; that they may come to an end: 'the prisoner in chains expects some time

---

157. J.T. Fitzgerald, *Cracks in an Earthen Vessel*, p. 62. See Fitzgerald's entire section on 'The Serene and Steadfast Sage', pp. 59-65. Phocion is described as one who embodies this ideal (Plutarch, *Phoc.* 36.1-37.1). Cf. Seneca, *Ep.* 85.41.

158. Cf. Epictetus, *Diss.* 1.30.2-3, where exile, imprisonment, bonds, and death are referred to as 'things indifferent'.

159. Similarly, in *Diss.* 2.6.25, Epictetus emphasizes that 'A platform and a prison is each a place, the one high, and the other low; but your moral purpose can be kept the same, if you wish to keep it the same, in either place.' Tertullian articulates a comparable position, when he writes, 'The Christian outside the prison has renounced the world, but in the prison he has renounced a prison too. It is of no consequence where you are in the world—you who are not of it...Let us drop the name of prison; let us call it a place of retirement' (*Ad Mart.* 2). Cf. Cyprian, *Ep.* 33.2.

to be set free; it is not impossible for the exile to return to his home; and he who is sick can hope until the end comes for recovery' (Dio Chrysostom, *Or.* 40).

'*Prison*' as Metaphor

> We men are in a prison all the time which we choose to call life. For this soul of ours, being bound and fettered in a perishable body, has to endure many things, and be the slave of all the affections which visit humanity; and the men who first invented a dwelling seem to me not to have known that they were only surrounding their kinds in a fresh prison; for, to tell you the truth, all those who inhabit palaces and have established themselves securely in them, are, I consider, in closer bonds in them than any whom they may throw into bonds. (Philostratus, *VA* 7.26)

Apollonius's soliloquy to his fellow prisoners shows how the metaphor of imprisonment might have been used to comfort those who faced physical incarceration by the Roman government. A common way to blunt the sorrow or pain which the imprisoned felt was to emphasize that their prison was only one type of prison, and that persons remained trapped regardless of their physical conditions.[160] In *VH* 1.39, Lucian refers to persons who live a luxurious life as 'roaming at large in a great prison that they cannot break out of'. In *Ep.* 24.17, Seneca emphasizes that one should not fear being put in chains, since one is never free from bonds: 'Behold this clogging burden of a body, to which nature has fettered me!' Plutarch emphasizes that 'nature leaves us free and untrammelled; it is we whobind ourselves, confine ourselves' (*Mor.* 601D).[161]

Dio Chrysostom makes a similar point in an even more commanding way, when he writes

> But much more do I marvel at and pity you for the grievous and unlawful slavery under whose yoke you have placed your necks, for you have thrown about you not merely one set of fetters or two but thousands, fetters by which you are throttled and oppressed much more than are those who drag themselves along in chains and halters and shackles. For they have the chance of release or of breaking their bonds and fleeing, but you are always strengthening your bonds and making them more numerous and stronger. (*Or.* 80)

160. See Dio Chrysostom, *Or.* 80.7. For a theological approach to this same argument, see Tertullian, *Ad Mart.* 2.
161. Cf. Plutarch, *Mor.* 554D.

Similarly, in *Or.* 30 (*Charidemus* 11–14), Dio Chrysostom presents Charidemus as claiming that because humans were hateful to the gods, they are now punished by them, on earth, for as long as each person should live. Charidemus emphasizes that it is the universe which is a prison:

> This place which we call the universe, they tell us, is a prison prepared by the gods, a grievous and ill-ventilated one…Then in addition to all this, because men cannot endure the bad air and changes of temperature, they devise for themselves other small prisons, namely their houses and cities…And the plants which grow all about us and the fruits of the earth…are just like the unappetizing and wretched food which is given to prisoners, but we nevertheless put up with it on account of the necessity which is upon us and our helplessness…Also, we are composed of the very things which torture us, namely, soul and body. For the one has within it desires, pains, angers, fears, worries, and countless such feelings; and by day and by night it is ever racked and wrenched by them.

Charidemus continues the metaphor, emphasizing that persons are not freed from the prison, generally, until they bear someone to be punished in their stead. He emphasizes that the prisoners do not stay voluntarily but that many are bound fast by a single chain (body and soul). The methaphor goes even further, when Charidemus claims that 'since the poor are leaner, the bond which lies about each of them is looser and easier', whereas the fetters pinch the rich and stout (17–24). Here is where Charidemus pivots from what initially appears to be a negative description of fetters and imprisonment to an understanding of how one might best endure and appreciate his or her confinement.

Also common in antiquity was the metaphor of the body as 'prison',[162] with Platonic thought undergirding this concept.[163] As Plato emphasized, 'if we are to ever know anything absolutely, we must be free from the body and must behold the actual realities with the eye of

162. E.g., Plato, *Cra.* 400C. Here Socrates refers to the Orphic poets and their belief that the body is 'an enclosure to keep it [the soul] safe, like a prison'. Cf. Plato, *Phd.* 62B, for the discussion that human beings are in a sort of prison; and Philo, *Somn.* 1.139.

163. See the discussion of Plato in Plutarch, *Mor.* 607D. Note that the author of the second-century Christian work *Epistula ad Diognetum* presumes that his audience will accept this doctrine, and then proceeds to extend this Platonism into the Christian realm: 'The soul has been shut up in the body, but itself sustains the body; and Christians are confined in the world as in a prison but themselves sustain the world' (6.6).

the soul alone' (*Phd.* 67D). Persons ranging from Cicero to Philo, from the Essenes to Plutarch, referred to the body as a prison which guarded both the mind and the soul. Josephus described the Essenes, for instance, in a manner which he thought would strike home with his Greek readers. The Essenes are seen as 'sharing beliefs with the sons of Greece', particularly in their understanding of the soul:

> Emanating from the finest ether, these souls become entangled, as it were, in the prison-house of the body, to which they are dragged down by a sort of natural spell; but when once they are released from the bonds of the flesh, then, as though liberated from a long servitude, they rejoice and are borne aloft. (*War* 2.154-55).

Philo refers to the mind as being 'cabined and cribbed' in the body, like a prisoner in a jail (*Ebr.* 101). This metaphor naturally developed more and more extensions on the basic theme. Philo encourages his readers to 'Depart, therefore, out of the earthly matter that encompasses thee: escape, man, from the foul prison-house, thy body...and from the pleasures and lusts that act as its jailers' (*Mig.* 9).[164] Various permutations of this perspective existed in ancient philosophy. Thus, when Cicero speaks with God, asking whether his father and others who have passed away were really still alive, God answers, 'Surely all those are alive who have escaped from the bondage of the body as from a prison; but that life of yours, which men so call, is really death' (*Rep.* 6.14.14).

In describing the body as a prison and in describing what is involved in freeing oneself from this prison, a number of writers, philosophers, and theologians point to the relationship between the will of God and the will of the individual.[165] Philo writes, 'It is not possible that he whose abode is in the body and the mortal race should attain to being with God; this is possible only for him whom God rescues out of the prison' (*Leg. All.* 3.14.42).[166] Epictetus offers a similar perspective in *Diss.* 1.9.16-26, admonishing those humans who realize both that they have a kinship to the gods and that the body is like a fetter fastened about them

---

164. Philo develops this central theme and works playfully with the metaphor to the point where it is often difficult to understand how the metaphor relates to the reality to which it is pointing. Cf. *Deus Imm.* 111–15. Philo concludes his admonitions here by writing, 'Follow indeed, if thou canst, a life-purpose which is unchained, liberated and free. But, if it be that thou art snared by the hook of passion, endure rather to become a prisoner than a prison-keeper.'

165. On free will, see John T. Fitzgerald, *Cracks in an Earthen Vessel*, pp. 70-87.

166. Cf. Philo, *Rer. Div. Her.* 84–85.

(cf. *Diss.* 1.9.11). Epictetus is presented as saying, 'Men, wait upon God. When He shall give the signal and set you free from this service, then shall you depart to Him; but for the present endure to abide in this place, where He has stationed you.' Cicero presents a divine figure as agreeing, saying that unless God frees a person from 'the prison of the body', that person cannot attain to the afterlife (*Rep.* 6.15.15). The true wise man, Cicero says, 'will not break the bonds of his prison-house—the laws forbid it—but as if in obedience to a magistrate or some lawful authority, he will pass out at the summons and release of God' (*Tusc.* 1.30.74).[167]

Conversely, although Seneca also sees the soul as being bound in confinement, he holds suicide forth as a possibility. He writes,

> Let the soul depart as it feels itself impelled to go; whether it seeks the
> sword, or the halter, or some draught that attacks the veins, let it proceed
> and burst the bonds of its slavery. Every man ought to make his life
> acceptable to others besides himself, but his death to himself alone. The
> best form of death is one we like. (*Ep.* 70.12-13)

Visitors and Bribery[168]

In Lucian's *Toxaris* 31–32, Demetrius's friendship with the imprisoned Antiphilus leads him to work near the prison, to earn money (both to bribe the jailer and to give to Antiphilus), to spend time with his friend, and even to sleep in front of the prison door. Later, when he is unable to visit Antiphilus in prison, he incriminates himself in a crime which he did not commit, so that he might be imprisoned with his friend (32). Even when he himself fell ill, he took care of Antiphilus so that he would suffer as little distress as possible.

On Friendship is, appropriately, the subtitle of Lucian's *Toxaris*. By describing what Demetrius underwent to help his imprisoned friend, Lucian offers the readers a paradigm of friendship; an example of the lengths to which friendship must go. Seneca would agree with such a

---

167. Cf. Seneca, *Ep.* 26.10.

168. B.M. Rapske, 'The Importance of Helpers to the Imprisoned Paul in the Book of Acts', *TynBul* 42 (1991), pp. 3-30, looks at 'prison-helpers' in the Greco–Roman world, primarily focusing on how our knowledge of them illuminates passages in Acts. Rapske presents a number of interesting examples from antiquity, and summarizes with a simple thesis: 'If, as we are frequently advised, the prisoner Paul went from victory to victory, we may be sure from this study that he did not do it alone' (p. 29). For lengthier discussions of how persons abandoned the imprisoned and ministered to the imprisoned, see, respectively, chs. 3 and 5 of this work.

paradigm: friendship is not self-centered but is directed to the other. The wise person desires friends, Seneca writes, not

> 'That there may be someone to sit by him when he is ill, to help him when he is in prison or in want'; but that he may have someone by whose sickbed he himself may sit, someone a prisoner in hostile hands whom he himself may set free. He who regards himself only, and enters upon friendships for this reason, reckons wrongly. The end will be like the beginning: he has made friends with one who might assist him out of bondage; at the first rattle of the chain such a friend will desert him. (*Ep.* 9.8)[169]

Similarly, the author of Hebrews sees friendship, or rather 'brotherly love' (φιλαδελφία) in terms of reaching out to others. One concrete way in which Christians are called to do this is by 'remembering those who are in prison, as though in prison with them' (13.3a). This admonition is parenetic, reminding the readers of something with which they themselves were familiar, since previously they had 'had compassion on the prisoners' (Heb. 10.34). In early Christianity, Ignatius similarly warns the Smyrnaeans to beware of 'those who have strange opinions concerning the grace of Jesus Christ...for love they have no care, none for the widow...none for the prisoner, or for him released from prison, none for the hungry or thirsty' (*Smyrn.* 6.2).

It is not difficult for most moderns to imagine visitors in ancient prisons: in his *Crito* and *Phaedo*, Plato sketched a picture of the imprisoned Socrates surrounded by friends. This image itself was familiar to persons in the Hellenistic era. After Peregrinus, for instance, had climbed onto the pyre, and while his Cynic companions stared at his burning figure, a sarcastic Lucian railed at their piety, saying,

> Let us go away, you simpletons. It is not an agreeable spectacle to look at an old man who has been roasted, getting our nostrils filled with a villainous reek. Or are you waiting for a painter to come and picture you as the companions of Socrates in prison are portrayed by him? (*Peregr.* 37).

Numerous discussions and narratives exist which describe how relatives and friends visited and comforted their loved ones. When Furius of Heraclia spoke out against the evils of Verres and was thus imprisoned, 'day and night his mother sat weeping by his side in the prison' (Cicero, *Verr.* 2.5.43). Similarly, Anthia visited her sweetheart Habrocomes in

---

169. See also the verse in Petronius, *Satyricon* 80: 'The name of friendship endures so long as there is profit in it...While my luck holds you give me your smiles, my friends; when it is out, you turn your faces away in shameful flight.'

prison, where together they 'lamented their catastrophe' (Xenophon, *An Ephesian Tale* 7.2). In Pliny, *HN* 7.36.121, we hear of a plebian woman, who had just given birth, who visited her mother in prison. She was searched by the doorkeeper to prevent her taking food to her mother, but 'she was detected giving her mother sustenance from her own breasts'.[170] The disciples of John the Baptist had contact with their leader when he was imprisoned (Mt. 11.2-6). And we are told that when Agrippa was imprisoned under Tiberius, his friends and his freedmen were allowed to visit him; they brought him his favorite foods, brought garments which they made into a bed, and did whatever service they could (Josephus, *Ant.* 18.204).[171]

Apollonius, similarly, offered to be of whatever service he could to the imprisoned Musonius. Philostratus says that when Musonius was in prison, during the time of Nero, Apollonius wrote, 'I would fain come unto you, to share your conversation and your lodgings, in the hope of being some use to you' (*VA* 4.46). Musonius, however, thought that it would be better if they did not talk openly with one another. As a result, they wrote letters, carrying on 'a correspondence through Menippus and Damis, who went to and fro the prison'.

Visitors, however, were not always friends or relatives of the imprisoned. We are told that pagans visited imprisoned Christians to try to persuade them away from their faith (*The Martyrdom of Pionius* 12). In addition, persons who might not have enjoyed each other's company outside of prison might have seen each other inside:

> Aristogeiton, the informer, was about to be put to death in prison, sentence having been passed upon him, and he wanted Phocion to come to him; but Phocion's friends were averse to his going to see such a wicked man. 'And where', said he, 'could anyone converse with Aristogeiton with greater pleasure.' (Plutarch, *Mor.* 188B)

It should also be noted, however, that visiting the imprisoned was no simple act of charity. Often risk and danger were involved. Association with the imprisoned drew suspicion to oneself, and this often led to one's death.[172]

---

170. Pliny continues by remarking that the daughter's act was seen as so noble that she was rewarded by the release of her mother.

171. Agrippa was allowed even to bathe every day.

172. See Dio, 58.3.7, 58.11.5-6, Philostratus, *VA* 4.46, Tacitus, *Ann.* 6.5.9. In particular, see Chapter 3 of this work for an extended discussion on the abandonment of the imprisoned.

The imprisoned were visited primarily during the day. In *The Acts of Thomas* 154, we hear of a young man named Vazan who stayed too late and accidentally (?) was locked in prison for the night. In Lucian, *Tox.* 30, Demetrius initially could not visit Antiphilus, because he arrived at the prison in the evening, and it was already locked up.[173] Afterwards, however, he could visit his friend during the day, but when night came, he had to sleep outside (31).[174] It is not surprising, however, that visiting hours might be cut short for various reasons. When a brigand died in the prison, 'a close guard was instituted, and not one of those who sought admission could enter the gaol any longer' (*Tox.* 32).

The early Christians saw prison visitation as particularly important. Tradition even has the admonition to visit the imprisoned extending back as far as Jesus himself.[175] Perhaps it is not all that surprising, then, that the first Christians had a reputation among pagans for their eagerness to serve their imprisoned brothers and sisters. Lucian, *Peregr.* 12–13 mentions that when rescue attempts for Peregrinus did not work, Christian widows and orphans waited near the prison where he was incarcerated, while officials—having bribed the guards—slept inside. Meals were then brought in, books were read aloud, and persons visited this Palestinian (?) prison from as far away as cities of Asia.

Visitation apparently became so standard that church officers needed to encourage Christians to visit with moderation. Thus, around 250 CE, Cyprian wrote to presbyters and deacons, asking them to let Christians know that their

> eagerness must be cautiously indulged, and not in crowds—not in numbers collected together at once, lest from this very thing ill-will be aroused, and the means of access be denied, and thus, while we insatiably wish for all, we lose all...by thus changing the persons and varying the people that come together, suspicion is diminished (*Ep.* 4.2).

There is also an interesting tradition, throughout the Apocryphal Acts of the Apostles, of women—most often wives of leading pagan political officials—visiting the different imprisoned apostles. In *The Acts of Paul*, numerous women visit Paul: Thecla; Artemilla, whose husband was

173. Cf. Achilles Tatius, *Clit. and Leuc.* 6. 14; Plato, *Phd.* 59D.

174. See Lucian, *Peregr.* 12 below, where Christian officials were able—through bribes—to spend time with Perogrinus in prison; keeping watch and ensuring that he might sleep.

175. Mt. 25.36-44: 'I was naked and you clothed me, I was sick and you visited me, I was in prison and you came to me...'

Hieronymus the governor of Ephesus; and Eubula, the wife of a freedman of Hieronymus. This last woman is said to have sat beside Paul 'night and day' (7). Furthermore, Artemilla and Eubula go so far as to imply that they could bring a smith to free Paul from his chains, so that he might baptize the two of them. Later in this same document, when Paul was in Philippi, deacons from Corinth delivered a letter to him, 'who was in prison because of Stratonice, the wife of Apollophanes' (*The Acts of Paul* 8). Although these visitations reflect aspects of historical reality,[176] it is also possible that the authors of the Apocryphal Acts are flirting with the pagan romance-novel genre (with abstinence, as opposed to sexual union, driving at least parts of the story).[177] Thus, for instance, we find Aegeates, a judge, unable to understand why his wife has given up marital intercourse (*The Acts of Andrew* 3–4) and now spends time in prison with the apostle Andrew.[178]

Sometimes it is said that visitation was allowed through the power of a supernatural being. In *The Passion of Andrew* 28–30, Jesus made invisible to their enemies both Iphidama and her mistress Maximilla. Once they were covered and invisible,[179] they then visited Andrew in prison.[180]

Just as Lucian made fun of Christians' gullibility in their serving the imprisoned Peregrinus (*Peregr.* 12–13),[181] so Christians themselves eventually came to mock the behavior of those imprisoned who expected to be treated in a particularly special manner. Defending the Montanist practice of fasting, Tertullian strikes out against some of the Christians of his day: 'Plainly your habit is to furnish cookshops in the prisons to untrustworthy martyrs, for fear they should miss their accustomed

---

176. Christian women, married to pagans, did visit imprisoned Christian men. In discussing the problems which an unbelieving husband could create for a Christian wife, Tertullian, *Ad Ux.* 4, refers to the hesitancy which such husbands would have if they knew that their wives were going to 'kiss the martyr's bonds' or to 'exchange the kiss' in prison.

177. In comparing the elements of the Acts with that of pagan novels, B.P. Reardon, 'Aspects of the Greek Novel', *Greece and Rome* 23 (1976), pp. 118-31, is illuminating.

178. Cf. *The Acts of Andrew* 14.

179. Cf. *PGM* 1.96-108, in 'Escapes Aided by the Supernatural' below.

180. Cf. *The Acts of Thomas* 154.

181. C. Osiek, 'The Ransom of Captives: Evolution of a Tradition', *HTR* 74 (1981), pp. 365-86, presents an interesting discussion on how Christians, particularly Christians from the city of Rome, raised money to ransom those of their brothers and sisters who were imprisoned or enslaved.

usages, grow weary of life, and be stumbled at the novel discipline of abstinence' (*De Ieiun.* 12).[182]

For most Christians, however, visitation affected them in much the same way as it affected anyone who was imprisoned; it was an important sign of support: 'For a few days, then, we were comforted by the visits of our brethren. The consolation and the joy of the day removed all the agony we endured at night' (*The Martyrdom of Saints Montanus and Lucius* 4.7).[183]

Often bribes were necessary if one wished to visit the imprisoned. Bribes also served other functions. In some cases, a large enough bribe could free the imprisoned (thus leaving only the poor in prison).[184] In other cases, bribery enabled individuals to sleep with friends in prison, to spend time with them, or to bring them food.[185] A bribe of a silver mirror brought Thecla into prison, where she sat and heard Paul proclaim 'the mighty acts of God' (*The Acts of Paul* 3.18). Charisius's wife, Mygdonia, was prepared to give ten denarii to the jailers so as to see Judas Thomas (*The Acts of Thomas* 118). Later in *The Acts of Thomas* 151, Mygdonia, Teria and Marcia offered the prisonkeeper 363 staters of silver so as to see Thomas. And in caring for their Christian sisters and brothers in prison, the deacons Tertius and Pomponius also bribed the soldiers to allow the Christians to go to a better part of the prison to refresh themselves for a few hours (*The Martyrdom of Perpetua and Felicitas* 3).

Probably the best description of bribery comes in Cicero, *Verr.* 2.5.44 (also see 43), where it is said that 'every groan and pang meant a scheduled profit' for the prison warden. Here Cicero presents the prison warden as a person hawking his wares, almost like an over-aggressive salesperson or a carnival worker:

182. Tertullian then goes on to discuss the case of Pristinus, a Christian prisoner who became so used to the food, the baths, and the visitors, that he did not want to die when the time came. As a result, his friends needed to gorge him with drugged wine, to ensure that his execution actually would occur.

183. In writing to martyrs, Tertullian acknowledges that prisoners' needs extended beyond care of their physical needs: 'Other things, hindrances equally of the soul, may have accompanied you as far as the prison gate, to which also your relatives may have attended you' (*Ad Mart.* 1).

184. E.g., Josephus, *War* 2.273. These situations need to be distinguished from those in which the paying off of a fine would result in the freedom of a friend or relative (cf. Lucian, *Tim.* 49).

185. E.g., Lucian, *Peregr.* 12; *Tox.* 31; Philostratus, *VA* 36.

'So much for leave to see him—so much to be allowed to bring in food and clothing'—and everyone paid up. 'Well now, what offers for making an end of your son with one blow of my axe—no long suffering, no repeated blows, no feeling of pain as he gives up the ghost?' Yes, the lictor got his money for this too.

Cicero goes on to say that the bribes continued even after the death of the prisoner. The corpses were thrown to the wild beasts, unless the relatives paid for permission to bury them. Cicero then ends this discussion in section 45, writing, 'All these negotiations being concluded and settled, they were taken from prison and bound to the stake'.

Bribery became such a commonplace that it is somewhat a misnomer for us to even use the English word. For the keepers of the prisons, bribes came to be expected. This is discussed in *The Martyrdom of Pionius* 11.3-4:

When they were all gathered together the gaolers realized that Pionius and his group were not accepting the things brought to them by the faithful... Hence the gaolers became angry, because they used to benefit by whatever came in to the prisoners. So in their anger they cast the prisoners into the inner part of the prison because they received no gifts from them.[186]

This is not to claim, however, that guards were always willing to take bribes. In *The Martyrs of Lyons* 57–60, it is said that after Christians were strangled in prison, they were thrown to dogs to be eaten. Both revenge and mockery seemed to lie behind the guards' refusal to accept money in exchange for the charred and ripped pieces of the head and of the rest of the body.

Similarly, Cicero writes that the parents of some prisoners under Verres were 'forbidden access to their sons, forbidden to bring their own children food and clothing' (*Verr.* 2.5.45).[187] No bribe would have been high enough for guards to risk their lives in defying Verres.[188]

Prison Guards and Prison Breaks
There are reports of decent prison guards in antiquity. We are told that during the reign of Tiberius, Antonia ensured that the soldiers and

186. Cf. Libanius, *Or.* 45.10. Here the jailer, who provided one lamp for all of the imprisoned, expected payments or bribes from all of the prisoners. Those without money were whipped and flogged.

187. Cf. Cicero, *Verr.* 2.5.8.

188. Cf. Josephus, *Ant.* 185–86 (also see *War* 1.663). Here Antipater seeks, to no avail, to bribe the jailer into letting him go free. After the jailer reports Antipater's plans to Herod the king (Antipater's father), the imprisoned was executed.

centurion guarding her husband Agrippa were 'of humane character' (Josephus, *War* 18.203). It is even reported that when these guards heard that Tiberius had died, they initially went so far as to rejoice at the news of the emperor's death and, being on friendly terms with Agrippa anyway, treated him to feasting and drinking (*War* 18.231-32). Numerous examples exist of guards treating prisoners with dignity, even with care.[189]

Guards' trust of prisoners often developed in proportion to the amount of time prisoners spent incarcerated. Philo presents Joseph as a sort of trustee, who gained this position of influence through the favor of the jailkeeper (*Jos.* 81). Similarly, *The Martyrdom of Perpetua and Felicitas* 9.1 reports that

> an adjutant named Pudens, who was in charge of the prison, began to show us great honour, realizing that we possessed some great power within us. And he began to allow many visitors to see us for our mutual comfort.

This same work mentions that Perpetua convinced the officer of the prison that because she and her companions were to die on the emperor's birthday, it would be to his advantage if the prisoners looked healthy. Thus, the soldier ordered that they be treated more humanely and he even allowed persons to visit the prison, so that the prisoners might eat with them.[190] The officer's motives might not have been of the most altruistic sort. If he were to send weak, emaciated, sickly-looking prisoners to battle the beasts—particularly on this the emperor's birthday—he might have faced the wrath of the emperor if not that of the Roman spectators.[191]

Although there were fair guards, it is not to be assumed, however, that prison guards in general were hard-working civil servants, eager for justice to be served and for penal reform to occur. It was not part of their job to be empathetic.[192] As one of the assistants to the prison

189. Josephus notes that he himself had been treated well, 'receiving every attention', while under guard. Vespasian was responsible, however, for much of this treatment, even providing Josephus with a virgin and native of Caesarea as his wife (*Life* 414). In *War* 5.544-45, Josephus's mother, in prison, is said to have had the opportunity to talk to her warders. And in Philostratus, *VA* 7.38, we are told that an emissary of Aelian entered prison and informed Apollonius that 'word has been given to the chief jailor to supply you with everything which you may want'.

190. The adjutant of the prison, we are also told, was himself a Christian (16.4).

191. See Petronius, *Satyricon* 45.11 and 12, where fans of matches in the amphitheater criticize both the producers and participants.

192. E.g., in describing Musonius, Philostratus notes that 'he would have died for

guards said to Felicitas, while she was having birth pains, 'You suffer so much now—what will you do when you are tossed to the beasts?' (*The Martyrdom of Perpetua and Felicitas* 15.5). Furthermore, although prison guards frequently took bribes in allowing prisoners certain comforts, numerous actions and comforts were considered outside the pale. Thus, prison officers were to be punished if they were 'bribed to keep someone in custody without chains, or allowed a weapon or poison to be brought into the prison' (*Dig.* 48.3.8, cf. 48.8.10).

It is difficult to know who or what sort of persons served as guards in Roman prisons. Julius Firmicus Maternus's *Ancient Astrology: Theory and Practice*,[193] a handbook on astrology from the fourth century, proclaims that those who are born when Mars is in a particular relation to the sun 'will be public executioners, jailers, or prison guards, or prison officials trained to beat prisoners with whips, and similar professions' (Book 4, 5.26). Those who have the ascendant in the seventh degree of Gemini also will be prison guards (Book 8, 21.4).[194]

A more accessible discussion of those who served as prison guards can be found in the letters of Pliny (*Ep.* 10.19-20). Here we are told that, rather than transfer soldiers to guard duty in prisons, public slaves (*servi publici*)—an unreliable lot—were used as guards.[195] John E. Stambaugh writes (with respect to Rome) that

> Routine police activities were distributed among several of the annually elected magistrates. The aediles had general responsibility for keeping public order, and three minor magistrates, the *triumviri capitales*, were in charge of arrests, prisons and executions. The latter were relatively inexperienced junior magistrates just starting their public careers. They had a staff

all his gaoler cared' (*VA* 4.35). Eusebius describes guards' attacks against prisoners 'in word and in deed' (*Hist. eccl.* 8.10.3).

193. Julius Firmicus Maternus, *Ancient Astrology: Theory and Practice* (trans. J.R. Bram; Park Ridge, New Jersey: Noyes Press, 1975).

194. It is interesting to note that there appears to be little relationship between those who are born in successive degrees in the ascension of Gemini: those with the ascendant in the sixth degree will be inspired seers; those who have the ascendant in the eighth degree will be either musicians or they will be trumpeters who will die in war.

195. As to the roles of public slaves, also see T. Wiedemann, *Greek and Roman Slavery* (London: Routledge & Kegan Paul, 1981), pp. 159-62, and A.H.M. Jones, *The Greek City from Alexander to Justinian* (Oxford: Clarendon Press, 1940), pp. 212-13, 349.

of public slaves to assist them and to do the dirty work of torture and executions, but they did not really have the capacity to deal with major disturbances.[196]

These may very well have been the sorts of persons to whom Pliny was referring.

Although Trajan tells Pliny that relying on slaves instead of soldiers serves a number of purposes, the core of his reasoning seems to be typically Roman, centering on the fact that such a policy was 'the custom of the province' (and that changing such a practice might set a dangerous precedent). However, the fact that Pliny initially ordered some soldiers to be on guard with the slaves, and that he considered replacing the slaves with soldiers, are but two signs which might indicate that Pliny was used to seeing soldiers in this position.[197]

Soldiers did serve in policing roles within the city. Since the time when Augustus organized the praetorian guard, the night watch, and the urban cohorts, military units began to play greater and greater roles in the policing of the city. Soldiers were even employed at the spectacles and games, to ensure that order reigned and that no riots would break out. Tacitus (*Ann.* 13.24-25) mentions that Nero, later in 55 CE, withdrew the troops from the games, both because of the poor influence that such events had on the guards and in order to see if the masses would show self-control. The relationship between state (public) prisons and the military can be seen in numerous ways. Soldiers most often

196. J.E. Stambaugh, *The Ancient Roman City* (Baltimore: The Johns Hopkins University Press, 1988), p. 125. Also see E. Echols, 'The Roman City Police', *Classical Journal* 53 (1958), pp. 377-385, and W. Nippel, 'Policing Rome', *JRS* 74 (1984), pp. 20-29.

197. Based on Pliny's letter to Trajan, *Ep.* 10.77, and its response, *Ep.* 10.78, G.R. Watson, *The Roman Soldier* (Ithaca, New York: Cornell University Press, 1969), p. 146, writes that 'of course, centurions were widely used as security police'. R. MacMullen, *Soldier and Civilian in the Later Roman Empire* (Cambridge, MA: Harvard University Press, 1963), p. 152, discusses how 'civilian turned soldier, soldier turned civilian, in a *rapprochement* to a middle ground of waste and confusion'. Although MacMullen focuses on the timespan from 200–400 CE, he shows that soldiers did serve as police before then (see pp. 50-53). It is very difficult, however, to know how this system functioned. As H. Zwicky, *Zur Verwendung des Militärs in der Verwaltung der römischen Kaiserzeit* (Zurich: Buchdruckerei Winterthur AG, 1944), p. 83 writes, 'Über die Organisation und den Umfang dieser Stationen sind wir schlecht unterrichtet' (cf. p. 76 and pp. 82-84).

were said to be the ones who incarcerated the prisoners,[198] who escorted them to the tribunal,[199] who tortured the prisoners (e.g. *b. Ber.* 61b), and who executed them.[200] Similarly, soldiers served in other comparable roles. They might have been employed in 'watching the crosses, to prevent anyone taking down a body for burial'.[201] In Josephus, *Ant.* 18.230,[202] Agrippa's 'house arrest' was supervised by a centurion, and in *The Martyrdom of Saints Montanus and Lucius* 3.1, these two write: 'imprisoned under the authority of the local magistrates, we got the news of our sentence from the soldiers'. In *The Martyrdom of Perpetua and Felicitas* 3.6, Perpetua describes one of the difficulties of imprisonment as being 'the extortion of the soldiers'.

Whoever the guards were, they generally are portrayed as a dangerous crew. In the world of ancient dream interpretation, it was said that if one dreamt of public executions or jailers, delay and pain was to come to that individual (Artemidorus, *Oneirocritica* 3.60). Most prison guards were seen as violent and cruel. In *Jos.* 81 and 84, Philo describes why this is so:

> Everyone knows how full of inhumanity and cruelty gaolers are; pitiless by nature and case-hardened by practice, they are brutalized day by day towards savagery, because they never even by chance see or say or do any kindness, but only the extremes of violence and cruelty...Custom has a

198. Cf. *The Martyrdom of Saints Ptolemaeus and Lucius* 11; *The Martyrs of Lyons* 14 and 17; *The Martyrdom of Bishop Fructuosus* 1.2-3; *The Martyrdom of Saint Conon* 2; *The Martyrdom of Saints Marian and James* 2; *The Martyrdom of Saints Montanus and Lucius* 4.1; and Libanius, *Or.* 45.5.

199. Cf. *The Martyrs of Lyons* 30; and *The Martyrdom of Saints Montanus and Lucius* 6.3.

200. Only governors had the *ius gladii* (right to execute) and only they, similarly, had access to or command over soldiers. Therefore, as J.S. Pobee writes, 'execution was in the hands of the military' (*Persecution and Martyrdom in the Theology of Paul* (JSNTSup, 6; Sheffield: JSOT Press, 1985), p. 5. It is not surprising, then, that a soldier of the guard was the one sent to behead John the baptizer (Mk 6.27). We are told in *The Acts of Paul* 11.5 (*The Martyrdom of Paul*), that 'when the executioner struck off his (Paul's) head, milk spurted upon the soldier's clothing'. Cf. *The Martyrdom of Saints Carpus, Papylus, and Agathonice* 40; *The Martyrdom of Pionius* 21; *The Martyrdom of the Saints Justin, Chariton...*(Recension C) 6; and *The Martyrdom of Potamiaena and Basilides* 3.

201. Petronius, *Satyricon* 111. Also see *The Martyrs of Lyons* 59, where soldiers guarded charred corpses—corpses partially eaten by dogs—so as to keep the bodies from being buried.

202. Cf. *War* 18.195.

wonderful power of forcing everything into the likeness of nature. Gaolers
then spend their days with footpads, thieves, burglars, men of violence and
outrage, who commit rape, murder, adultery and sacrilege, and from each
of these they imbibe and accumulate something out of their villainy, out of
which miscellaneous amalgam they produce a single body of evil, a fusion
of every sort of pollution.

Each guard may have been 'a single body of evil, a fusion of every
sort of pollution', but those characteristics are not entirely surprising,
considering the consequences the guards would face, if they did not
keep the prisoners under control. The proconsul in *The Passion of
Andrew* 31 has four of his cohorts go off to the prison to deliver a
message to the jailer, warning him of the consequences of his behavior:

Right now, secure the door for which you are responsible! See that you do
not open it for any of the dignitaries even if you are won over by intimida-
tion or bribery—not even if I should come myself—or you will be missing
your head!

Jailers had reason to be nervous. Though they were responsible for the
prison itself, they were also responsible to magistrates. Thus, in *The Acts
of Thomas* 153, we see a jailer interrupting a late-night gathering of
Christians in prison, saying, 'Put away the lamps, lest anyone accuse (us)
to the king.' According to the book of Acts 12.19, the sentries who
were on duty the night Peter escaped from prison were put to death
by Herod. Thus, it is not surprising in Acts 16.27 that the Philippian
jailer sought to turn his sword upon himself when he believed that his
prisoners had escaped. The magistrates may have dealt him a harsher
punishment.[203]

Because they were rarely befriended by prisoners, guards often were
killed during prison escapes. This makes sense, since those who broke
out of prison were to be killed if they were caught.[204] In Lucian, *Tox.*
33, the prisoners used a file, 'cut the chain to which they were all attached
in a row, with their fetters strung upon it, and so set them all free;
whereupon they easily killed the guards, who were few, and escaped
together'.

At the same time, however, some prisoners found that good relations

---

203. This is codified in *Dig.* 48.3.12 and 48.3.14, which describes under what
circumstances guards are punished.
204. *Dig.* 47.18.1. Also see W. Rein, *Das Criminalrecht der Römer von Romulus
bis auf Justinianus* (Lepizig: K. F. Köhler Verlag, 1884), pp. 762-65.

with guards actually afforded them the opportunity to escape.[205] Under a type of house arrest in 220 BCE, Cleomenes managed to spread a rumor among those guarding him that he was going to be set free by the king. At a party where he entertained those who were attending him, he also sent meat, garlands, and wine to the guards. Once the guards were drunk, Cleomenes and his group went running from the house, with none of the guards even noticing their escape (Polybius, 5.39.1-3).

Polybius goes on to say that the revolt which Cleomenes hoped to initiate did not find followers. Although he and his group then sought to free those in prison (not under house arrest) to join them, the guards of the prison heard the news and secured the prison. With no alternative, Cleomenes and his cohorts 'died by their own hands like brave men and Spartans' (Polybius, 5.39.3). Attempted prison escapes, thus, were not always successful.[206] Livy reports that although Damocritus the Aetolian chief had escaped from prison by night, his capture was so certain that he took his own life (37.46.5).

Elsewhere Tacitus acknowledges an incident where those who were being dragged off to prison began to shout to bystanders and onlookers, claiming that the same fate would befall them. With these persons doing

> anything and everything that could arouse odium or sympathy, alarm or indignation, the crowd flew to the rescue, forced the guard-room, unchained the prisoners, and now took into fellowship deserters and criminals condemned for capital offences (*Ann.* 1.21).

Prison escapes were often more systematically engineered by persons outside the prison.[207] The ancient maxim, 'The prisoner cannot free

---

205. E.g., Ammianus Marcellinus, 28.6.24, recounts a certain Flaccianus who was somehow able to escape, after having bribed the guards.

206. Plutarch describes an example of a prison break foiled by the guards in *Agis and Cleomenes* 37.4-5. Livy, 32.26.17-18, describes precautions taken by guards so as to avoid a prison break. Cf. Livy 34.44.7-8, 29.22.10. In *b. ʿErub.* 21b, we are told that the prison keeper did not allow Rabbi Joshua to take the imprisoned Rabbi Akiba a certain quantity of water. Rather, the prison keeper poured out half of it, concerned that the water would be used in undermining the prison.

207. *Dig.* 48.4.4 reports that those who helped a convicted person escape from prison would face capital punishment. The classic example of those who sought to engineer an escape can be seen in the descriptions of Socrates' friends (cf. Plato, *Cri.* 44B–46B; and Xenophon, *Ap.* 23). Sometimes outsiders, however, would not need to engineer an escape. If they had enough power or influence, they could facilitate the freedom of prisoners in other ways. Thus, Josephus describes himself as liberating almost 190 children and women who had been imprisoned (*Life*, 419). In *Life* 450, he

himself from jail',[208] appears to have been grounded in the reality of the day. Prisoners ran a risk if they tried to escape from prison,[209] and often they needed the assistance of outsiders. We are told that on the night when the Spartans shut the Etruscans up in prison under a strong guard, the Etruscan women—after many prayers and entreaties—were allowed to enter the prison and speak to their husbands. Then their plan went into effect:

> When they had gone inside they bade their husbands to change their clothing quickly, leaving their own for their wives, and then, putting on their wives' garments, to depart with their faces covered. This done, the women waited there, prepared to face all terrors, but the guards were deceived and allowed the men to pass, supposing, of course, that they were women (Plutarch, *Mor.* 247B–C).[210]

A more action-filled escape is related in Plutarch, *Mor.* 598. In this episode, a certain Phyllidas calls the jailer at a late hour, and tells him that the Polemarchs have asked for the release of a particular prisoner. The jailer sees through the charade, and rattles off a list of questions concerning this Phyllidas's intentions. His final question is 'What token of authority do you bring?'

> 'This is my authority', said Phyllidas, and, as he said it, ran him through the body with a cavalry lance he held, striking down a vile fellow, on whom not a few women trod and spat the next day...We then split down the gaol door and first called out the name of Amphitheus and then those of the rest with whom we were severally connected. Recognizing our voices they leapt joyfully from their pallets, dragging their chains; and those whose feet were confined in the stocks stretched out their arms and cried out, begging not to be left behind.

relates an incident in which he saw three crucified prisoners who were friends of his. They were removed from the cross, with one actually surviving. Josephus also notes that Salome 'released the prisoners whom Herod had ordered to be put to death, telling them that the king had changed his mind and now dismissed them all to their homes' (*War* 1.666).

208. This expression is quoted twice in the *Babylonian Talmud*: in *b. Ber.* 5b and in *b. Ned.* 7b.

209. *Dig.* 48.3.13. Here Callistratus described the legal penalties incurred in one's trying to escape from prison. Callistratus notes that informers who expose such a 'conspiracy should receive a lighter penalty'.

210. Cf. Plato, *Cri.* 53D, where Socrates discusses 'the ludicrous way in which you ran away from prison by putting on a disguise, a peasant's leathern cloak or some of the other things in which runaways dress themselves up'.

Other escapes were not quite so dramatic. Plutarch says that Demosthenes,

> out of shame at the charge under which he lay…and owing to the weakness of his body, which could not endure confinement, ran away, through the carelessness of some of his keepers and the connivance of others (*Dem.* 26.2).

Furthermore, Socrates' friends express no doubt that if Socrates had ever wanted to escape or leave prison, it would be possible.

Finally, both by those inside and outside the prison, both by pagans and Christians, supernatural forces were summoned to aid in escape.[211] Escapes by such means are frequently mentioned. The Greek magical papyri[212] contain a number of spells enabling the imprisoned to find a way to freedom. The spell in *PGM* 1.96-102 is intended to summon an assistant for the imprisoned. This assistant is to 'free from bonds a person chained in prison, he opens doors, he causes invisibility so that no one can see you at all…' Whether or not spells came with an assistant, they pretty much had the same effect. Another pagan magical text— later employed by imprisoned Christians—can be seen in *PGM* 13.289-96. After the initial praise to the deity comes the petition in lines 294-96: 'Let every bond be loosed, every force fail, let all iron be broken, every rope or every strap, let every knot, every chain be opened, and let no one compel me…' Furthermore, outsiders—perhaps friends or relatives—also had access to a charm with which they could free others (or themselves). *PGM* 12.16-78 claims that

> If you want to do something spectacular and want to free yourself from danger, stand at the door and say the spell, and having said it, go out, adding: 'Let the bonds of him, NN, be loosened, and let the doors be opened for him, and let no one see him.'

---

211. Cf. Lucian, *Nav.* 42; *Menippus* 6. For a complete discussion of the role of the supernatural in escapes, see R. Kratz, *Rettungswunder: Motiv-, traditions- und formkritische Aufarbeitung einer biblischen Gattung* (Las Vegas: Peter Lang, 1979), pp. 351-445. Also see O. Winreich, 'Türöffnung im Wunder-, Prodigien- und Zauberglauben der Antike, des Judentums und Christentums', in *idem et al.* (eds.), *Genethliakon W. Schmid zum 70: Geburtstag* (Tübinger Beiträge zur Altertumswissenschaft, 5; Stuttgart, 1929), pp. 200-264.

212. References to the magical papyri all come from the translations in H.D. Betz (ed.), *The Greek Magical Papyri in Translation* (Chicago: The University of Chicago Press, 1986). The Greek texts can be found in K. Preisendanz (ed.), *Papyri Graecae Magicae: Die griechischen Zauberpapyri* (Stuttgart: Teubner, 2nd edn, 1973, 1974).

The charm continues: 'You may even prove that it happens. Bind some-one securely and shut him in a house. Stand outside and say the spell six or seven times thus...'

In addition to these charms and spells, there are a number of others which could be used to open doors.[213] One involved evoking the proper names, the names being AIA AINRYCHATH and ACHEBYKROM (*PGM* 13.327-34); one involved 'taking the navel of a male crocodile (he means pondweed) and the egg of a scarab and the heart of a baboon (he means perfume of lilies)'[214] (*PGM* 13.1065-1075); one involved taking 'from a firstborn ram an umbilical cord that has not fallen to the ground, and after mixing in myrrh, applying it to the door bolts when you want to open a door' and then saying the proper spell (*PGM* 36.312-20).

In the first centuries of the first millennium, practitioners of magic were severely punished, since magic spells were considered efficacious.[215] *The Martyrdom of Perpetua and Felicitas* 16.2 relates that the military tribune treated the Christians in a particularly harsh manner, because 'on the information of certain very foolish people he became afraid that they would be spirited out of the prison by magical spells'.

Tales of prison escapes which involve the manipulation of the super-natural occur often in ancient popular literature. Philostratus employs a graphic visual aid, demonstrating Apollonius's true freedom in prison, when he shows Apollonius laughing at his fetters, taking his leg out of them and then putting them back on again (*VA* 7.28). Examples of supernatural involvement in prison escapes are scattered throughout Christian texts, particularly in the canonical and the Apocryphal Acts.

Three incidents stand out in the Acts of the Apostles: 1) in Acts 5.19-20 an angel of the Lord opens the prison doors and commands the apostles to go out and to speak words of life in the temple; 2) in Acts 12.6-19 an angel of the Lord also appears to the imprisoned Peter and,

213. Prayers or spells often resulted in the opening of doors. In Paul's reference to 'opening a door' in Col. 4.3 ('Pray for us also, that God may open to us a door for the word, to declare the mystery of Christ, on account of which I am in prison'), the double entendre may have been intentional.

214. The technical terms and in-house argot used here, for instance, show some of the difficulties involved in understanding these spells.

215. See S.R. Garrett, *The Demise of the Devil: Magic and the Demonic in Luke's Writings* (Minneapolis: Fortress Press, 1989), pp. 11-19. Also see C.R. Phillips, 'The Sociology of Religious Knowledge in the Roman Empire to AD 284', in W. Haase (ed.), *ANRW*, II 16.3 (New York: de Gruyter; 1986) esp. pp. 2711-32.

even though Peter is chained to guards on either side of him, even though sentries are guarding the door of the prison, Peter is freed and able to walk out; and 3) after an evening of Paul and Silas praying and singing in a Philippian prison, an earthquake shakes the foundations of the prison, forcing all the doors open and resulting in everyone's fetters being unfastened (Acts 16.25-26).

The accounts from the Apocryphal Acts are even more fantastic. A common theme centers on imprisonment's inability to hamper the apostles' work and ministry. Thus, the apostles—although spending time in prison—seem to have the ability to leave when they want to. Paul's prayer in *The Acts of Paul* 7 results in 'a youth very comely in grace' coming and loosing Paul's chains. Shortly after breaking out of prison (and after baptizing Artemilla in the sea), Paul then breaks back into prison while the guards remain sound asleep. Similarly, in *The Acts of Thomas* 119–22, after Judas Thomas has left prison and baptized a believer, he returns to the prison, finding 'the doors open and the guards still asleep'.

The Acts of Thomas mentions supernatural release from prison a number of other times. Judas Thomas answers how he was brought out of the prison, by saying merely, 'My Lord Jesus is more powerful than all powers and kings and rulers' (119). This approach to prison escape also is seen later in the text. When a youth, Vazan, visited Judas Thomas and stayed too late—so that the jailers had already locked the doors of the prison and gone to sleep—Judas says 'Believe in Jesus, and thou shalt find the doors open!' (*The Acts of Thomas* 154). Later in the narrative, ready to accept his martyrdom and to seal himself back in prison, Judas Thomas says 'My Saviour, who didst endure much for our sakes, let these doors become as they were, and (let them be sealed) with their seals!' (*The Acts of Thomas* 161).[216]

Although there are numerous accounts of supernatural and miraculous escapes which made guards appear foolish, *The Acts of Andrew and Matthias* 19 presents one supernatural escape which resulted even in the death of the guards. Andrew, after he had gone to the prison to free Matthias, 'saw seven guards standing at the door of the prison guarding

---

216. All the opening and sealing of the prison doors in this work results in a humorous ending where the guards go to the king and complain indignantly that although they close and lock the doors, the 'sorcerer' somehow manages to get out. The upshot of the discussion is that King Misdaeus visits the prison where he, of course, finds the doors sealed and accuses the guards of spreading lies.

it. He prayed silently, and the seven guards fell and died.' Then, 'when he came to the prison door, Andrew marked it with the sign of the cross and it opened automatically'. This prison break, the reader is told, resulted in Andrew's release of 248 men and 49 women (21).

6. *Conclusion*

Ancient legal texts and the limited references to imprisonment in the New Testament present a narrow and potentially misleading picture of ancient prisons and prison life. Images of incarceration in the Roman world are strewn throughout a wide variety of ancient texts. Individuals in the first century, like individuals today, may not have been familiar with all of the legislation involved in imprisonment. However, through a wide variety of popular sources, they would have had concrete impressions of what prisons were like and of what prisoners experienced. Although this first chapter has sought to paint a picture of various images of imprisonment, these images, as stated earlier, cannot simply be transposed to the Pauline epistles. However, in the chapters which follow, it will be shown that Paul's rhetoric and experiences in prison are illuminated by the broader context of prison life in antiquity. Imprisonment influenced both the apostle and his relationships with individual church communities.

Chapter 2

PAUL'S CHOICE AND THE RHETORIC OF VOLUNTARY DEATH

For to me to live is Christ and to die is gain.
If it is to be life in the flesh, that means fruitful labor for me. Yet which I
shall choose I cannot tell.

—Phil. 1.21-22

1. *Introduction*

In the midst of Paul's discussion on whether he will live or die in prison
(Phil. 1.18b-26), the exclamation καὶ τί αἱρήσομαι οὐ γνωρίζω
(1.22b) juts out of the text. It is difficult to know what Paul meant when
he wrote this: the Greek phrase τί αἱρήσομαι is both ambiguous and
enigmatic. Whereas the RSV translates it as 'which I shall choose I
cannot tell',[1] the NRSV has 'I do not know which I prefer' (the *preference* being between living and dying). The implications of these different
translations might not be apparent immediately, but it is fair to say that
the RSV presents Paul as believing that he has a *choice* in whether he
lives or dies. The NRSV, conversely, does not necessarily imply that Paul
himself has any say in the matter.

Although most commentators have held that Paul's imprisonment left
him with no ability to make a choice or decision regarding his own
life—that this decision was left to the whims of the Roman state—such a
position does not do justice to Paul's language, to the rhetorical strategy
of this letter,[2] or to Paul's presence in prison. Claiming that Paul had

---

1.   Most translations are similar to the RSV: 'I do not know which I should
choose' (NJB); 'I do not know which to choose' (NASB); 'What I shall choose I wot
not' (KJV).

2.   The emphasis on rhetoric in this chapter focuses on the section from Phil. 1.1–
3.1. Thus, the thesis of this chapter does not depend on either the integral or the com-
posite nature of Paul's letter to the Philippians. In general, however, this work as a
whole assumes the integrity of the letter. There have been a number of compelling

only a 'preference' as to whether he might live or die fails to acknowledge Phil. 1.18b-26 as a significant part of Paul's moral exhortation to the Philippians. Stated positively, Paul's deliberations on his own life and death serve a mimetic purpose. By pointing both to his own desires and to his subsequent decisions, Paul presents a pattern of behavior which he expects the Philippian community to follow.

To grasp the significance of Phil. 1.22b, initially it is helpful to look briefly at the phrase τί αἱρήσομαι, and then to examine how 1.18b-26 has been understood within its immediate literary context. These discussions of previous scholarship will serve to introduce an analysis both of the rhetoric of Phil. 1.18b-26 and of its role within the epistle.

2. *Philippians 1.22b: Choice versus Preference*

Phil. 1.22b contains one of the murkiest and yet least discussed phrases in the entire corpus of Paul's letters: τί αἱρήσομαι. Linguistic evidence by itself offers no conclusive ruling on how this phrase might be understood. However, a brief overview of how αἱρήσομαι has been interpreted here, and of how the term is used elsewhere, can identify the major interpretative difficulties.

Much of the difficulty in interpreting 1.22b stems from Paul's choice of verbs: αἱρήσομαι has proved to be a stumbling block for many interpreters of this passage. Commentators have responded to this verb with silence, with incredulity, and with imagination.

Many discussions of Philippians manage to avoid Phil. 1.22b, collapsing it with—and then focusing on—those verses which frame it.[3] Thus, in

arguments which chdefend the integrity of Philippians: R. Jewett, 'The Epistolary Thanksgiving and the Integrity of Philippians', *NovT* 12 (1970), pp. 40-53; W.J. Dalton, 'The Integrity of Philippians', *Bib* 60 (1979), pp. 97-102; D.E. Garland, 'The Composition and Unity of Philippians: Some Neglected Literary Factors', *NovT* 27 (1985), pp. 141-73; D.F. Watson, 'A Rhetorical Analysis of Philippians and its Implications for the Unity Question', *NovT* 30 (1988), pp. 57-88; L. Alexander, 'Hellenistic Letter-Forms and the Structure of Philippians', *JSNT* 37 (1989), pp. 87-101; B.J. Capper, 'Paul's Dispute with Philippi: Understanding Paul's Argument in Phil. 1–2 from his Thanksgiving in 4.10-20', *TZ* 49 (1993), pp. 193-214; and D.A. Black, 'The Discourse Structure of Philippians: A Study in Textlinguistics', *NovT* 37 (1995), pp. 16-49.

3.   E.g., D.E. Garland's exposition in 'Philippians 1.21-26 The Defense and Confirmation of the Gospel', *RevExp* 77 (1980), p. 334; and B. Byrne, 'The Letter to the Philippians', in R.E. Brown *et. al.* (eds.), *The New Jerome Biblical Commentary* (Englewood Cliffs, NJ: Prentice–Hall, 1990), p. 793.

his Philippians commentary, although H.C.G. Moule does say that οὐ
γνωρίζω might be translated best by the English phrases 'I *recognize*
not' or 'I do not see clearly', he does not, however, mention the first
part of the verse (τί αἱρήσομαι).[4]

Most commentators simply deny that Paul had any kind of choice.
According to this type of interpretation, Paul actually did not mean what
he wrote; the choice he refers to is actually not his own to make. Thus,
Ralph P. Martin shifts rapidly from v. 21 to v. 23, only briefly alluding
to the troubling verse which intervenes. Paul, he writes, balances

> only theoretical issues, because his life is still at risk and at the mercy of
> his captors. Yet he knows, as a Christian and an apostle, that his life stands
> in the field of God's providential ordering and control, where no evil force
> can touch him except by divine permission.[5]

Others, like G.B. Caird, have interpreted 1.22b by saying that this is not
what Paul meant to write: 'Paul is not claiming that he actually has a
choice. The decision lies with his Roman judge. His dilemma is that he
does not know which verdict to hope for.'[6] Other scholars spiritualize
Paul's words. Fred B. Craddock writes,

> Since Paul is neither judge nor jury but the one on trial, what possible
> meaning could there be in his struggle with his choice? Were any of us to
> get a letter from a friend on trial and the friend confided that deciding
> whether to be sentenced or to be set free was most difficult, we would
> begin to wonder about our friend's mental state. Has Paul suffered too
> much, too long? In one sense, of course, Paul has absolutely no decision;
> he awaits the decision of others. In another sense, though, Paul can take
> the initiative, walk into his own future, embrace rather than resist necessity,
> and be on top rather than beneath his situation.[7]

---

4.   H.C.G. Moule, *Philippians* (Cambridge: Cambridge University Press, 1903),
p. 53.

5.   R.P. Martin, *Philippians* (NCB; Grand Rapids: Eerdmans, 1980), p. 77. Ernst
Lohmeyer presents a similar position in *Die Briefe an die Philipper, an die Kolosser
und an Philemon* (Göttingen: Vandenhoeck & Ruprecht, 1930), p. 61.

6.   G.B. Caird, *Paul's Letters from Prison* (Oxford: Oxford University Press,
1976), p. 113. Cf. A.F.J. Klijn, *De Brief van Paulus aan de Filippenzen* (Nijkerk:
Uitgeverij, G.F. Callenbach N.V., 1969), p. 40; M.A. Getty, *Philippians and Philemon*
(NTM, 14; Wilmington, DE: Michael Glazier, 1980), p. 19; and R.T. Fortna,
'Philippians: Paul's Most Egocentric Letter', in R.T. Fortna and B.R. Gaventa (eds.),
The Conversation Continues: Studies in Paul and John in Honor of J. Louis Martyn
(Nashville: Abingdon Press, 1990), p. 222.

7.   F.B. Craddock, *Philippians* (Interpretation; Atlanta: John Knox, 1985), p. 29.

Those who deny that Paul had any sort of 'choice' as to whether he might live or die draw a picture of the imprisoned apostle submissive to the Roman authorities, to the will of God, or to a type of fate.

Those scholars who have taken the verb αἱρήσομαι literally[8] are few in number. Joachim Gnilka appears to take it literally, but it is not entirely clear how he then develops the rest of his interpretation:

> This faces him [Paul] with a personal choice. The decision is a difficult one, yet he demands it of himself. But is it really his affair to lay down which way he should take? In the spirit of prayer Paul breaks through the outward human situation and places himself before God, in whose sight he wishes his decision to be made. The Roman judges, in their dignity and power, are puppets in the hands of him whom Paul calls his God.[9]

For Gnilka, then, Paul's choice appears to involve giving himself over to God's will. Although Gnilka is attentive to the Greek word which Paul uses, although Gnilka acknowledges that a 'choice' is involved, Paul's choice, in effect, is to declare himself as a passive actor in a Roman drama directed by God.

In a somewhat similar interpretation, Jean-Francois Collange argues that Paul's choice would be, in effect, that of Jesus. However, 'the apostle had nothing "from the Lord" to declare (cf. 1 Cor. 7.10-13) concerning the options "to live or to die".' Collange claims that αἱρήσομαι should perhaps be taken interrogatively. Philippians 1.22b might then read, '"What shall I choose? I cannot say", or "I have nothing to declare about this matter"'.[10] In effect, Collange takes the choice away from Paul and gives it to Jesus. Because Paul has not been told from the Lord what to choose, Paul does not know what he himself will choose.

There are obvious difficulties with each of these positions. Although Paul elsewhere refers to his dependence on God, it is striking in this passage that submission to God—contrary to Gnilka—is *not* the focus. Paul's 'choice' relates to life and death, not to faith in God. Similarly, if Paul's choice—as Collange argues—was dependent on guidance from Jesus, it is odd that Paul does not develop this more in this passage. However much Paul appealed to the Lord for guidance, the text gives

8.   The literal meaning of the verb is 'choose'; 'prefer', as discussed below, is a derivative meaning.

9.   J. Gnilka, *The Epistle to the Philippians* (trans. R.A. Wilson; New York: Herder and Herder, 1971), p. 26.

10.   J.F. Collange, *The Epistle of Saint Paul to the Philippians* (trans. A.W. Heathcote; London: Epworth Press, 1979), pp. 63-64.

us no reason to believe that that is an issue here.

Dealing head-on with the troubling verb αἱρήσομαι, Arthur J. Droge believes that Paul uses this particular verb deliberately. Paul is not writing about his having only a *preference* for being free or being executed: this is no passive Paul; Paul is writing about *his* having the *choice* of living or dying.

Thus, in a series of writings from 1988 through 1992,[11] Droge places the discussion of Phil. 1.22 within the context of first-century Greco–Roman philosophy. Examining the various philosophical discussions of suicide in antiquity, starting with Plato's *Phaedo*, and then looking at the Cynics, at the Epicureans and—in particular—at the Stoics (discussing Cicero, Seneca and Marcus Aurelius), Droge analyzes Phil. 1.22 in light of these discussions and texts. Paul's musings here are seen as similar to that of the philosophers of his day: 'Paul's yearning for death...is best explained as his reflection on the possibility—indeed, the desirability—of suicide.'[12] With reference to 1.22, Droge writes

> I take this to mean what it says, that the question of life or death is a matter of Paul's own volition, not something to be imposed on him from the outside. And if it is a matter of Paul's own choosing, then it appears that he is reflecting on the possibility of suicide.[13]

Droge's observations raise important questions about Paul's use of what has been seen as a very peculiar verb.

Interpretative difficulties in Paul's letter to the Philippians often have been explained away by assuming that Paul digressed often, that he wrote parts of the letter at different times, or that he had written three previous epistles (no longer extant) which were edited into the epistle which we now possess. More often than not, such explanations point to our unfamiliarity not only with ancient society, but also with ancient rhetoric and epistolography. Similarly, in looking at Phil. 1.22b, it is important to be prudent and not simply dismiss Paul's use of the verb αἱρήσομαι in favor of what might be seen as fitting best in this particular context. In

11. A.J. Droge, '*Mori Lucrum*: Paul and Ancient Theories of Suicide', *NovT* 30 (1988), pp. 263-86; 'Did Paul Commit Suicide?', *BibRev* (1989), pp. 14-21; 'Suicide', in D.N. Freedman (ed.), *The Anchor Bible Dictionary*, VI (New York: Doubleday, 1992), pp. 225-31; and A.J. Droge and J.D. Tabor, *A Noble Death: Suicide & Martyrdom Among Christians and Jews in Antiquity* (San Francisco: Harper & Row, 1992), esp. pp. 113-28.

12. Droge, '*Mori Lucrum*', p. 264.

13. Droge, '*Mori Lucrum*', p. 279.

Phil. 1.22b, Paul could have chosen to use the future forms of the verbs βούλομαι or θέλω. However, he did not. He used the verb αἱρήσομαι.

Liddell and Scott's *Greek–English Lexicon* defines αἱρέω as 'to take with thehand, grasp, seize', with the primary medial form of the verb meaning 'to take for oneself, choose'.[14] The verb refers to an intentional, directed action; one made on behalf of the person who performs the action.

Students are quick to translate this verb (in its middle form) as *either* 'to choose' or 'to prefer' on the basis of lexicons such as Bauer–Arndt–Gingrich, which offer both of these English verbs as possible translations of the Greek.[15] At times, it is *possible* to translate αἱρέομαι with the English verb 'prefer'. That which one *chooses* is often that which one *prefers*; choice is generally made on the basis of preference. This is not to say that αἱρέομαι can be translated with either of these English verbs, or that either translation is valid. Choosing reflects a preference, but that is not to say that preferring reflects a choice (or the ability to make a choice).

Although the Greek word αἱρέομαι can have the connotations of both 'choosing' and 'preferring', to translate this term with the English verb 'prefer' results in ambiguity. When αἱρέομαι is translated as 'prefer', persons who do not know Greek are left unsure of whether the preference reflects the actual ability to make a choice.

Other than in Philippians 1.22, the middle form of this verb is used only two other times in the New Testament: in 2 Thessalonians and in Hebrews. In 2 Thess. 2.13, Paul employs the aorist form to emphasize that '...God chose (εἵλατο) you from the beginning, to be saved...' In a participial form of the verb in Heb. 11.25, it is said that Moses 'chose (ἑλόμενος) rather to share ill-treatment with the people of God than to enjoy the fleeting pleasures of sin'. Both of these instances support the definition of this verb found in Liddell and Scott: the actors are 'choosing', they are 'taking for themselves'.

A survey of Greek texts demonstrates that these New Testament examples represent typical Greek usage of this verb.[16] One representative

14. LSJ, I, pp. 41-42.
15. BAGD, p. 24.
16. Cf. Appian, *BCiv.* 4.16.117; Demosthenes, *Or.* 15.3; Dio Chrysostom, *Or.* 53.8.7; Plato, *Symp.* 213E; *Plt.* 265B; Plutarch, *Mor.* 620B; Polybius, *Hist.* 31.23.12; and Xenophon, *An.* 1.3.6. The majority of the examples listed here refer to the present middle or future middle first person singular form of the verb αἱρεομαι. This, of course, is similar to Paul's use of αἱρήσομαι in Phil. 1.22b.

example comes from Dio's *Roman History*. During a speech before the senate, where it appeared as if Caesar were retiring from sole leadership, Caesar stated that if this action were to result in his death, he would accept it: 'If some disaster should befall me...with entire willingness I make my choice (αἱροῦμαι) to die even before my time as a private citizen, in preference to living forever as the occupant of a throne' (53.9.3). Caesar is not saying that he would commit suicide, but he is acknowledging his actions and accepting the consequences of them. He emphasizes that because he is going through with his plan (to retire), if some disaster resulted because of this plan, he—in effect—would choose this death.

If the use of this verb in 2 Thessalonians and Hebrews illuminates its use in Phil. 1.22b, and if, in addition, these examples reflect typical Greek usage, it would be wise to translate Paul's words not as 'what I prefer', but rather as 'what I will choose'. The difference is a significant one.

Having seen some of the ways in which the Greek phrase τί αἱρήσομαι has been interpreted by modern commentators, and having seen some of the ways in which the verb αἱρέομαι was employed by ancient writers, it is important to examine the broader context of this expression (and of Phil. 1.18b-26) before advancing any conclusions on how this enigmatic passage might be understood. Regardless of whether Paul is discussing what might be referred to as 'suicide', Droge's observations have served to draw attention, as never before, to a passage which often has been ignored: Phil. 1.18b-26.

What Droge does not do, however, is look at this passage within its immediate literary context. His focus is on 'the choice', not on how 'the choice' functions or why it is even discussed here. Leaving aside for a moment the question of what sort of choice Paul might be referring to, it is important to shift to a question concerned more with Paul's rhetoric: How does Phil. 1.18b-26 function within the context of this letter?

3. *The Literary Context of Philippians 1.18b-26*

In this passage, the apostle Paul is frank, perhaps surprisingly so: he finds dying to be more desirable for himself, although his living is more necessary for the community. Most scholars place this passage within the larger context extending from Phil. 1.12-26: whereas 1.12-18a describes the circumstances of Paul's imprisonment, 1.18b-26 functions primarily to share information about Paul's disposition, emotions and feelings.

With this view, Phil. 1.27-30 is presented as then initiating a new section of the letter, one which focuses more on the Philippian community. In looking at Phil. 1.27-30, Gerald F. Hawthorne thus writes, 'After having discussed his own affairs and their consequences, and after having disclosed his own innnermost feelings, Paul turns now, as is his custom, to give instructions to the entire community.'[17] G.B. Caird sees a similar shift in Paul's thought. In discussing Phil. 1.27–2.4, Caird emphasizes that

> Thus far Paul has concentrated on his own condition and prospects, because he knows that these are uppermost in the minds of his friends and that their greatest need is to be assured that he is in good heart. But now the pastor in him comes to the fore.[18]

Although readers such as Hawthorne and Caird have focused on the shift or disjuncture between Phil. 1.18b-26 and 1.27-30, other interpreters have been careful to emphasize the transitions which span these passages.[19] Jean-Francois Collange, presenting Phil. 1.12-26 under the heading 'The Apostle's Circumstances',[20] recognizes that there are both literary and substantive relations between this section and that which follows (1.27–2.18):

> When he has given news of his own situation Paul turns, as vv. 24b-26 have already foreshadowed, to the community at Philippi. It too has its problems—adversaries ('*antikeimenoi*', 1.28) troubling it and its unity threatened by the rivalries to which it is a prey (1.27; 2.1ff.).[21]

Ernst Lohmeyer focuses, in particular, on what he sees as the substantive similarities between Phil. 1.12-26 and 1.27–2.16. He labels 1.12-26 as 'The Martyrdom of Paul' and 1.27–2.16 as 'The Martyrdom of the Community'.[22] Because Lohmeyer persistently sees the presence of martyrdom in this epistle (he refers to other sections of the letter with titles like 'Helpers in Martyrdom', 'Dangers in Martyrdom', etc.), it is

---

17. G.F. Hawthorne, *Philippians* (WBC, 43; Waco, TX: Word Books, 1983) p. 54. Cf. J.L. Houlden, *Paul's Letters from Prison* (Baltimore: Penguin Books, 1970), pp. 61-65.

18. Caird, *Paul's Letters from Prison*, p. 114.

19. In addition to the examples which follow, also see Martin, *Philippians*, p. 80; and M. Silva, *Philippians* (WEC; Chicago: Moody Press, 1988), pp. 17-18, who focuses on the transitional word μόνον in 1.27, seeing it as functioning in an exceptive or adversative sense (as a qualification of that which precedes).

20. Collange, *Philippians*, p. 51.

21. Collange, *Philippians*, p. 71.

22. Lohmeyer, *Philipper*, p. 70.

not surprising that he would recognize a link between 1.12-26 and 1.27–2.16.

Unlike Lohmeyer, who sees the bridge between 1.18b-26 and 1.27–2.16 in terms of a continuing theme, Loveday Alexander sees the relation between these sections more in terms of formal criteria: Paul's letter to the Philippians has the same form as Hellenistic 'family letters'.[23] Thus, Phil. 1.12-26 is seen as typical 'reassurance about the sender' and Phil. 1.27–2.18 is a 'request for reassurance about the recipients'.[24] These two passages are related primarily in that they are a part of a larger letter whose purpose is to strengthen 'the "family" links between the apostle and the Christian congregation in Philippi'.[25]

In describing how Phil. 1.18b-26 functions within the letter, numerous interpreters have focused on this passage as background information for that which follows: Paul informs the Philippians of his own situation and his personal reflections before he proceeds with the rest of the epistle. Other Pauline interpreters, however, have emphasized that this passage also sets a tone for the rest of the letter: just as Paul either suffered or served as a martyr, so will the Christian community at Philippi.

Phil. 1.18b-26 does need to be understood in light of that which precedes it. The passage which serves to introduce the subject of Paul's imprisonment—Phil. 1.12-18a—is indeed linked to 1.18b-26 through both subject matter and vocabulary.[26] At the same time, however, Phil. 1.18b-26 needs to be understood in light of that which follows. Loveday Alexander points us in the right direction, asking us to see the primary context of Phil. 1.18b-26 as that of a 'family letter'.

4. *Paul's Rhetorical Strategy in Philippians*

Loveday Alexander describes Philippians as a family letter or a 'Verbindungsbrief'.[27] Ancient theorists did not recognize specifically the

23. L. Alexander, 'Hellenistic Letter-Forms', pp. 87-101.

24. L. Alexander, 'Hellenistic Letter-Forms', p. 94.

25. L. Alexander, 'Hellenistic Letter-Forms', p. 95.

26. All of Phil. 1.12-26 deals with the nature of Paul's imprisonment and the continuation of his mission. Furthermore, the demonstrative pronoun τοῦτο (1.19) points the reader back to 1.12-18, and the word προκοπή, which appears only here in Paul, both opens and closes this section (1.12 and 1.25).

27. Alexander, 'Hellenistic Letter-Forms', pp. 87-101. Cf. J. White, *Light from Ancient Letters* (Philadelphia: Fortress Press, 1986), p. 197, for a discussion of 'family letters'.

'family or household letter', but they 'could have isolated the family letter as a type analogous to the friendly letter: A letter for maintaining the affection and social relationships of the household'.[28] Thus, although Stanley K. Stowers refers to Philippians as 'a hortatory letter of friendship',[29] instead of as a 'family or household letter', both he and Alexander would agree that the letter's primary function is to maintain or strengthen the relationships between persons who care for each other.

What did such letters look like? Stowers lists a number of examples of family letters and letters of friendship in *Letter Writing in Greco–Roman Antiquity*.[30] The textbook example of such a letter is that of Pseudo-Demetrius:

> Even though I have been separated from you a long time, I suffer this in body only. For I can never forget you or the impeccable way we were raised together from childhood up. Knowing that I myself am genuinely concerned about your affairs, and that I have worked unstintingly for what is most advantageous for you, I have assumed that you, too, have the same opinion of me and will refuse me in nothing. You will do well, therefore, to give close attention to the members of my household lest they need anything, to assist them in whatever they might need, and to write to us about whatever you should choose.[31]

The particular concerns expressed in this epistle might vary from concerns found in other family/friendly letters. However, these letters serve similar purposes. Just as family/friendly letters today often primarily serve to express interest both in the maintenance of the relationship and in communication between the parties, so, for such letters in antiquity,

28. S.K. Stowers, *Letter-Writing in Greco–Roman Antiquity* (LEC, 5; Philadelphia: Westminster Press, 1986), p. 71. Also see Stowers's remarks concerning Cicero on pp. 74-75 and his remarks on 'Letters of Friendship' on pp. 58-70.

29. 'Friends and Enemies in the Politics of Heaven', in J.M. Bassler (ed.), *Pauline Theology. I. Thessalonians, Philippians, Galatians, Philemon* (Minneapolis: Fortress Press, 1991), pp. 105-121. Here, on p. 107, Stowers remarks on the irony that modern commentators of Philippians have failed to notice that 'scholars of ancient letter writing have long identified Philippians as a letter of friendship (φιλικὸς τύπος)'. In a previous work (*Letter-Writing in Greco–Roman Antiquity*), Stowers himself had written that 'Although there are no letters of friendship in the New Testament, some letters employ commonplaces and language from the friendly letter tradition' (p. 60).

30. Stowers, *Letter-Writing*, esp. pp. 58-76.

31. *Ancient Epistolary Theorists* (trans. A.J. Malherbe; SBLSBS, 19; Atlanta: Scholars Press, 1988), p. 33.

often 'there is no isolable message or body apart from the corres-pondents' interest in each others' welfare'.[32]

In showing the similarities between Philippians and other family letters, Alexander initially focuses on a group of four Hellenistic family epistles.[33] Taking the entire pattern of formal characteristics from one of these letters—that of Apolinaris to his mother[34]—Alexander shows that Paul's letter to the Philippians follows this same pattern. Both have an address and greeting, a prayer for the recipients, reassurance about the sender, a request for reassurance about the recipients, information about the movements of intermediaries, an exchange of greetings with third parties, and a closing wish for health.[35]

These elements, one might argue, are characteristic of a great many letters. Although many of Paul's letters share these elements, in Philippians they do seem central. On a very practical level, Alexander's proposal does make sense of the basic structure of Philippians.

Alexander qualifies her study, referring to the small number of letters employed. However, as she writes, 'The group contains sufficient struc-tural parallelism to make it interesting for our purpose. We are not trying to argue that all family letters follow this pattern, simply that the pattern exists.'[36] There is, in any case, a need to further qualify this formal analysis. Family letters may focus primarily on the act of com-munication between the members of the family. Phil. 1.12-26 may reflect 'reassurance about the sender' and Phil. 1.27–2.18 may be a 'request for reassurance about the recipients'.[37] At the same time, however, there is much more at stake in each of these sections: there is ethical reasoning; there is moral admonition; there is theological reflection. A stark formal analysis runs the risk not only of reducing each section of the letter to particular predictable elements, but also of failing to note ways in which the sections are themselves interrelated.

An examination of the rhetorical strategy of yet another family letter,

---

32. White, *Light from Ancient Letters*, p. 197.

33. Alexander, 'Hellenistic Letter-Forms', pp. 90-94. The letters she employs are second-century papyri, brought together in White, *Light from Ancient Letters*, pp. 196-97.

34. This second-century (CE) letter is presented in White, *Light from Ancient Letters*, pp. 196-97 (n. 104B = P. Mich. VIII 491).

35. Alexander, 'Hellenistic Letter-Forms', p. 94.

36. Alexander, 'Hellenistic Letter-Forms', p. 90.

37. Alexander, 'Hellenistic Letter-Forms', p. 94.

Cicero, *Ad Quintum Fratrem* 1.3,[38] will go far in enabling us to understand both how family letters do employ rhetoric and how Phil. 1.18b-26 functions within Philippians as a whole.

The letter is fascinating. Accused of a crime, a man writes to 'family'. He starts the letter with an extensive thanksgiving, rejoicing for the recipient and expressing his desire that they see one another. He talks about strife and difficulties resulting from his current situation. Emphasizing the partnership shared with the letter's recipient, the accused continues the letter explaining that he remains alive only for the sake of his 'family'. Admonitions for the future are given, the family is warned of possible strife which might occur, and then the letter concludes with a reference to a gift which the accused received from the family. The writer is thankful, but he also emphasizes that the gift was more than enough. Good wishes end the epistle.

Those elements of the letter are, in short, a fair summary of Cicero's epistle to his brother Quintus (*QFr.* 1.3). As is evident to anyone who has read Paul's letters, the apostle's letter to the Philippians has remarkable similarities to this particular epistle from Cicero.

Literary dependence is unlikely: there is no reason to assume that Paul modeled his Greek epistle on that of Cicero's Latin one. Cicero's letter to Quintus, however, can help us understand better both rhetorical conventions and moral dispositions with which Paul's audience may well have been familiar. As Abraham J. Malherbe writes,

> Ancient writers had an interest in what constituted the proper subject matter and style of a letter, and Paul's letters will be illuminated by their prescriptions for letter writing as well as by the letters of the men who were familiar with the theory.[39]

Cicero's epistle is an excellent example not just of a family letter, but also of epistolographic style and of moral exhortation. At the very least, it is significant to note that here we have two examples of family letters, both written by accused criminals, and both which explicitly discuss the choice between living and dying.

Paul's choice between life and death, discussed in Phil. 1.18b-26, is illuminated by an examination of Cicero's discussion of the same in chs. 2

---

38. It may be noted that this letter also reflects a number of the elements of the basic formal pattern identified by Alexander.

39. *Social Aspects of Early Christianity* (Philadelphia: Fortress Press, 2nd edn, 1983), p. 58.

and 5 of his epistle. Before discussing the rhetorical strategy Cicero
employs, a short summary of *QFr.* 1.3 will help in setting the context.

Having been forced into exile, Cicero starts this letter to his brother
Quintus emphasizing not only that he was not angry with him, but also
that he had always found in Quintus 'all that is honourable and
pleasant'(1). From here, Cicero pivots into an apology, recognizing that
his exile had hurt Quintus: 'In me you have found grief for my degradation, apprehension of your own, yearning, mourning, abandonment'
(1.3.1). Cicero writes that he has missed his brother greatly and then
emphasizes that he would have preferred death over life in this present
situation, but for the sake of his brother, he chose to remain alive: 'But I
call all the gods to witness that the one argument which called me back
from death was everybody's saying that no small portion of your life
was vested in mine. And so I behaved like a fool and a criminal...' (2)
After accounting for the fact that he had not written recently, Cicero
stresses that he has missed his brother and all that they shared together.
Quintus is 'one who in affection is almost a twin, in deference a son, in
counsel a father. What has ever given me pleasure without your sharing
it, or you without my sharing it' (3).

The letter then turns to a discussion of Cicero's desire for Quintus to
proceed to Rome (4). Although enemies of Cicero may face Quintus
there, Quintus is to rouse himself and show his strength: '...but if you
are free from your own particular danger, you will of course do whatever you think can be done in my interests' (5). In this context, Cicero
again states his desire to leave life, but emphasizes, 'Whatever happens,
as long as you have need of me, or see any danger ahead, so long shall I
remain alive; longer than that I cannot brook my present life' (5). Cicero
writes that he does not want to tarry (in this life) 'any longer than either
your needs or any trustworthy hope shall necessitate' (6). He then
acknowledges 'a bill of exchange' and the other resources and money
which Quintus has provided for him, emphasizing that 'For myself the
sum I now have in hand is sufficient for what I have in view. For whether
I am restored or given up in despair, I shall need nothing more' (7).

Quintus is warned that Cicero's enemies are apt to attack him when
they see that his supplications and acquittal will 'excite compassion' for
Cicero (8). Cicero realizes that he and his brother have lost friends because
of their 'endless calamities' (9), and he concludes the letter, wishing that
his brother 'Be as brave as the nature of the case permits' (10).

Cicero describes not only his own situation and the actions of the recipient of the letter, but he is also, and primarily, concerned with the relationship between himself and his brother. That, of course, is typical of family letters. Although Cicero is discussing a variety of issues— ranging from death to his being recalled, from the money he has received to expectations for his brother—the emphasis on the fraternal relationship runs throughout the letter. It is within the context of this familial relationship that Cicero's reflections on life and death can best be understood.

Twice in this letter Cicero discusses taking his own life. In the first instance (2), he refers to a situation from the past, when he had wanted to commit suicide, but did not. In the second instance, he sees taking his own life as a possibility in the future. As for the present, Cicero writes, 'No wisdom, no philosophy, is strong enough to bear such a weight of woe' (5).

Cicero's discussions here could be seen as little more than musings about suicide. Such musings would find a home in the philosophy of this time period.[40] These discussions, however, are much easier to understand if one notes how they function rhetorically within Cicero's epistle. In other words, regardless of what Cicero may have regretted not having done in the past, regardless of what he might do in the future, why does he mention taking his life within this particular letter? In determining how these discussions function within the epistle as a whole, it is helpful to look at each in context.

After emphasizing his respect for Quintus, Cicero tells of the anguish he felt, that his brother was forced to see that he had lost prestige (1). Cicero felt so much anguish that he desired to take his own life:

> But I call all the gods to witness that the one argument which called me back from death was everybody's saying that no small portion of your life was vested in mine. And so I behaved like a fool and a criminal. For had I died, my death in itself would be sufficient proof of my brotherly affection for you. As it is, I have made the mistake of depriving you of my aid while I am yet alive, and causing you, while I am yet alive, to need the aid of others (2).

It should be noted initially that Cicero does not explicitly say that he was going to put himself to death: he only says that he was 'called back from death'. Yet he is clearly referring to suicide. This can be seen not only in an extended discussion later in the epistle (1.3.5-6), but also in

---

40. Cf. Droge and Tabor, *A Noble Death*, pp. 17-51.

QFr. 1.4.4. Here Cicero writes, 'The tears of my family prevented me from putting myself to death, which was certainly the course best adapted to the retention of my honour and my escape from unendurable sufferings.'

Although Cicero wanted to take his own life, for the sake of his brother (as described in 1.3.1), he did not. Cicero made his choice not on the basis of his own preference, but on the basis of what was necessary and important for his brother Quintus. Thus, the discussion of his 'suicide plans' in 1.3.2 serve at least two purposes: 1) they present Cicero as a person who is willing to forego his own desires for the sake of his brother's will; and 2) they explain why, in spite of Cicero's own desires, he remains both alive and dependent on 'the aid of others'.

Similarly, after Cicero encourages Quintus, who will be in Rome, to act on his behalf, he again states his desire for death, but emphasizes, 'Whatever happens, as long as you have need of me, or see any danger ahead, so long shall I remain alive; longer than that I cannot brook my present life' (5). This section of the letter is followed by a discussion of the financial support which Quintus has provided for him (7).

Although Cicero is quick to write that he has no more need of money, and although his language implies uneasiness or apprehension about his dependence on financial support, Cicero's rhetoric of suicide—at the very least—shelters him from potential criticism about these financial matters. He has stated openly that he wants to die and, as soon as Quintus no longer needs him, Cicero will indeed choose death. Then any concern about financially supporting the exiled Cicero would be gone: there would be no need to write 'bills of exchange', there would be no need to 'draw upon your own and your son's very life-blood' (7).

Cicero remains alive for the sake of his brother and that alone. At least that is what he emphasizes in 1.3.2: 'the one argument which called me back from death was everybody's saying that no small portion of your life was vested in mine'. In 1.3.6, however, Cicero emphasizes that he will remain alive 'no longer than either your needs or any *trustworthy hope* shall necessitate'.[41] 'Trustworthy hope', Cicero now writes, provides another condition whereby he would consider remaining alive. Such 'trustworthy hope', it seems, depends on Quintus' arguing in Rome on his behalf.

Thus, Cicero implies that at least one of the consequences of his still being alive is that his brother should help him. As he writes,

41. Emphasis mine.

2. *Paul's Choice and the Rhetoric of Voluntary Death*   111

> But if you are free from your own particular danger, you will of course do
> whatever you think can be done in my interests. And as to that, there are
> many who write long letters to me and make it plain that they have their
> hopes; but I cannot discern myself what I am to hope for, seeing that my
> enemies are exceedingly powerful, while my friends have in some cases
> deserted, in other cases actually betrayed me, perhaps because they are
> terribly afraid that my recall would imply a censure upon their scandalous
> conduct.

When Cicero refers to the necessity of trustworthy hope (*firma spes*) in
1.3.6, Quintus must have read that in light of 1.3.5, where his brother
just emphasized that his hope cannot rest in former friends: Cicero's
hope rests in Quintus alone. Just as Cicero had made a sacrifice—
remaining alive for the sake of Quintus and, thus, 'behaving like a fool
and a criminal'—so he calls on his brother to support him by working in
his 'interests'. Cicero appears to assume that this will happen, going so
far as to warn Quintus that persons will attack him all the more fiercely
when he defends Cicero (1.3.8).

Would Cicero actually have committed suicide? He writes that he
would have. Was he actually planning on it in the future? He writes that
he was. For the sake of his brother, however, he did not take his own
life. It is not that Quintus *asked* Cicero not to; it is rather that, as Cicero
claims, 'everybody said' (*omnes...dicebant*) that Quintus would be
distraught if Cicero did kill himself. Cicero then writes that he would
prefer to take his own life and that he would do so, when Quintus told
him that he no longer had need of him. In its simplest form, the admonition sounds odd: 'Whenever you want me to kill myself, just tell me.'
This reduction, at the very least, points us to the rhetorical purpose which
Cicero's discussion of suicide serves within the context of the letter.

In this letter, Cicero needs to respond to his brother's financial
support: a recent letter from Quintus must have mentioned a bill of
exchange (1.3.7). By emphasizing that he had desired to kill himself in
the past, Cicero protects himself from potential criticism that he was
exploiting others for whatever financial support he was receiving (the
support would have been unnecessary if he were dead). Even more than
this, Cicero's not having taken his own life—he is quick to point out—
shows that he has placed his brother's desires before his own.

Out of concern for Quintus, Cicero writes, he decided not to kill
himself. Thus, whatever burden resulted from his still being alive rests on
Quintus's shoulders. At the same time, Cicero implies that his not having
taken his own life has resulted in an even greater burden for Quintus.

Cicero will take his own life in the future, unless Quintus either needs him or gives him reason for 'trustworthy hope'. He places his fate in his brother's hands. No melancholy discussion of suicide, Cicero's words serve to remind his brother of the significance of their relationship: they function as a call to action.

Philippians 1.18b-26 is seen most often as a description of Paul's temperament in prison: Paul is musing about the relative worth of life and death. Although Paul does discuss these options, Phil. 1.18b-26—as part of a family letter—also addresses the apostle's relationship with those persons to whom he is writing. Within the larger scheme of the rhetoric of Philippians, Paul's discussion of life and death serves a mimetic purpose. Like Cicero's discussion of suicide, Paul's words are a call to action.

Initially, summarizing key points in Phil. 1.18b-26 is helpful in examining the overall rhetorical strategy of this passage. The pericope begins with a discussion of σωτηρία:

> Yes, and I shall rejoice. For I know that through your prayers and the help of the Spirit of Jesus Christ this will turn out for my deliverance (εἰς σωτηρίαν), as it is my eager expectation and hope that I shall not be at all ashamed, but that with full courage now as always Christ will be honored in my body, whether by life or by death (1.18b-20).

Some commentators have argued that the expression 'this will turn out for my deliverance' refers to Paul's release from prison.[42] Although it is possible that the Greek word σωτηρία could refer to a deliverance from prison, and although it is tempting to read v. 20 in light of vv. 25-26, Moisés Silva has shown convincingly that such an interpretation 'runs against insurmountable difficulties'. Silva presents a number of reasons why the Greek word σωτηρία should be understood as referring to 'salvation' (or 'vindication')[43] and not to 'release (from prison)':[44]

1. Initially, Silva emphasizes that Paul links his adversity with his deliverance. The demonstrative pronoun τοῦτο in 1.19 points the reader back to 1.12-18, to the description of what Paul has experienced and that which his imprisonment has affected. As Silva writes,

> It is not merely that he will be delivered, but that his adversity *will result* in his deliverance. It makes little sense to say that what Paul has suffered

---

42. For a thorough discussion of this stance, see Hawthorne, *Philippians*, p. 40.

43. Cf. Martin, *Philippians*, p. 75.

44. The following arguments are developed from those discussed in Silva, *Philippians*, pp. 76-79.

(whether the imprisonment itself or the work of his opponents) will lead to his release (p. 76).

In emphasizing that Paul is discussing 'salvation' and not 'release from prison', Silva notes the 'conceptual parallelism' between v. 12 and v. 19:

| 1.12 | τὰ κατ' ἐμὲ | εἰς προκοπὴν τοῦ εὐαγγελίου | ἐλήλυθεν |
| 1.19 | τοῦτο | εἰς σωτηρίαν | ἀποβήσεται |

Paul is convinced, through the help of the Spirit and through the prayers of the Philippians, that that which Paul has suffered will result in his salvation.

2. Regardless of what happens in prison, regardless if he lives or dies (1.20), Paul expects and hopes for this σωτηρία. Σωτηρία here, thus, should not be linked with freedom or deliverance from prison.

3. Philippians 1.19 shares remarkable verbal similarities with Job 13.16 (LXX).[45] In ch. 13, Job is pleading before God and he cries out that 'this will turn out for my salvation (τοῦτό μοι ἀποβήσεται εἰς σωτηρίαν) since deceit will not come before him'. Paul's words ('this will turn out for my salvation') are exactly the words of Job. In a letter in which quotations from the Hebrew Scriptures play no major role,[46] in an epistle in which allusions from the Hebrew Scriptures might well have been lost on its readers, it is unlikely that Paul is employing this expression as a quotation or a Scripture proof. Regardless, the verbal similarities between Paul's and Job's words point to the possibility of Paul's interpreting his own situation in light of Job's. If Paul is referring to Job, he is referring to a context in which Job's 'eternal destiny' is at stake.

4. Finally, Silva sees the Greek expression κατὰ τὴν ἀποκαραδοκίαν καὶ ἐλπίδα μου ('according to my eager expectation and hope') as most appropriate for a discussion of salvation: 'Why Paul would use such (soteriologically) charged terms in describing his desire to be released from prison defies explanation.'[47]

Thus, although the word σωτηρία could be employed to refer to a

45. For a more thorough discussion of the relationship between these passages see R.B. Hays, *Echoes of Scripture in the Letters of Paul* (New Haven: Yale University Press, 1989), pp. 21-24.

46. L.M. White, 'Morality between Two Worlds: A Paradigm of Friendship in Philippians', in D.L. Balch *et al.* (eds.), *Greeks, Romans, and Christians: Essays in Honor of Abraham J. Malherbe* (Minneapolis: Fortress Press, 1990), pp. 205-206, emphasizes that Paul's letter to the Philippians, written to a primarily Gentile community, has 'little that is Jewish in its content, its tone, or its ethical exhortation'.

47. Silva, *Philippians*, p. 77.

physical deliverance (for instance, from prison), within the context of this letter, 'the primary reference is to Paul's perseverance in faith: the magnification of Christ—not his own freedom or even his life—is Paul's salvation'.[48] Whether he lives or dies in prison, it will result—regardless—in his salvation.[49]

Paul continues this section of the letter by pointing to the advantages of both living and dying. It is not as if Paul is trying to make himself out as indifferent to whether he lives or dies. He is not indifferent to death: death is 'gain'; death is 'far better'. Paul shows a distinct preference:

> For to me to live is Christ, and to die is gain. If it is to be life in the flesh, that means fruitful labor for me. Yet which I shall choose I cannot tell. I am hard pressed between the two. My desire is to depart and be with Christ, for that is far better (1.21-23).

Although Paul lets the Philippians know that his own preference is for death, he concludes his deliberations by writing that he is convinced that he will remain with them:

> To remain in the flesh is more necessary on your account. Convinced of this, I know that I shall remain and continue with you all, for your progress and joy in the faith, so that in me you may have ample cause to glory in Christ Jesus, because of my coming to you again (1.24-26).

In Phil. 1.18b-26, Paul writes that regardless if he lives or dies in prison, he hopes and expects that salvation will follow. Looking at life and death, he is torn between the two. He says he does not know which he will choose, but he goes on to imply that it is death which he prefers. Finally, Paul emphasizes that because his living is more necessary on account of the Philippians, he will 'remain and continue' with them.[50]

---

48. Silva, *Philippians*, p. 78. Cf. R.F. Hock, 'Philippians', in J.L. Mays (ed.), *Harper's Bible Commentary* (New York: Harper & Row, 1988), p. 1221; and B. Witherington, III, *Friendship and Finances in Philippi: The Letter of Paul to the Philippians* (The New Testament in Context; Valley Forge, PA: Trinity Press International, 1994), p. 46.

49. A first-century discussion of another prisoner, Socrates, offers an interesting analogue to Paul's words here. Epictetus writes, 'Socrates does not save his life with dishonour (Σωκράτης δ' αἰσχρῶς οὐ σῴζεται)...this man it is impossible to save by dishonour, but he is saved by death, and not by flight (τοῦτον οὐκ ἔστι σῶσαι αἰσχρῶς, ἀλλ' ἀποθνήσκων σῴζεται, οὐ φεύγων) (Epictetus, *Diss.* 4.1.164-65).

50. S.E. Porter, 'Word Order and Clause Structure in New Testament Greek: An Unexplored Area of Greek Linguistics Using Philippians as a Test Case', *FN* 6 (1993), p. 199, offers a helpful syntactical analysis of this passage in a discussion of the function of the infinitives ζῆν (1.22) and ἐπιμένειν (1.24). As he writes, 'the

If it were simply the case that Paul was debating with himself whether he preferred to live or to die, one can scarcely imagine that he would have expressed a clear preference. But Paul does express a preference: death. It needs to be asked not why Paul preferred this, but why he wrote it to the Philippians. How does this fit into the rhetoric and argument of this letter?

In 1.22, Paul writes, 'which I shall choose I cannot tell'. In 1.21 and 23, he seems to show a clear preference for death. However, because it is 'more necessary'[51] to remain alive on account of the Philippians (1.24), Paul then resolves the tension created in 1.22 and announces that he will 'remain and continue with you all' (1.25).

Just as Cicero stressed that he remained alive only for Quintus' sake, so Paul emphasizes that he will remain alive for the sake of the Philippians. Both Cicero and Paul stifled their own preferences but made their choices and decisions on the basis of what was necessary for the persons to whom they were accountable. In Paul's letter to the Philippians, even more than in Cicero's letter to Quintus, the motivation behind such rhetoric is apparent: Paul's own deliberation is presented as exemplary to the Philippians.

Almost immediately after Paul's discussion of life and death (1.18b-26), he expresses his hope that he may hear that the Philippians 'stand firm in one spirit, with one mind striving side by side for the faith of the gospel' (1.27). Paul writes such a statement, knowing full well that to 'stand firm...striving side by side' involves more than each individual's pursuing her or his own desires or goals.[52] Thus, when Paul continues with his concern for the unity of the Philippians, he writes,

subject grammaticalized by the infinitive appears to serve often as a topic marker that enhances the focus upon a subject already raised (and not yet discussed) by giving it a verbal aspectual semantic weight'.

51. Droge, *'Mori Lucrum'*, pp. 282-84, offers a particularly interesting discussion of the role of this expression in Greek philosophy.

52. E.M. Krentz, 'Military Language and Metaphors in Philippians', in B.H. McLean (ed.), *Origins and Method: Towards a New Understanding of Judaism and Christianity* (Festschrift J. C. Hurd; JSNTSup, 86; Sheffield: JSOT Press, 1993), pp. 112-13 and 120-27, emphasizes that Paul's language here reflects the sorts of military metaphors which would have been familiar to the Philippians. 'Standing firm', for example, 'describes the attitude of the soldiers drawn up in line...Nothing leads to more certain defeat than having one or another soldier break the line and allow the enemy to pour through' (p. 120). The military metaphors, thus, are particularly relevant in a discussion of the importance of unity.

> Complete my joy by being of the same mind, having the same love, being in full accord and of one mind. Do nothing from selfishness or conceit, but in humility count others better than yourselves. Let each of you look not only to his own interests, but also to the interests of others (2.2-4).

Lest his readers not grasp the point which Paul is making, he offers an example of one who made the ultimate sacrifice: Christ Jesus. Here Paul introduces and then quotes a pre-Pauline hymn:[53]

> Have this mind among youselves,[54] which is yours in Christ Jesus, who, though he was in the form of God, did not count equality with God a thing to be grasped, but emptied himself, taking the form of a servant, being born in the likeness of men. And being found in human form he humbled himself and became obedient unto death, even death on a cross (2.5-8).

Wayne A. Meeks points to this Christ drama as the model for the reversal of values which Paul expects from the Philippians:[55]

> It is Christ's own obedience to the point of death and subsequent exaltation, in short the Christ drama encapsulated in the hymn (2.6-11), that is the basis and model. The analogy is reinforced in Paul's description of Epaphroditus' experience, for Epaphroditus is mediator between Paul and the Philippians not only in his practical service but also here in Paul's rhetoric. His obedience to Christ's task (τὸ ἔργον Χριστοῦ) led him μέχρι θανάτου ('to the point of death', 2.30)—like Christ's own obedience (2.8).[56]

---

53. Cf. E. Lohmeyer, *Kyrios Jesus, Eine Untersuchungen zu Phil 2, 5-11* (Heidelberg: Carl Winter, 2nd edn, 1961), p. 7; and Martin, *Carmen Christi: Philippians ii.5–11 in Recent Interpretation and in the Setting of Early Christian Worship* (Cambridge: Cambridge University Press, 1967), pp. 36-39.

54. Collange, *Philippians*, p. 79, notes the assonance between the Greek word for 'humility' (ταπεινοφροσύνη) in 2.3, and the verb often translated as 'have this mind' (φρονεῖτε) in 2.5. Martin, *Philippians*, p. 89, explains the implications of this well: 'The message would be clear to the readers: let your attitude to and regard for others (*phronein*) be humble (*tapeinos*), and that means a total lifestyle of *tapeinophrosyne*.'

55. W.A. Meeks, 'The Man from Heaven in Paul's Letter to the Philippians', in B.A. Pearson (ed.), *The Future of Early Christianity: Essays in Honor of Helmut Koester* (Minneapolis: Fortress Press, 1991), pp. 329-36, focuses on the paraenetic use of this hymn and the 'generative image' of Christ. Focusing less on 'moral reasoning' and more on ancient discussions of friendship, L.M. White, 'Morality between Two Worlds', p. 213, argues that 'Paul has grounded the fundamental ethical imperative of the Christian's social relationships within the community in the Greek ideal of virtue (friendship) exemplified in Christ's own actions'.

56. Meeks, 'The Man from Heaven', p. 335. Cf. S.J. Kraftchick, 'A Necessary

Just as Christ Jesus was humble unto death, so Epaphroditus 'nearly died for the work of Christ, risking his life' to complete the Philippians' service to Paul (2.30). Paul presents Christ Jesus and Epaphroditus as examples of those whose obedience brought them either to embrace death or to come near death. They emptied themselves in their service for others. Similarly, Paul presents Timothy as one 'who will be genuinely anxious for the welfare' of the Philippians, because he looks after not his own interests but those of Jesus Christ (2.20-22).[57] Similarly, the apostle presents himself as one whose obedience (for the sake of the ἀπολογία τοῦ εὐαγγελίου) has brought him near death and, at the same time, has brought him back from the attraction of death, reminding him of his role in the 'progress and joy' of the Philippians' faith.

In setting the stage for the admonitions and rhetoric of 1.27–2.11, Paul presents the pattern of his own behavior in 1.18b-26 as a model for the Philippians. The Philippians faced their own problems and disagreements (1.28; 2.1-4, 14; 4.2-3), they encountered threats from outside (?) the community (3.2-21), and they—for the sake of their own community—needed to be reminded about the importance of self-sacrifice (1.27–2.11).

Thus, Paul is not simply sharing news.[58] His reflections here build on to that which immediately follows: the exhortation to unity. The apostle does not say, nor does he imply, that God is the one who will ensure that Paul remains and continues with the Philippians. Paul does not refer to what God will do:[59] Paul is the one with the choice. And just as

Detour: Paul's Metaphorical Understanding of the Philippian Hymn', *HBT* 15 (1993), p. 24.

57. Black, 'The Discourse Structure of Philippians', p. 23, also notes the emphasis on serving others found in the letter's salutation. Just as Christ Jesus is described as taking the form of a servant (2.7), so Timothy and Paul refer to themselves as 'servants of Christ Jesus' (1.1). What is particularly striking about this is that Paul usually refers to himself as an 'apostle'. Note Black's discussion ('Discourse Structure of Philippians', pp. 38-39) entitled 'News about Paul's Companions', where he discusses Timothy, Epaphroditus, and the internal structure of 2.19-30.

58. Alexander, 'Hellenistic Letter-Forms', pp. 87-101, presents a compelling analysis of Philippians as a family letter, but in describing 1.12-26, she does not acknowledge how these verses set the stage for the argument in the rest of the letter. Rather, she describes these verses only in terms of Paul's reassurance to the Philippians that all is fine with him: 'After reassuring his converts about his own position, Paul expresses his own need for reassurance about their welfare' (p. 95).

59. *Contra* Garland, 'Defense and Confirmation', p. 334, who takes the decision

Paul's deliberations and choice led him to affirm that he would remain and continue with the Philippians, so each of the Philippians is encouraged to 'look not only to his own interests, but also to the interests of others' (2.4).[60]

Philippians 1.18b-26 has not often been linked to Paul's admonition to unity in 1.27–2.11. When it is assumed that Paul was unsure of whether he *preferred* to live or to die, the apostle is robbed of personal initiative and is seen only as a passive figure. Paul, however, does not use verbs like βούλομαι or θέλω; he uses the verb αἱρήσομαι and, by doing so, presents himself as an example for his factious sisters and brothers, thereby initiating the pattern of 'life for others' which subsequently runs throughout the epistle.[61]

Paul's presentation of incidents from his own life to illustrate the importance of living 'life for others' is not unique to Philippians. In 1 Corinthians 9, he also emphasizes that he had relinquished his own rights for the sake of the community. 1 Corinthians 9, like Phil. 1.18b-26, is not a digression or an aside by Paul: the passage is not merely a defense of Paul's apostleship. The context of 1 Corinthians 9—between two chapters concerned with eating sacrificial meat—points to its rhetorical function. As Wendell Lee Willis points out

> Chapter 9 presents the life of Paul as an example for Christian conduct. This appeal to the normative character of his own conduct may be understood as but the development of the point which is implicit in 8.13 and which is then summarized in the exhortation of 11.1. In 1 Corinthians 9 Paul calls attention to his own willingness to forego his apostolic rights (9.1-5), although he can certainly establish them (9.5-14).[62]

out of Paul's hands and places it in God's: 'While his personal preference is for death (something far better), he concludes that it will be overruled in God's providence by the necessity that he return to the Philippians to strengthen their faith (1.24-26). This conclusion is based on the prior conviction that God always acts for the best interest of His people as a whole.'

60. Capper, 'Paul's Dispute with Philippi', p. 210, writes that Paul's 'rhetoric is designed to humble the Philippians—he will set aside his own desires and make his bold apostolic decision not to die, but to be resurrected to further ministry *for their sakes*, in order to continue ministering as the "missionary" of the Philippian church'.

61. Cf. L.T. Johnson, *The Writings of the New Testament: An Interpretation* (Philadelphia: Fortress Press, 1986), p. 348.

62. *Idol Meat in Corinth: The Pauline Argument in 1 Corinthians 8 and 10* (SBLDS, 68; Chico, CA: Scholars Press, 1985), p. 273.

Where Paul's behavior serves as exemplary in the middle of the argument in 1 Corinthians, it initiates the pattern of life for others which we see in Philippians. J. Paul Sampley sees such behavior as central to Paul's moral understanding:

> Throughout his letters, Paul regularly counsels care for the well-being of the community and shows great concern for the individual members of the body, even the weakest among them. But wherever there is a tension between an individual's or a subgroup's rights and the well-being of the community, he sides with the community and calls for the individual or subgroup to go along with the larger community.
>
> Paul exemplifies this principle in his open reflection about his death in his Letter to the Philippians. He can see some advantage in death: he could be eternally with Christ, which appeals to him (Phil. 1.21, 23). But his own desires, as powerful as they may be, are not the only or even the primary consideration. When he asks himself how his death might affect his partners in the gospel he knows that 'to remain in the flesh is more necessary on account of you' (1.24). Therefore, he directly and firmly announces his plan: 'Persuaded of this, I know that I shall remain and stay on with you all, for your advancement and joy in the faith' (1.25). Paul always expects of his followers this respect for what is good for the community.[63]

5. *Imprisonment and Voluntary Death*

If the apostle, as Sampley writes, 'directly and firmly' announced his plan to remain in the flesh—if Paul decided to not choose death— readers still need to ask themselves, in what respects *could* Paul have 'chosen' death? How would an expression like 'choosing' death have had credibility? Why should we believe that the Philippians might have taken Paul's words seriously?

As quoted above, Arthur Droge sees the issue as to *how* Paul chose death as fairly clear-cut:

> I take this to mean what it says, that the question of life or death is a matter of Paul's own volition, not something to be imposed on him from the outside. And if it is a matter of Paul's own choosing, then it appears that he is reflecting on the possibility of suicide.[64]

---

63. J.P. Sampley, *Walking between the Times: Paul's Moral Reasoning* (Minneapolis: Fortress Press, 1991), pp. 42-43.

64. '*Mori Lucrum*', p. 279.

In a subsequent work on the same subject, Droge has taken some of the passion out of his original proposal, now referring to Paul's choice as reflecting not 'suicide', but 'voluntary death'. In *A Noble Death*, Droge and Tabor deliberately avoid

> using the word *suicide*, a recent innovation and pejorative term, preferring instead the designation *voluntary death*....to describe the act resulting from an individual's intentional decision to die, either by his own agency, by another's, or by contriving the circumstances in which death is the known, ineluctable result.[65]

What such a definition gains in its inclusiveness, it loses—naturally enough—in its precision. Simply for the purpose of organization, it is helpful to break this category down into two sets. As used here, the expression 'active voluntary death' will refer to the result of a person taking his or her own life by means of his or her own hands. The expression 'passive voluntary death' will refer to the result of a person accepting death as a consequence of other actions which they willfully have taken.

What Droge originally referred to as 'suicide' can also be seen as active voluntary death. Droge sees the justification for Paul's consideration of suicide as 'the troubles that vex his earthly life': imprisonment (Phil. 1.7, 13, 14, 17); afflictions (1.17; 4.14), the struggle of life (1.30), grief (2.27), 'humiliation, deprivation, and hunger' (4.11-12).[66] Droge also refers to the other Pauline letters, claiming that 'death is a gain for Paul not only because it means union with Christ but also because it brings deliverance from life's miseries'.[67]

Although Paul himself experienced his share of miseries, if one is looking for motives as to why he may have desired to take his own life, it is important to look not only at his letters but also at ancient texts which discuss the horrors of prison. Suicide in prison occurred often. As described in Chapter 1, despair, shame, fear of a worse fate, and fiscal concerns all led numerous prisoners to take their own lives.[68] Writing from prison, Paul may well have been exploiting his readers' familiarity with this phenomenon. Because suicide occurred frequently in ancient prisons, the imprisoned clearly had 'a choice'.

Suicide, however, was not the only choice the imprisoned could

65. Droge and Tabor, *A Noble Death*, p. 4.
66. Droge and Tabor, *A Noble Death*, p. 121.
67. Droge and Tabor, *A Noble Death*, 122.
68. See Chapter 1, 'Suicide'.

embrace. Numerous persons chose to die through a type of passive voluntary death, an unwillingness to be fully cooperative during trial.

One imprisoned figure who was remembered in this way, one classical figure who was unwilling to compromise his integrity in the courtroom, was the philosopher Socrates. Xenophon presents Socrates as saying,

> If I am going to offend the jury by declaring all the blessings that I feel gods and men have bestowed on me, as well as my personal opinions of myself, I shall choose (αἱρήσομαι) to die rather than to live begging meanly and thus gaining a life far less worthy in exchange for death (*Ap.* 9; adaption of Loeb translation).

Plato offers a similar speech attributed to Socrates:

> I did not think at the time that I ought, on account of the danger I was in, to do anything unworthy of a free man, nor do I now repent of having made my defence as I did, but I would rather choose (αἱροῦμαι) to die after such a defence than to live after a defence of the other sort (*Ap.* 38E; adaption of Loeb translation).

This image of Socrates was not confined to Xenophon's and Plato's descriptions of him. During the first century CE, Epictetus highlighted the portrayal of Socrates as one who chose to die rather than to desert his station.[69] A.A. Long sees Epictetus's Socrates as 'the Stoics' patron saint'.[70]

In antiquity, then, there was a standard portrayal of the philosopher Socrates, considering his choice between life and death: life (a possible acquittal) was his, if he offered a defence involving wailing and lamenting, saying what the jury wanted to hear; death was his if he spoke the truth with integrity. Epictetus said that death was that which had the potential to save Socrates. As mentioned above, in *Diss.* 4.1.164-65, Epictetus writes, 'Socrates does not save his life with dishonour [Σωκράτης δ' αἰσχρῶς οὐ σῴζεται]...this man it is impossible to save by dishonour, but he is saved by death, and not by flight [τοῦτον οὐκ ἔστι σῶσαι αἰσχρῶς, ἀλλ' ἀποθνῄσκων σῴζεται, οὐ φεύγων].'

Christians in the first century would likely have been familiar with the

---

69. Epictetus, *Diss.* 1.9.22-24. Cf. *Diss.* 2.2.8-20. Here Socrates is described as deliberately provoking his judges.

70. A.A. Long, 'Socrates in Hellenistic Philosophy', *Classical Quarterly* 38 (1988), pp. 150-51. Note also that Paul, in Philippians, frequently employs Stoic ideas and ideals. In particular, see T. Engberg-Pedersen, 'Stoicism in Philippians', in T. Engberg-Pedersen (ed.), *Paul in Hellenistic Context* (Minneapolis: Fortress Press, 1995), pp. 356-90.

typical descriptions of the canonical philosopher of their day.[71] The fact
that he was imprisoned and that he discussed choosing death over life
would not have fallen on deaf ears. Regardless, as readers of the Gospels
know, Socrates was not the only figure whose courtroom defence led to
his death. In Mk 15.2-5,[72] the governor Pontius Pilate asked Jesus,

> 'Are you the King of the Jews?' And he answered him, 'You have said
> so.' And the chief priests accused him of many things. And Pilate again
> asked him, 'Have you no answer to make? See how many charges they
> bring against you.' But Jesus made no further answer, so that Pilate
> wondered.

Jesus' impetuous answer, followed by silence, did not positively impress
the authorities. Pilate responded to the silence by crucifying the accused.

Regardless of the harshness of the consequences, regardless of Jesus'
having been crucified, this dominical precedent of silence found numerous
followers among early Christians. Particularly in the second and third
centuries, Christians 'believed that they had to re-enact the death of
Jesus in order to become true disciples. His death was the paradigm.'[73]
As Droge writes,

> It appears that the courtroom in particular was the breeding ground of
> spontaneous acts of self-destruction. Not only individuals but also whole
> groups of Christians would give themselves up in the heat of the moment
> at 'unfair sentences' handed down by the Romans.[74]

When Christians responded to all questions with the answer ἐγὼ
Χριστιανός εἰμι, when they were silent during their trials, or when

71. See K.O. Sandnes, 'Paul and Socrates: The Aim of Paul's Areopagus
Speech', *JSNT* 50 (1993), pp. 13-26, esp. pp. 20-25; E. Benz, 'Christus und Sokrates
in der alten Kirche: Ein Beitrag zum altkirchlichen Verständnis des Märtyrers und des
Martyriums', *ZNW* 43 (1950-51), pp. 195-224; K. Döring, *Exemplum Socratis:
Studien zur Sokratesnachwirkung in der kynische-stoischen Popularphilosophie der
frühen Kaiserzeit und im frühen Christentum* (Wiesbaden: Franz Steiner Verlag,
1979); A. von Harnack, *Sokrates und die alte Kirche* (Gissen: J. Richer, 1900); and
I. Opelt, 'Das Bild des Sokrates in der christlichen lateinischen Literatur', in H.D.
Blume and F. Mann (eds.), *Platonismus und Christentum: Festschrift für Heinrich
Dörrie* (Jahrbuch für Antike und Christentum; Münster Westfalen: Aschendorfsche
Verlagsbuchhandlung, 1983).
72. Cf. Mt. 27.11-13 and Lk. 23.1-4. When Herod is the interrogator in Lk. 23.9,
Jesus—here also—is said to have been silent.
73. Droge and Tabor, *A Noble Death*, p. 131.
74. Droge and Tabor, *A Noble Death*, p. 132. Cf. R.L. Fox, *Pagans and
Christians* (San Francisco: Harper & Row, 1986), pp. 442-43.

they engaged before the tribunal (or in the courtroom) in what Roman magistrates saw as impetuous or impious behavior, they were following their Lord and—in effect—choosing death.[75]

Thus, it is not surprising that Christians may have developed a reputation for being non-cooperative: Marcus Aurelius saw Christians' willingness for death as a result of 'obstinate opposition';[76] some fifty years earlier Pliny also had pointed to the Christians' 'stubbornness and inflexible obstinacy' (*pertinacia et inflexibilis obstinatio*).[77] Pliny saw this reluctance and stubbornness as justifiable grounds for executing the Christians.[78]

The pattern of 'inflexible obstinacy' during trial extended for Christians back to their Lord. However, fairly early in the church some Christians chose another path. Perhaps they were concerned with their own lives. Perhaps they were concerned with the survival of Christianity. Perhaps they were more optimistic about the role and intentions of the Roman government. Perhaps they simply felt the need to reconcile their Christian world with the Roman world. During their trials, these Christians chose no passive death; they chose to offer a defence for Christianity.[79]

One of the best examples of this attitude in early Christianity can be seen in 1 Peter. Here Christians are called to 'be subject for the Lord's sake to every human institution, whether it be to the emperor as supreme, or to governors' (2.13-14). Christians are exhorted not just to make a defence but to make it in a respectful manner: 'Always be prepared to make a defence to any one who calls you to account for the hope that is in you, yet do it with gentleness and reverence' (3.15).

In general, Paul seemed optimistic about the role of the Roman

---

75. In H. Musurillo, *The Acts of the Christian Martyrs* (Oxford: Clarendon Press, 1972), there are numerous examples of accused Christians who said nothing and did nothing to defend themselves. Cf. Droge and Tabor, *A Noble Death*, esp. pp. 132-55.

76. *Med.* 11.3.

77. *Ep.* 10.96.

78. Different views on how Christian obstinacy affected Romans and magistrates are presented in G.E.M. de Ste Croix and A.N. Sherwin-White, 'Why Were the Early Christians Persecuted?—An Amendment', *Past and Present* 27 (1964), pp. 23-33.

79. Note, in Philostratus, *VA* 4.46, the imprisoned Musonius is presented as writing to Apollonius (who had wanted Musonius to escape from prison). Musonius responds, 'Socrates was put to death, because he would not take the trouble to defend himself, but I shall defend myself'.

government. In Rom. 13.1-7, he called 'every person to be subject to the governing authorities'. In v. 4, he even stressed that rulers, as servants of God, 'do not bear the sword in vain'. This sort of optimism can be seen also in Philippians. In Philippians, Paul faced a choice between life and death. Perhaps this choice, more simply stated, was between an active defence (which also involved an ἀπολογία τοῦ εὐαγγελίου, 1.16) and no defence at all (*in imitatio Christi*). Neither silence nor obstinacy would have gone far either in preserving his life or his mission. Paul's choosing to defend himself seems very plausible.

6. Conclusion

Although the imprisoned had few liberties, they could choose between life and death. Often when prisoners were tired of living, or when the shame, fear and despair of imprisonment had become overwhelming, they chose death by committing suicide. Sometimes, however, prisoners embraced death in a less direct manner. Some, like Jesus and Socrates, did not testify aggressively on their own behalf. They did not defend themselves in court nor did they say what they knew would lead to their acquittal and, in effect, they chose death by accepting the consequences of their actions. Plato, Xenophon and Epictetus all presented Socrates as acknowledging that the decisions he had made led him to choose death.

Thus, in a discussion of life and death, when Paul wrote 'which I shall choose I cannot tell' (1.21-22), the Philippians would have been conscious that the incarcerated frequently chose death in prison. When the Philippians read those words, the choices available to the apostle would have been obvious to them. Like so many imprisoned philosophers and political figures of his day, Paul could have committed suicide. Like both Jesus and Socrates, Paul could have remained silent or not defended himself before the Roman officials. Paul, after all, saw death as 'gain' and as 'far better' than life. There is no reason to believe that Paul's words would not have sounded reasonable to the Philippians.

Paul, however, goes on to stress that he would not choose death: 'remaining in the flesh' is 'more necessary' for the sake of the Philippians' 'progress and joy in the faith' (1.24-25). Just as Cicero emphasized that, regardless of his own desire to commit suicide, he remained alive for the sake of his brother Quintus, so Paul emphasizes that, regardless of his desire to 'depart and be with Christ', his choice needed to reflect what was best for the gospel and for the Philippians.

Just as Christ Jesus 'emptied himself, taking the form of a servant' (2.7), just as Epaphroditus 'nearly died' for the sake of the community (2.30), just as Timothy was anxious for the welfare of the Philippians— looking after not his own interests, but those of Jesus Christ—so Paul himself put aside whatever desires he himself may have had. Paul, Jesus, Epaphroditus and Timothy stand as examples to the Philippians, who are admonished to 'do nothing from selfishness or conceit, but in humility count others better' than themselves (2.3).

In Phil. 1.18b-26, Paul is not simply musing out loud on whether he would 'prefer' life or death. Rather, Paul is referring to a situation where he has a choice. By employing the rhetoric of voluntary death, by letting his readers know that he does have a choice—with a preference which, for their sake, he will not choose—Paul presents a pattern of behavior which he expects the Philippian community to follow. Paul is talking about making a choice, against his own preference, for the sake of others. He expects his readers to do the same.

Chapter 3

THE PHILIPPIANS' GIFT TO THE IMPRISONED APOSTLE: THE FUNCTION OF PHILIPPIANS 4.10-20

Not that I seek the gift; but I seek the
fruit which increases to your credit.
—Phil. 4.17

1. *Introduction*

Thrown into the darkness of prison, the incarcerated in antiquity were concerned not only about their future, but about their fate within the prison itself. Death, disease and starvation were common; weakness and shattered nerves were the norm. The imprisoned, however, were not always forced to face these torments alone. Visitors to prison—bearing bribes for the guards and aid for the prisoners—often made incarceration more tolerable, if not more humane. Sometimes they brought food and clothing. Sometimes they enabled the incarcerated to move to a better part of the prison. Sometimes they brought only moral support.[1]

Although New Testament writings emphasize the importance of Christians visiting the imprisoned (e.g., Mt. 25.36-44 and Heb. 13.3), that which was involved in these visits is probably best seen in later narratives from the second and early third centuries. Lucian's *The Passing of Peregrinus* and *The Martyrdom of Perpetua and Felicitas*, for example, both present vivid descriptions of the lengths to which Christians would go in supporting the imprisoned. What is explicit in these narratives, however, is left only implicit in epistles like that of Paul to the Philippians. Paul does not elaborate on how Epaphroditus—the Philippians' 'messenger and minister' to his need—served him in prison.[2] Likely there was no need for a detailed written explanation. Since Epaphroditus himself was the bearer of this letter, he could elaborate orally both on

1. See 'Visitors and Bribery', in Chapter 1.
2. Phil. 2.25-30; 4.10-20.

Paul's situation and on his own activities.[3]

With no need for Paul to belabor the obvious, the letter to the Philippians itself shows few traces of Epaphroditus's visit. Even then, we know less about the visit itself than we do about Paul's interpretation of it. One thing the apostle does mention, though, is a gift (δόμα) which Epaphroditus had brought from the Philippians.[4] Because prisoners generally depended on some form of outside assistance, a gift would not have been seen as unusual. What has been seen as unusual, however, is that Paul's discussion of this gift does not occur explicitly until near the end of the letter (Phil. 4.10-20). Thus, it has often been asked why Paul would not have discussed it earlier.

A variety of answers have been offered. Perhaps these verses originally constituted an independent note. A later editor may have combined this note with fragments from one or more other epistles in order to create the canonical letter which we now have.[5] Perhaps, as another proposal goes, Phil. 4.10-20 was a personal message which Paul added to a letter written by his scribe.[6] Or perhaps, as others argue, the recognition of thanks occurs where it does because that is when Paul remembered to mention the gift.[7]

---

3.   The person who carried the letter often supplemented the written message with additional information. Cf. Col. 4.7-9; Cicero, *Fam.* 1.5b.1; 1.8.1; 3.1.2; 3.5.1; 11.20.4; 11.21.5; 12.6.1; etc. Also see M.M. Mitchell, 'New Testament Envoys in the Context of Greco–Roman Diplomatic and Epistolary Conventions: The Example of Timothy and Titus', *JBL* 111 (1992), pp. 641-62.

4.   Although C.O. Buchanan, 'Epaphroditus' Sickness and the Letter to the Philippians', *EvQ* 36 (1964), pp. 158-63, argues that the gift was a financial one, Paul does not say directly what this gift was. He refers to it only as τὰ πάρ ὑμῶν (4.18).

5.   See B.D. Rahtjen, 'The Three Letters of Paul to the Philippians', *NTS* 6 (1959–60), pp. 167-73; W. Schenk, *Die Philipperbriefe des Paulus* (Stuttgart: Kohlmanner, 1984), pp. 334-36; and J.-F. Collange, *The Epistle of Saint Paul to the Philippians* (trans. A.W. Heathcote; London: Epworth Press, 1979), pp. 3-15. Despite there being no textual evidence for this hypothesis, partition theories have found widespread support. One of the most striking disadvantages of the partition theory is its implicit assumption that the redactor would have been so clumsy (or at least clumsier than Paul), that he or she would have left obvious seams in the newly-created letter.

6.   C.J. Bahr, 'The Subscriptions in the Pauline Letters', *JBL* 87 (1968), pp. 27-41; and P.T. O'Brien, *The Epistle to the Philippians: A Commentary on the Greek Text* (Grand Rapids, MI: Eerdmans, 1991), p. 17. Without the autograph copy of the letter or other (compelling) ancient examples of this practice, this intriguing hypothesis is impossible to prove.

7.   J. Eadie, *A Commentary on the Greek Text of the Epistle of Paul to the*

Other interpreters have sought to see these verses within the rhetoric of the letter as it now exists. Perhaps Paul was perturbed with the Philippians, who had taken so long to respond to his need (4.10), and so he finished the letter with a 'sarcastic rebuke'.[8] Or perhaps Paul left this discussion of the gift to the letter's end, because he was concerned with his self-reliance and did not want to accept gifts from others: he was appreciative, but somewhat indignant that the Philippians had not respected his desire to be independent.[9]

If Paul was trying to be sarcastic, if he was concerned with his self-reliance, it would be odd that he would rejoice at the Philippians' renewed concern on his behalf (4.10) and praise them for sharing his affliction (4.14). At the very least, it would be surprising that he would refer to their history of 'giving and receiving' (4.15-16) without reprimanding them. It does not appear that Paul is seeking to highlight ways in which the Philippians' support of him had faltered (either in frequency or in intent).

Philippians (Edinburgh: T. & T. Clark, 1896), p. xxxi, writes, 'The transitions depend upon no logical train—as the thoughts occurred they were dictated. And we can never know what suggested to the apostle the order of his topics.' Cf. W. Hendriksen, *Exposition of Philippians* (Grand Rapids, MI: Baker Book House, 1962), pp. 37-38.

W.J. Dalton, 'The Integrity of Philippians', *Bib* 60 (1979), p. 98, basically in agreement with Eadie's position, sees the random nature of the letter as related to Paul's incarceration: 'The letter was written from prison, hardly a place conducive to elegant composition. Paul, as he faced death, had a good deal more on his mind besides the orderly composition of Philippians.'

8.   T.W. Manson, 'St Paul in Ephesus: The Date of the Epistle to the Philippians', *BJRL* 23 (1939), p. 190. Cf. R.T. Fortna, 'Philippians: Paul's Most Egocentric Letter', in R.T. Fortna and B.R. Gaventa (eds.), *The Conversation Continues: Studies in Paul and John in Honor of J. Louis Martyn* (Nashville: Abingdon Press, 1990), p. 231 n. 8. Against Manson and Fortna, it must be noted that if we take Paul at face value in Phil. 4.10, he does recognize that the Philippians had been concerned. There is no need to assume that Paul is being sarcastic here.

9.   G.F. Hawthorne, *Philippians* (WBC, 43; Waco, TX: Word Books, 1983), p. 195. D.E. Garland, 'The Composition and Unity of Philippians: Some Neglected Literary Factors', *NovT* 27.2 (1985), p. 153, writes that 'The self-conscious style that characterizes 4.10-20 reveals Paul's discomfort about the gift, and this may also explain why the thank you comes at the end of the letter. Paul is undeniably sensitive about matters of money.'

L. Alexander, 'Hellenistic Letter-Forms', p. 97, argues similarly, emphasizing that Paul had 'his own ideological reasons for unease at being in receipt of financial support from one of his churches, when he had refused such help from other churches'.

The gift Epaphroditus brought was of no minor importance or significance. Many even see the gift as the impetus behind Paul's letter to the Philippians: 'There is general agreement that the immediate occasion of the letter is the receipt of a pecuniary gift that had been delivered by Epaphroditus to Paul in captivity (2.25-26; 4.14, 18).'[10] If the gift is so significant, however, why does Paul discuss it explicitly only at the letter's end?[11] What is he trying to express?

On the most basic level, this chapter will argue that Paul's discussion of the gift intentionally occured at the end of the letter, so that he could shape how the Philippians viewed that which they had sent to him. This was not simply a present. Paul was in prison. As a prisoner, he would have needed support from outside of the prison. And the Philippians' gift to him likely provided him with his basic needs. Paul, however, does not want the Philippians to see their gift merely as support for the imprisoned. Paul wants them to see it as an opportunity for them to grow together through their shared commitment to the gospel.

In understanding how Phil. 4.10-20 fits into the rhetoric of the epistle as a whole, it is illuminating to look at a comparable discussion in Cicero, to understand the controversy and shame involved in imprisonment, and to see the role of the gospel within Paul's rhetoric.

2. *Cicero's QFr. 1.3 and the Belated Thanks*

Why does Paul discuss the Philippians' gift at the end of the letter? In seeking to answer that question, it is puzzling that scholars have compared Philippians to modern letters[12] and to ancient 'thank you notes',[13]

---

10. D.A. Black, 'The Discourse Structure of Philippians: A Study in Textlinguistics', *NovT* 37 (1995), p. 19.

11. An explicit discussion of the gift may appear only in Phil. 4.10-20, but as P. Schubert, *Form and Function of the Pauline Thanksgivings* (BZNW, 30; Berlin: Töpelmann, 1939), pp. 74-77, has demonstrated, the epistolary thanksgiving of Philippians (1.3-11) clearly refers to the gift and alerts readers not only to the gift but to other key themes in the epistle. Also see Black, 'The Discourse Structure of Philippians', pp. 24-25. Note also that the gift is alluded to in Paul's discussion of Epaphroditus in Phil. 2.25-30.

12. Those commentators who see the content of Phil. 4.10-20 as inappropriate at the end of a letter seem to focus on epistolary conventions from their own century. As O'Brien, *Philippians*, p. 17 n.25, writes, 'The idea that a "thank you" note must appear first in a letter is a modern presupposition.'

13. G.W. Peterman, '"Thankless Thanks": The Epistolary Social Conventions

but not to comparable ancient letters.

Although there are very few extant letters written from ancient Roman prisons, Philippians can be illuminated through a comparison with Cicero's letter to his brother Quintus (*QFr.*) 1.3. Here, as described in the preceding chapter, Cicero writes from exile. Like Paul's letter to the Philippians, this is a friendly and family letter, written by a person both accused of a crime and, at least for the present, physically ostracized from society. Like Paul, Cicero praises the letter's recipient, discusses their relationship, points to enemies whom the recipient might face, and then, near the letter's end, responds to financial support received.

After a section in which he expressed the desire to take his own life, Cicero discusses a bill of exchange which his brother had drawn up for him:

> Why, then, did you write to me about a bill of exchange? As though I was not being supported as it is by your resources. And it is just there that I see and feel, alas, what a crime I have committed, seeing that you are forced to satisfy your creditors by drawing upon your own and your son's very life-blood, while I have squandered to no purpose the money I had received from the treasury on your account. Anyhow the amount you mentioned in your letter has been paid to M. Antonius, and the same amount to Caepio. For myself the sum I now have in hand is sufficient for what I have in view. For whether I am restored or given up in despair, I shall need nothing more. As to yourself, if there is any trouble, you should, I think, apply to Crassus and to Calidius (1.3.7).

Comparing Paul's acknowledgment of the Philippians' gift (Phil. 4.10-20) with this section of Cicero's letter to Quintus, a number of similarities can be noted in the manner in which both Cicero and Paul discuss the gifts. Neither explicitly offers thanks. Each emphasizes that there has been a history of support by the addressee. Each acknowleges that the addressee is sharing his troubles.[14] And each sees the gift as sufficient for his needs.[15] Furthermore, both Cicero and Paul point to sources of

in Philippians 4.10-20', *TynBul* 42.2 (1991), pp. 261-70. Peterman's analysis focuses on the difficulties which have arisen from the absence of any direct word of thanks in Phil. 4.10-20. Comparing these eleven verses with epistolary conventions of thanks in the first century, Peterman's analysis is excellent, but is not concerned with the role 4.10-20 plays in the epistle as a whole.

14. Paul writes, 'It was kind of you to share my trouble' (Phil. 4.14), whereas Cicero, in very rhetorical language, sees the true crime being committed as his need to draw on his brother's and nephew's money (1.3.7).

15. 'I have received full payment, and more; I am filled...' (Phil. 4.18). Cicero,

support, other than themselves: Cicero tells Quintus, 'As to yourself, if there is any trouble, you should, I think, apply to Crassus and to Calidius'; Paul emphasizes to the Philippians that 'my God will supply every need of yours' (4.19a).

Although these two sections share a number of similarities, perhaps even more interesting than the discussions of financial support themselves is the placement of these sections within the larger rhetorical structure of the epistles. Before looking more carefully at Paul's rhetoric, it is helpful to see how Cicero's discussion of the bill of exchange functions within the letter as a whole.

Cicero's letter serves a number of purposes: it discusses his relationship with his brother Quintus; it emphasizes that Cicero would have taken his own life, if he had not been concerned for Quintus's welfare; and it recognizes the bill of exchange which Quintus negotiated. In a number of respects, this is a typical family letter.

In the beginning of the letter, Cicero expresses his love for his brother and explicitly discusses the qualms which his brother may have had with him: 'In you I have always found all that is honourable and pleasant; in me you have found grief for my degradation, apprehension of your own, yearning, mourning, abandonment' (1.3.1). Cicero goes on to emphasize that it is his love for Quintus which kept him from taking his own life (even when he saw suicide as preferable to exile). By not taking his own life, however, he became dependent on Quintus. Thus, he expresses regret that he, who had helped others, now was forced to be dependent on them:

> I have made the mistake of depriving you of my aid while I am yet alive, to need the aid of others, so that my voice, which had so often been the salvation of the most complete strangers, should fail of all times in the hour of domestic danger (1.3.2).

Acknowledging his dependence on Quintus, Cicero also stresses the depth of this relationship:

> When I miss you, is it only a brother that I miss? No, it is one who in affection is almost a twin, in deference a son, in counsel a father. What has ever given me pleasure without your sharing it, or you without my sharing it? (1.3.3)

similarly, writes, 'For myself the sum I now have in hand is sufficient for what I have in view...I shall need nothing more' (1.3.7).

The two brothers were so close that Cicero even feared that if they had met, Quintus would not have been able to tear himself away (1.3.4). Following this discussion, Cicero repeats a theme brought up earlier in the letter: his desire, 'in this down-trodden and desperate condition', to take his own life. Only after all this rehearsal of their relationship, does Cicero discuss the bill of exchange which Quintus had negotiated on his behalf.

Why does Cicero discuss this bill only near the end of the letter? One reason, apparently, is out of awkwardness concerning his relationship with Quintus: Cicero has caused his brother feelings of 'grief', 'apprehension, yearning, mourning, abandonment' (1.3.1); he has called upon Quintus to bring him out of exile (1.3.5, 8-10); he has become financially dependent on him (1.3.2, 7); he has created a situation where Quintus would be attacked 'all the more fiercely' (1.3.9). As a result of all of this, because he had been deserted and betrayed by friends (1.3.5) and is now awkwardly dependent on Quintus, Cicero does not discuss the gift until after he is able to place the entire situation in context. The bill of exchange, itself, is not the focus of the letter, but—as Cicero acknowledges—it represents the brothers' relationship in some important ways.

Before Quintus read this epistle, he might have had a variety of feelings about Cicero's exile and the pressures which it placed upon his own shoulders. Quintus may have been a devoted brother, but Cicero's exile had created problems for him. However, by the time Quintus had read Cicero's remarks on the bill of exchange (1.3.7), the context in which the financial support was to be understood was obvious. In 1.3.1-6, Cicero expresses a great deal of care for Quintus. He sees himself and Quintus as sharing all things, and he stresses—twice—that he would currently have no need for financial support if he had taken his own life. For Quintus's sake, however, he had remained alive. The support makes sense within their relationship.

In analyzing Philippians (and wanting to see it as a compilation of three redacted letters), Jean-Francois Collange poses two rhetorical questions: 'Is a place at the end of a letter at all likely for an expression of thanks?...Would Paul have waited so long before expressing his thanks?'[16] After looking at a letter such as Cicero's, where thanks for financial support is postponed, one might well answer Collange's questions in the affirmative.

---

16. Collange, *Philippians*, p. 5.

3. *Abandonment of the Imprisoned*

Like Cicero's letter to Quintus, Paul's letter to the Philippians begins with a strong emphasis on the love which he had for them.[17] He thanks God in his remembrance of them (1.3), he holds them in his heart (1.7), and he yearns for them all 'with the affection of Jesus Christ' (1.8). Later in the letter, Paul even refers to these Christians as his 'joy and crown' (4.1). Based on the glowing words which Paul uses to describe the Philippians, readers often have seen this relationship as one of the best, if not the best, which Paul had with his churches.[18]

Just as Cicero had had a strong relationship with his brother Quintus, so Paul had had a strong relationship with the Philippians. However, there is one significant difference. Cicero emphasizes that his exile has made him 'down-trodden and desperate' (1.3.6) and has brought shame and grief upon his brother. Quintus might have seen the bill of exchange as a burden borne by him because of his brother's exile. Quintus might have seen it as drawing upon his 'very life-blood'. But Cicero's discussion of the bill of exchange, near the end of the letter, occurs only after he can describe the bill in a more positive context. The bill functions as a sign of their relationship.

Does Paul's discussion of the Philippians' gift serve a similar function? Is it placed at the letter's end so that Paul could encourage them to see the gift within a positive context? On the one hand, Paul shows no sign of shame (cf. Phil. 1.20) and no reason to believe that imprisonment has changed his relationship with the Philippians. Conversely, he almost goes to extremes to show how their partnership had remained the same.[19]

On the other hand, regardless of the present state of his relationship with the Philippians, Paul would have known that imprisonment, like exile, strained and changed relationships between people. Paul had undergone numerous imprisonments, he was said to have imprisoned others, and he would have been conscious of the fragility of relationships between those in prison and those outside. Prisoners faced disease, hunger, torture and lack of sleep. They had reason to fear other prisoners, guards, the prisonkeeper or the local magistrate. And they had concerns both

17. See 'Paul's Rhetorical Strategy in Philippians' in Chapter 2.

18. The title of R. Pesch's 1985 monograph illustrates well how most interpreters have understood Paul's relationship with the Philippians: *Paulus und seine Lieblingsgemeinde* (Herderbücherei, 1208; Freiburg: Herder & Herder, 1985).

19. See below.

about the future and about their loved ones. Before looking more closely at Paul's understanding of the gospel in Philippians, it is important to examine one other concern the imprisoned had: the fear that they would go through that ordeal alone. Outsiders often rejected the imprisoned.

In antiquity, those who were free responded to the imprisoned in a variety of ways. Although numerous examples have been preserved of family and friends who visited the incarcerated, it is not always possible to determine whether such visitations reflect historical reality, a norm or exemplary exceptions. Demetrius's service and loyalty to the imprisoned Antiphilus,[20] for example, point not to typical prison visitation, but to the highest ideals of friendship.

Often, family, friends and associates fell short of these ideals; abandoning, deserting, or forgetting about the imprisoned. Sometimes they simply did not invest the time to continue the relationship, sometimes they feared being implicated through association, and sometimes they were shamed because of their friend's circumstances.

In *Ep.* 9.8, Seneca counters an Epicurean position when he writes that the wise person desires to be friends, not 'with one who might assist him out of bondage; at the first rattle of the chain such a friend will desert him'.[21] Some persons did not invest the time or effort to support the imprisoned.

Similarly, when the author of Hebrews appeals to his readers' past actions (10.33) and encourages them to 'remember those who are in prison, as though in prison with them' (13.3a), such admonitions may point to a concurrent ambivalence about this sort of ministry.[22] If human nature is such that Jesus' closest disciples could deny him, so as to avoid his fate (Mt. 26.69-75), early Christians' abandonment of others is understandable; it does not seem particularly odd.

Visitors to prison often implicated themselves in criminal activity. In the third and fourth centuries, for instance, numerous Christians were condemned simply because of their presence during the trials of their brothers and sisters in the faith.[23] Similarly, in Eusebius, *De mart.*

---

20. Lucian, *Tox.* 27–34.

21. *Ep.* 9.8.

22. G.W. Buchanan, *To the Hebrews* (AB, 36; Garden City, New York: Doubleday, 1972), p. 230, writes, 'when some people were suffering and dying for their faith, there was a strong tendency to deny association with them…and in this way to avoid similar fates'.

23. R.L. Fox, *Pagans and Christians* (New York: Harper & Row, 1986), p. 442

Palaest. 3, after Agapius and Dionysius helped six fellow Christians who were imprisoned, they attracted so much attention that they themselves were condemned and beheaded. In *Ep.* 4.2, Cyprian goes so far as to discuss the manner in which Christians should engage in prison visitation to ensure that 'suspicion is diminished'.

Pagans, of course, faced similar pressures.[24] Brian M. Rapske points to a number of examples where 'helping the prisoner could pose significant threats to the safety and well-being of the helper'.[25] Although Philostratus's *Life of Apollonius* post-dates Paul's epistles, it does provide concrete descriptions of the dangers faced if one assisted the incarcerated. It is said, for instance, that the imprisoned Musonius thought that it would be wise if Apollonius not visit him, 'in order that both their lives might not be endangered'.[26] Elsewhere, Apollonius instructs his sidekick Damis to follow him 'in the guise of one not sworn to my philosophy, but just attached to me for other reasons'.[27] This, Apollonius implies, will keep Damis from being arrested. Philostratus also describes how fear of association with Apollonius (before his arrest) reduced the number of his followers from thirty-four to eight.[28]

Distance between the incarcerated and their friends and family resulted not only from the fear of those who were free, but also from the shame which seemed to be an inevitable part of incarceration. Regardless of why prisoners found themselves in prison, their mere presence there often was seen as pointing to unscrupulous, immoral or illegal activity. Thus, in *Ap.* 28B, Plato has an imaginary interlocutor ask Socrates that which was on the minds of many: 'Are you then not ashamed, Socrates, of having followed such a pursuit, that you are now in danger of being put to death as a result?' Regardless of whether one was actually guilty of any crime, imprisonment in itself was seen as reason for shame.[29]

Understandably, then, prisoners often felt shamed. Demosthenes, 'out

refers to the courtroom as 'a great breeding ground of spontaneous Christian protest'.

24. E.g., Tacitus, *Ann.* 6.5.9; Dio, 58.3.7; 58.11.5-6; Plutarch, *Dion* 57.5.

25. B.M. Rapske, 'The Importance of Helpers to the Imprisoned Paul in the Book of Acts', *TynBul* 42.1 (1991), esp. pp. 23-26.

26. Philostratus, *VA* 4.46.

27. *VA* 7.15.

28. *VA* 4.37.

29. Cicero, *Cat.* 2.27, refers to the '*carcer*' as the place 'where following the ordinances of our ancestors, we exact the penalty for heinous crimes when they have been exposed'. If this reflects an image typical of that which was in people's minds, it would not be surprising that prisoners might feel shame.

of shame at the charge under which he lay', ran away from prison.[30] Escape, however, was not always so easy. Trapped in prison, the incarcerated sometimes let the feelings of shame overwhelm them. Suicides often were committed, in noble attempts to avoid the shame involved with criminal proceedings.[31]

Friends and family also were ashamed by the imprisonment of loved ones. The prisoner Ignatius expresses gratitude to the Smyrnaeans, since they treated his 'bonds with neither haughtiness nor shame' (10.2). Elsewhere he refers to Christians who do not care for the imprisoned as having 'strange opinions concerning the grace of Jesus Christ' (*Smyrn.* 6.2). Shame often caused family and friends to withdraw from the imprisoned and, ironically, one of the best descriptions of this is found in 2 Timothy, a letter purporting to be from the pen of the imprisoned Paul.[32]

After presenting himself as an example of one who is not ashamed to follow that for which God has appointed him, Paul then points to such persons as Phygelus and Hermogenes who 'turned away' from him (1.15). These are contrasted with Onesiphorus—and his household— who 'was not ashamed' of Paul's chains (1.16). Timothy is then encouraged to do his best to present himself 'to God as one approved, a workman who has no need to be ashamed, rightly handling the word of truth' (2.15).

In 2 Timothy, a natural reaction to imprisonment—shame—is aggressively countered. This letter emphasizes that however shameful Paul's imprisonment may have been perceived as being, the grounds for the imprisonment were not shameful. The imprisonment was 'for the gospel' (1.8).

Regardless if we see Phygelus and Hermogenes (2 Tim. 1.15) as obscure historical figures[33] or as fictional negative examples,[34] they do

---

30. Plutarch, *Dem.*, 26.1.

31. Cf. Suetonius, *Tib.* 61.4. See 'Suicide', in Chapter 1.

32. Although the issue of pseudepigraphy would affect some concerns in the study of 2 Timothy, the issue is not central to the discussion here. The author of the epistle—regardless if it were the apostle, a disciple of his, or someone else—wanted readers to believe that he was Paul himself. Out of convenience, then, I will refer to him as 'Paul'. For further discussions of pseudepigraphy and 2 Timothy, see the excellent study by M. Prior, *Paul the Letter-Writer and the Second Letter to Timothy* (JSNTSup, 23; Sheffield: JSOT Press, 1990).

33. J.N.D. Kelly, *A Commentary on the Pastoral Epistles* (Grand Rapids: Baker Book House, 1981), p. 169.

34. B. Fiore, S.J., *The Function of Personal Example in the Socratic and Pastoral*

represent figures who abandoned the imprisoned apostle. Similarly, Demas, 'having loved this present world', deserted Paul and went to Thessalonica (2 Tim. 4.10a). For that matter, it is said that no one supported Paul. All deserted him at his first defence (2 Tim. 4.16).

Phygelus, Hermogenes and Demas stand out as individuals who had abandoned Paul. However, it is difficult to know both why they did so and what it would take before an early Christian community, as a whole, might do the same. Church members in the twentieth century often fail to agree on what constitutes faithful obedience to the gospel. If Christians today came to be in jail, because their religious convictions led them to handcuff themselves either to a nuclear power facility or to an abortion clinic, there would be other Christians who might have serious reservations about supporting these people in jail. These Christians might have theological differences or they might have different views on how their theology should be embodied or demonstrated. Similarly, some of the first Christians may have seen Paul as a fanatic; disagreeing with that which he did or said which resulted in his imprisonment.

Although writings like Lucian's *The Passing of Peregrinus* present Christians as bumbling yokels who would fall all over themselves to help the imprisoned, the author of 1 Peter affirms that Christians needed to 'suffer' for the right reasons: 'By no means let any of you suffer as a murderer, or thief, or evildoer, or a troublesome meddler; but if anyone suffers as a Christian, let him not feel ashamed, but in that name let him glorify God' (1 Pet. 4.15-16). Tertullian, looking at the same issue from a different perspective, emphasizes to pagan readers that church funds were used to support only those Christians who were punished for a particular manner of criminal activity: 'Any who may be in mines, islands or prisons, provided that it is for the sake of God's school (*dumtaxat ex causa dei sectae*), become the pensioners of their confession (*alumni confessionis suae fiunt*).'[35] Christians realized that if they were to have any integrity among themselves, or any credibility within the broader Roman society, their support for the imprisoned needed to reflect discrimination. Although we see this in Tertullian's time, it is even more likely that the nascent churches, with no policies, would have had trouble determining what was involved and to whom they were accountable, in their allegiance to the imprisoned.

Prisoners in antiquity often were deserted or forgotten. Paul himself

---

Epistles (Analecta Biblica, 105; Rome: Biblical Institute Press, 1986), pp. 200, 205.

35. *Apol.* 39.6. Cf. *Apostolic Constitutions* 4.1.9.

was remembered as having been abandoned in prison. Although the Philippians had supported Paul, both through a gift and through the presence of Epaphroditus, it would have been prudent for Paul to anticipate that, at least in the future, some Philippians would have had qualms, apprehensions, or concerns about supporting him as a prisoner. Paul anticipates such concerns.

4. *The Philippian Partnership in Paul's Imprisonment*

The apostle whom the Philippians had supported in his preaching, mission work and new church development was now incarcerated. This peripatetic preacher, their partner, was now locked up in prison. Paul would have realized the potential that his imprisonment had to change his relationship with the Philippians. They might come to feel shame. They might avoid contact with him out of fear for themselves. Or they might come to believe that Paul's imprisonment served no purpose or was unrelated to their Christian faith. The Philippians still supported Paul, but just as Cicero reassured Quintus of the strength of their relationship, so Paul reassured the Philippians of the strength of their partnership.

Paul opens his letter in a unique manner: he uses the all-inclusive word πᾶς to address his readers. In 1.1b, Paul makes clear that he is addressing all of the Christians in Philippi: πᾶσιν τοῖς ἁγίοις ἐν Χριστῷ Ἰησοῦ τοῖς οἶσιν εν Φιλίπποις. What is unique about this address is that Paul explicitly refers to 'all' Christians only rarely in his epistles. David Alan Black notes that

> The salutation in Romans is the only other place where Paul emphasizes 'all' his readers in a particular locale. The reason for doing so seems to be that the apostle desires to give a unity to a Roman Christian community that consists of churches meeting in various private homes.[36]

Immediately following the salutation in Paul's letter to the Philippians is the thanksgiving. Here, in that part of the letter which highlights the epistle's major themes, the apostle repeatedly emphasizes that he is addressing *all* of the Christians in Philippi:

> ...always in every prayer of mine for you all (ὑπὲρ πάντων ὑμῶν) making my prayer with joy...It is right for me to feel thus about you all (ὑπὲρ πάντων ὑμῶν), because I hold you in my heart, for you are all

---

36. Black, 'The Discourse Structure of Philippians', p. 23 n. 21.

(πάντας ὑμᾶς ὄντας) partakers with me of grace...For God is my witness, how I yearn for you all (πάντας ὑμμᾶς) with the affection of Jesus Christ (1.4-8).

Paul emphasizes that their primary relationship—their partnership in the gospel—has not changed. His incarceration has worked for the progress of the gospel. And, thus, their service (or gift) to him can be seen as working for the progress of the gospel.[37]

The gospel, Paul reminds the Philippians in 4.15, had long been central to their relationship: 'in the beginning of the gospel', the church in Philippi was the only one to enter into partnership with Paul in giving and receiving. Throughout this epistle, Paul seeks to remind the Philippians of the centrality of the gospel in their relationship.[38]

After offering thanks for the Philippians' partnership with him 'in the gospel from the first day until now' (1.5), Paul, two verses later, again refers to their partnership in the gospel. Here, however, they are described as partners (συγκοινωνοί) not only 'in the defense and confirmation of the gospel', but also in Paul's imprisonment (1.7).

Thus, in 1.12-18, Paul starts the body of the letter by emphasizing that his imprisonment had not affected the proclamation of the gospel. In 1.12, Paul's first words are defensive. However it may appear, Paul states, his imprisonment 'has actually (μᾶλλον) served to advance the gospel' (1.12). Regardless of whatever anyone else might have said or thought,[39] the goals of the partnership in the gospel—which the Philippians shared with him—had been advanced. Not only had the fact that Paul's chains, manifest ἐν Χριστῷ, 'been known throughout the whole praetorian guard and to all the rest' (1.13), but Christians had even become more confident as a result of this and were 'much more

37. See the discussion in P.T. O'Brien, 'The Importance of the Gospel in Philippians', in *idem* (ed.), *God who is Rich in Mercy: Essays Presented to Dr D.B. Knox* (Homebush West, NSW: Lancer Books, 1986), pp. 229-30.

38. See the illuminating study by B.J. Capper, 'Paul's Dispute with Philippi: Understanding Paul's Argument in Phil 1–2 from his Thanks in 4.10-20', *TZ* 49 (1993), pp. 193-214. In an interesting discussion of Chrysostom, Capper notes that the issue is not that no church 'gave' (ἔδωκεν) to Paul, but no other church 'shared' (ἐκοινώνησεν) with him (p. 199).

39. D.P. Ewald, *Der Brief des Paulus an die Philipper* (Lepizig: A. Deichert [Georg Böhme], 1908), p. 20, writes that μᾶλλον 'setzt voraus, dass der Ap wusste, wie man in Philippi seine Lage anders beurteilte'. Cf. D.E. Garland, 'The Composition and Unity of Philippians', p. 152; O'Brien, 'The Importance of the Gospel', pp. 220-24; and G.F. Hawthorne, *Philippians*, p. 34.

bold to speak the word of God without fear' (1.14). As Robert Jewett notes,

> The emphasis in Paul's expression, as shown by the word order, is that the 'manifestation of my chains' is really 'in Christ.' It is this which specifies what Paul had in mind when he stated that his fate had not jeopardized the mission. It follows that there were some in Ephesus who felt that the imprisonment was *not* a manifestation of Christ's saving activity and thus could not contribute to the spread of the gospel.[40]

In 1.15-18 Paul continues to discuss the effects his imprisonment had on the proclamation of the gospel. He recognizes that of those who preach Christ, some do it out of envy and strife, hoping to distress him in his imprisonment. Others, however, preach from good will, out of love, knowing that Paul was put in prison 'for the defense of the gospel' (1.15b). Regardless of persons' motives in preaching Christ, whether they preach 'in pretense or in truth' (1.18c), Paul finds Christ's proclamation as reason to rejoice (1.18a).

But Paul is not just communicating information about the dissemination of the gospel. Within the rhetoric of this letter, he is also employing 'those who preach Christ' (in 1.14-17) as examples for the Philippians.[41] In the thanksgiving, Paul has referred to the Philippians as partners in the 'defence and confirmation of the gospel' (1.7). Furthermore, he has prayed that the Philippians' 'love may abound more and more' (1.9). Thus, in 1.16, when Paul then writes that some persons 'preach Christ out of love, knowing that I am put here for the defence of the gospel', again Paul calls the Philippians to recognize that his imprisonment resulted from his relationship with Christ.

Paul is adamant with the Philippians that their partnership in the gospel had not been encumbered as a result of this imprisonment. Regardless if Paul himself had been affected by this change in circumstances, his rhetoric in 1.12-18 is reminiscent of that of other Hellenistic authors,

---

40. R. Jewett, 'Conflicting Movements in the Early Church as Reflected in Philippians', *NovT* 12 (1970), p. 367.

41. S.K. Stowers, 'Friends and Enemies in the Politics of Heaven: Reading Theology in Philippians', in J.M. Bassler (ed.), *Pauline Theology. I. Thessalonians, Philippians, Galatians, Philemon* (Minneapolis: Fortress Press, 1991), p. 115, emphasizes that 'The fundamental architecture of the letter is one of antithetical models, most often contrasting Paul and his enemies. The letter urges the reader to emulate one kind of behavior and avoid or oppose another kind.'

who portrayed the true philosopher or sage as one who would be unaffected by imprisonment.

It would be surprising if Paul had not been familiar with portrayals of the imprisoned Socrates. Plato and Xenophon, of course, had portrayed Socrates as continuing his life and mission within the prison walls. Furthermore, numerous Hellenistic authors continued to develop this portrayal, describing almost in mythic terms how Socrates' imprisonment hindered neither his teaching nor his writing. Some of his best discourses were said to have been composed while in prison.[42] Seneca even stressed that Socrates' imprisonment had come to affect all humanity: 'Socrates in prison discoursed, and declined to flee when certain persons gave him the opportunity; he remained there, in order to free mankind from the fear of two most grievous things, death and imprisonment' (*Ep.* 24.4).

Socrates was not the only person portrayed as having taken advantage of his imprisonment. Also in control of his own fate and purpose was the imprisoned Joseph, described by Philo, who assumed the same sorts of responsibilites he had had and would come to have outside of prison.[43] And, a few centuries later, the imprisoned Apollonius of Tyana was portrayed by Philostratus as one who was in charge of his own life, 'leading exactly the same life here as I would outside; for I converse about casual topics, and I do not need anything'.[44] Whether or not these later descriptions and dialogues accurately reflected the reality of these persons' incarcerations, they did reflect a standard philosophical position, heavily affected by Stoicism, which saw the 'sage' overcoming whatever may have stood in his way.[45]

---

42. E.g., Epictetus, *Diss.* 2.1.32; 2.6.26-27; and 2.13.24; Diogenes Laertius, 2.24; Plutarch, *Mor.* 607F; 466F; Cicero, *Tusc.* 1.40.96-97; and Seneca, *Ep.* 67.7.

43. Philo, *Jos.* 81–120.

44. Philostratus, *VA* 7.28.

45. For instance, Epictetus, *Diss.* 2.6.25-27, writes: 'A platform and a prison is each a place, the one high, and the other low; but your moral purpose can be kept the same, if you wish to keep it the same, in either place. And then we shall be emulating Socrates, when we are able to write paeans in prison...' Epictetus, *Diss.* 3.24.113-14, further emphasizes that if Zeus were to bring him to prison, it would not be because Zeus hates him, 'but because He is training me and making use of me as a witness to the rest of men'. For an extended discussion of this motif in Stoicism, see J.T. Fitzgerald, *Cracks in an Earthen Vessel: An Examination of the Catalogues of Hardships in the Corinthian Correspondence* (SBLDS, 99; Atlanta: Scholars Press, 1988), esp. pp. 59-70.

Regardless of whether Paul was drawing intentionally on a standard philosophical *topos*, he was seeking to show his 'partners in the gospel' that his incarceration was not in vain. It resulted in the progress of the gospel, it made persons aware of Christ, and, even more than if Paul had not been in prison, the incarceration gave Christians 'far more courage to speak the word of God without fear' (1.14c). Paul refuses to let any of the Philippians feel shame because of the potential offense of his imprisonment. John Calvin, in an extended discussion on Phil. 1.12-18 (specifically referring to those who preached Christ 'from envy and rivalry') describes this in ways in which few commentators have:

> We all experience in ourselves how much the flesh is offended by the low-liness of the cross. We allow, indeed, Christ crucified to be preached to us; but when He appears with His cross, then, as though struck at its novelty, we either avoid or abhor Him; and that not only in our own persons, but also in the persons of those who deliver to us the Gospel. It may have happened that the Philippians were somewhat discouraged at the persecu-tion of their apostle. And it is possible that those bad workmen, who looked for every opportunity, however small, of doing harm, did not refrain from triumphing over the calamity of the holy man, and so making his Gospel contemptible. If, however, they failed in this attempt, they might easily slander him as hated by the whole world, and at the same time make the Philippians afraid lest, by an unfortunate association with him, they should needlessly incur hatred among all. For such are the usual tricks of Satan. The apostle forestalls this danger when he states that the Gospel had been advanced by his bonds. The aim, therefore, of this account is to encourage the Philippians, that they may not be put off by his persecution.[46]

As R. Jewett has also emphasized, Paul 'was being charged with jeopardizing the mission by exhibiting a humility and suffering which were incompatible with the life of a Christian apostle'.[47]

The link between partnership, gospel, and imprisonment does not end with 1.12-18. Paul goes on to say that although he prefers death, he will remain with the Philippians for their 'progress and joy in the faith' (1.25). Regardless of how the Philippians may feel about Paul personally, he exhorts them to be true to the gospel and to their faith:

---

46. D.W. and T.F. Torrance (eds.), *Calvin's Commentaries: The Epistles of Paul the Apostle to the Galatians, Ephesians, Philippians and Colossians* (trans. T.H.L. Parker; Grand Rapids, MI: Eerdmans, 1965), p. 234.

47. R. Jewett, 'Conflicting Movements', p. 368.

> Only let your manner of life be worthy of the gospel of Christ, so that whether I come and see you or am absent, I may hear of you that you stand firm in one spirit, with one mind striving side by side for the faith of the gospel (τῇ πίστει τοῦ εὐαγγελίου; 1.27).

In Paul's last reference to the 'gospel', in his acknowledgment of the Philippians' gift , he again reminds them that they are a distinctive community. They had been active from the 'beginning of the gospel'; the only church involved in a partnership of giving and receiving (4.15). The Philippians had a history of giving (4.16), and their latest gift to Paul stands within this history. Because they recently shared in his trouble (συγκοινωνήσαντές μου τῇ θλίψει) (4.14), they are referred to as Paul's partners not only 'in the defence and confirmation of the gospel' but also in his imprisonment (1.7).

Although Paul often refers to the 'gospel' (εὐαγγέλιον) in this letter, the word itself is not defined. Paul uses the term, rather, to remind the Philippians of that to which they have committed themselves. The fact that Paul is incarcerated does not matter; the defence and progress of the gospel do matter.

So, by emphasizing that his imprisonment actually has aided their partnership in the gospel, is Paul merely trying to ensure that gifts from the Philippians continue to come? That does not appear to be the case. In Phil. 4.10-12, Paul makes it abundantly clear that he did not need the gift from the Philippians.[48] Similarly, in 4.17-18 Paul says that he has received 'full payment', and that he is 'filled': 'Not that I seek the gift; but I seek the fruit which increases to your credit.' The gift is not as important to Paul as the giving and, it is not surprising to note that the Philippians' concern and giving is described in Phil. 4.10 using the language of morality which runs throughout this epistle.

The language of morality is well understood, at least in part, through the term φρονέω. a term significant in Phil. 4.10, but which also runs throughout the epistle. Although this Greek word occurs only a total of

---

48. L.M. White, 'Morality between Two Worlds: A Paradigm of Friendship in Philippians', in D.L. Balch *et al.* (eds.), *Greeks, Romans, and Christians: Essays in Honor of Abraham J. Malherbe* (Minneapolis: Fortress Press, 1990), p. 214, writes that 'Given the tone of 4.10-12, where Paul "disdains" his financial distress, we may begin to suspect that the bonds of their friendship had become strained either by Paul's or Epaphroditus's situation.'

White explains this in part, writing, 'My own suspicion is that one or another of Paul's house church patrons (perhaps either Euodia or Syntyche) had decided no longer to support Paul, thus creating the sense of crisis and distress' (p. 214 n. 59).

thirteen times in the rest of the Pauline (and Deutero-Pauline) corpus, in Philippians stand ten uses of this verb. Throughout the letter, Paul calls the Philippians to moral thought and action.[49] In introducing the Christ hymn, he entreats them to 'Base your practical reasoning (τοῦτο φρονεῖτε) on what you see in Christ Jesus' (2.5).[50] Wayne A. Meeks writes that the model of the Christ hymn 'sets the terms of the thinking and acting expected of the Philippians in the face of conflict inside and hostility from outside the community'.[51] Paul emphasizes in Phil. 1.7 that he has the right frame of mind towards all of the Philippians (ἐμοι; τοῦτο φρονεῖν ὑπὲρ πάντων ὑμῶν) and, with Paul's behavior as exemplary, the Philippians are further called upon to have 'the same mind' (based on the model of Christ Jesus).

Thus, Paul expects that those who are mature will have the correct mindset (τοῦτο φρονῶμεν; 3.15). He encourages the Philippians to complete his joy by being both 'of the same mind' (τὸ αὐτὸ φρονῆτε) and 'of one mind' (τὸ ἓν φρονοῦντες; 2.2). And he entreats two specific members of the community, Euodia and Syntyche, to agree—to be of the same mind (τὸ αὐτὸ φρονεῖν)—'in the Lord' (4.2). As N.A. Dahl writes, 'This implies not ony that they should agree and live in harmony with each other but also that they ought to have the same concern in mind.'[52] Although the exhortation to Euodia and Syntyche (4.2) might be seen as forming an *inclusio* with Phil. 2.2—and these women's disagreement might have been the justification for this epistle—

---

49. W.A. Meeks 'The Man from Heaven in Paul's Letter to the Philippians', in B.A. Pearson (ed.), *The Future of Early Christianity: Essays in Honor of Helmut Koester* (Minneapolis: Fortress Press, 1991), p. 333, writes, 'this letter's most comprehensive purpose is the shaping of a Christian *phronesis*, a practical moral reasoning that is "conformed to [Christ's] death" in hope of his resurrection'. Also see R. Jewett, 'The Epistolary Thanksgiving and the Integrity of Philippians', *NovT* 12 (1970), pp. 51-52; Jewett's Tübingen dissertation, 'The Pauline Anthropological Terms: Their Use in the Struggle against Early Christian Heresy', 1966; and S.J. Kraftchick, 'A Necessary Detour: Paul's Metaphorical Understanding of the Philippian Hymn', *HBT* 15 (1993), p. 29.

50. Meeks 'The Man from Heaven', p. 332.

51. Meeks 'The Man from Heaven', p. 335.

52. N.A. Dahl, 'Euodia and Syntyche and Paul's Letter to the Philippians', in L.M. White and O.L. Yarbrough (eds.), *The Social World of the First Christians: Essays in Honor of Wayne A. Meeks* (Minneapolis: Fortress Press, 1995), p. 6. Dahl also speculates that 'Questions about who had suffered the most for her faith or who had contributed the most to the gift to Paul may perhaps have been part of their conflict' (p. 15).

Paul does focus on *phronesis* yet again, when acknowledging the Philippians' gift.[53]

A particularly striking feature of the epistle, after Paul's positive appraisal of himself and after his exhortations to the Philippians, is this language in Phil. 4.10. The one single example of the Philippians' use of their 'practical reasoning' is in their concern for the imprisoned apostle.[54] Paul writes (translated literally),

> I rejoiced in the Lord greatly that now at length you revived your thought
> for me (τὸ ὑπὲρ ἐμοῦ φρονεῖν), about which you indeed had thought
> (ἐφρονεῖτε), but you had no opportunity.

Previously, in Phil. 2.2, Paul had called on the Philippians to 'complete my joy (πληρώσατέ μου τὴν χαρὰν) by being of the same mind (τὸ αὐτὸ φρονῆτε)'. In Phil. 4.10, Paul now acknowledges that he can 'rejoice (ἐχάρην) in the Lord greatly', because of the Philippians' thought for him (τὸ ὑπὲρ ἐμοῦ φρονεῖν). Despite division within the community,[55] the Philippians' support of the imprisoned apostle is a concrete example of their having oriented their thought on the gospel.[56]

5. *Conclusion*

When Cicero received financial support from his brother Quintus, he responded in a letter, both by acknowledging the obvious—the changes which resulted from his exile—and by placing his response to the financial support near the end of the letter. The financial support was discussed only after Quintus would have come to see it as an important link to the goals which he and his brother shared.

When the imprisoned Paul received a gift from the Philippians, he, like Cicero, acknowledged this gift at the end of his letter to them; only after he had had the opportunity to place it within a broader context. What is interesting, however, is that Paul, unlike Cicero, did not explicitly acknowledge the obvious. Imprisonment, like exile, changed relations

53. Cf. J.P. Sampley, *Pauline Partnership in Christ: Christian Community and Commitment in Light of Roman Law* (Philadelphia: Fortress Press, 1980), esp. pp. 62-70. Also see Black, 'The Discourse Structure of Philippians', pp. 45-46.

54. M. Silva, *Philippians* (WEC; Chicago: Moody Press, 1988), p. 236.

55. See 'Paul's Rhetorical Strategy in Philippians', in Chapter 2.

56. Jewett, 'Conflicting Movements', pp. 374-75, argues that Paul discusses the gift in this manner so that the Philippians would not see 'their generosity as an individual virtue for which they could be proud'.

between people. The Philippians had supported Paul in the past. They were 'partners in the gospel'. But now that Paul was in prison, some would likely wonder if the basis for their partnership was gone.

Paul does not explicitly acknowledge this possibility. In the salutation and thanksgiving of the epistle, he is clearly addressing all of the Philippians. And, from the beginning of the body of the letter, he emphasizes that his change in circumstances has actually helped achieve the primary goal which he and all of the Philippians shared. Employing standard rhetoric of the day, Paul emphasizes that his imprisonment has served them in promoting the spreading of the gospel (esp. 1.12-18). Paul acknowledges his long-standing relationship with the Philippians, notes that he had not heard from them for a while, and expresses his appreciation for their gift. Perhaps most significantly, in a letter which focuses on the Philippians' sharing common goals, Paul describes their gift to him as the one concrete example of their correct mindset; of their concern for each other and the gospel.[57]

The Philippians might have understood Paul's imprisonment, and their support of him, in a variety of ways. Regardless of their original motivations in sending Epaphroditus with the gift, by the time they had read the end of the letter (Phil. 4.10-20), it would have been clear to them that Paul saw their gift as representing much more than the deliveries which pagans made to their imprisoned friends and loved ones. Their 'partnership in his imprisonment' represented both their Christian commitment to each other and their faith that Paul's incarceration truly was in service to the gospel. The Philippians helped Paul not by sending him a gift, but by showing that they had dedicated themselves to the gospel.

---

57. W.G. Scroggie, *Paul's Prison Prayers* (Grand Rapids, MI: Kregel Publications, repr., 1981 [1921]), p. 11, notes that Phil. 1.9 ('I pray that your love may abound yet more and more') 'is a generous recognition of the exercise of love on the part of the Philippians. But there is a hint also of its deficiency.'

Chapter 4

PAUL AS 'A PRISONER OF CHRIST JESUS':
MILITARY IMAGERY AND THE LETTER TO PHILEMON

And among the many Paul also was brought bound; to him all his fellow-
prisoners gave heed, so that Caesar observed that he was the man in
command. And he [Nero] said to him: 'Man of the great king, but (now)
my prisoner, why did it seem good to thee to come secretly into the empire
of the Romans and enlist soldiers from my province?'
—*The Acts of Paul* 11.3 (ca. 180 CE)

1. *Introduction*

Paul may have been a prisoner of Caesar. He may well have been a
prisoner of Nero's. He was undoubtedly a prisoner of the Roman
government. However, in Paul's letter to Philemon, he states neither
that he is a prisoner of the state nor that he is a prisoner of Nero: he is
Paul, δέσμιος Χριστοῦ Ἰησοῦ.[1]

As a prisoner—we know from Philippians and 2 Timothy—Paul faced
all sorts of difficulties, not the least of which must have involved, 'the
daily pressure' of 'anxiety for all the churches'.[2] Members of Paul's
churches, it would appear, did not always understand the apostle's
motives and they shamed him and were ashamed of him because of his
incarceration. Some Christians are remembered as having even abandoned him.[3] Just as apologists in the first centuries of Christianity

1. Phlm. 1 and 9.
2. 2 Cor. 11.28.
3. E.g. 2 Tim. 1.15; 4.10, 14-16. In 2 Timothy, even the addressee himself is
encouraged to 'not be ashamed of testifying to our Lord, nor of me his prisoner'
(1.8). Some Christians, it should be noted, might have abandoned Paul simply out of
concern for their own safety. B.M. Rapske, 'The Importance of Helpers to the
Imprisoned Paul in the Book of Acts', *TynBul* 42 (1991), esp. pp. 23-29, describes
the sorts of risks faced by those who helped the imprisoned.

needed to contend with accusations that their master died as a criminal under the Roman government, so the earliest Christian communities needed to wrestle with the fact that the apostle Paul had an identity as a prisoner. The imprisoned apostle, like the crucified messiah, was a stumbling block for a number of the first Christians.

Thus, when Paul opens his letter to Philemon by describing himself as δέσμιος Χριστοῦ ˙Ιησοῦ,[4] it is difficult to know what he is trying to communicate. Because this is such a rare appellation, when later Christian copyists encountered it, some changed it. Thus, in some manuscripts, Paul is presented as describing himself either as 'Paul, an *apostle* Χριστοῦ ˙Ιησοῦ,[5] or metaphorically as 'Paul, a *slave* Χριστοῦ ˙Ιησοῦ.[6] Regardless of the emendations made by later scribes, Paul did refer to himself as a 'prisoner' and the expression was novel. At the very least, the use of this appellation should make us ask why Paul would have employed such a potentially controversial title.

At the same time, however, we must admit that we have little evidence to know how the readers of this epistle would have reacted when Paul described himself so. Maybe he had used this title in their presence before. Maybe the title had a particular theological significance which both Paul and this community shared. Maybe the title was one given to Paul by members of this very church.[7] Unfortunately, we just do not know.

4. Verses 1 and 9 contain the earliest extant uses of this expression. Paul is referred to as a 'prisoner' also in 2 Tim. 1.8, in Eph. 3.1, and in Eph. 4.1. Cf. *3 Cor.* 3.1. These passages, at the very least, imply that Paul's use of this self-designation was widely known and used for a variety of purposes. The use in 2 Tim. 1.8 (particularly in light of the rest of the letter) points to Paul's status—as δέσμιος—as sometimes being a source of shame. The use in Eph. 3.1, in a letter written to Gentiles, emphasizes that Paul's status as a prisoner (ὁ δέσμιος τοῦ Χριστοῦ) was on their behalf. Although this chapter will look at Eph. 4.1 below, these later passages do little to illuminate the appellation in Philemon.

5. D*, the original scribe of Codex Bezae Cantabrigiensis. The miniscule 629 reads ἀπόστολος δέσμιος. Each of these readings seem to be modeled on those passages where Paul, or someone in his name, writes that he was called to be an 'apostle' (Rom. 1.1; 1 Cor. 1.1; and Gal. 1.1) or, more specifically, an 'apostle of Christ Jesus' (1 Cor. 1.1; 2 Cor. 1.1; Eph. 1.1; Col. 1.1; 1 Tim. 1.1; and 2 Tim. 1.1. Cf. Gal. 1.1; and Titus 1.1).

6. Miniscules 322, 323, 605, 945, and a few others present this reading. Cf. Rom. 1.1; Phil. 1.1; and Titus 1.1.

7. B.M. Rapske, 'The Prisoner Paul in the Eyes of Onesimus', *NTS* 37 (1991), p. 202, claims that because Paul starts his letter with this appellation, 'this suggests that the self-designation would not be a surprise to Philemon or the other addressees'.

In better understanding what Paul was trying to communicate, a variety of proposals have been advanced; proposals ranging from the absurd to the mundane: from those which have said that the meaning of the expression is entirely metaphorical, to those which have said that the meaning simply came from the physical state in which Paul found himself. Any reasonable proposal needs to span these extremes.

Paul's use of this phrase has been studied in light of such social events as triumphal marches and initiations into mystery cults. Although these social situations provide fascinating turf for understanding the expression, this chapter will focus primarily on the letter to Philemon itself, pointing to how Paul's use of other appellations informs our understanding of δέσμιος Χριστοῦ 'Ιησοῦ.

Why does Paul refer to himself with this expression? Many say that the obvious reason for this appellation is because of Paul's imprisonment.[8] The term describes where Paul is and what he is currently experiencing. Paul is neither simply using the expression metaphorically, nor referring to an abstract philosophical *topos*. He actually is incarcerated.[9] This can be seen in vv. 10, 13, and 22: Paul claims that, 'in chains' (ἐν τοῖς

Contra Rapske, this chapter will argue that the meaning of this epithet is illuminated through the context of the letter. Although the letter's recipients likely knew that Paul was imprisoned, we cannot be sure that the recipients would have already been familiar with this designation.

8. Almost all commentators agree with this. G. Kittel, *TDNT*, II, p. 43, writes 'there can be no doubt that the actual imprisonment of Paul everywhere underlies the usage'. Cf. R.P. Martin, *Colossians and Philemon* (NCB; London: Oliphants, 1974), p. 158; and P.T. O'Brien, *Colossians, Philemon* (WBC, 44; Waco, TX: Word Book, 1982), p. 271. A. Wilson, 'The Pragmatics of Politeness and Pauline Epistolography: A Case Study of the Letter to Philemon', *JSNT* 48 (1992), p. 113, notes that Paul would not have had to use this as a title, but it does allow him to both emphasize 'his social solidarity with Onesimus' and 'boost Philemon's status by diminishing his own'. By doing so, Wilson argues, Paul was deliberately employing politeness in his request.

9. *Contra* E.R. Goodenough, 'Paul and Onesimus', *HTR* 22 (1929), pp. 181-83. Goodenough claims that Paul must have been free, 'else he could not have offered to go bond for Onesimus' peculations...It is also strange that Paul could have entertained a fugitive slave' (p. 182). Although Goodenough believes that Paul must have been free and, thus, the appellation δέσμιος Χριστοῦ 'Ιησοῦ, like δοῦλος Χριστοῦ 'Ιησοῦ, should not be taken literally, his theory is based on a number of unstated—and fallacious—assumptions regarding both the operation of prisons and the purpose of Paul's rhetoric here.

δεσμοῖς),[10] he gave birth to Onesimus (v. 10); he mentions the possibility of Onesimus serving him during his 'imprisonment for the gospel' (ἐν τοῖς δεσμοῖς τοῦ εὐαγγελίου; v. 13); and, in the letter's conclusion, he then asks that the reader(s) of the letter prepare a guest room for him, 'for I am hoping through your prayers to be granted to you' (v. 22). One explanation of the term δέσμιος Χριστοῦ Ἰησοῦ centers on the fact that it states the obvious: Paul is incarcerated.

One could dismiss this term as little more than a statement of the obvious. Four factors, however, point beyond a purely mundane interpretation of the expression. First, when Paul wrote to the Philippians from prison, he did not refer to himself as δέσμιος Χριστοῦ Ἰησοῦ. His imprisonment did not *oblige* him to identify himself in terms of this situation.

Secondly, even without employing this title, there would have been plenty of opportunities for Paul to emphasize his imprisonment. Even if his readers had not previously known about his incarceration, Paul could have communicated that message either within the body of the letter,[11] or through the messenger delivering the letter.[12]

Thirdly, if Paul were simply communicating information, he could have stated that he was a prisoner in v. 1 and then said nothing more. However, Paul re-emphasizes the significance of this appellation, repeating it in v. 9.

Finally, and most obviously, the word δέσμιος should not be isolated from the genitive expression which qualifies it. Paul refers to himself as δέσμιος Χριστοῦ Ἰησοῦ. Paul's use of this expression is not so much to share information with Philemon's community as it is to appeal to them.

10. A classic example of *synecdoche*, the Greek word for 'chains' is often used when writers are referring to 'prisons'.

11. Cf. Phlm. 10, 13, 22. In Philippians, Paul refers to his imprisonment not through self-appellations but through a discussion within the letter itself (Phil. 1.12-26).

12. Epaphroditus (Phil. 2.25-30), Onesimus (Phlm. 12), or Tychicus (Col. 4.7) undoubtedly would have transferred all sorts of information in addition to that explicitly found in the letters which they delivered. See Chapter 5's discussion on ancient messengers. Cf. E.J. Epp, 'New Testament Papyrus Manuscripts and Letter Carrying in Greco-Roman Times', in B.A. Pearson (ed.), *The Future of Early Christianity: Essays in Honor of Helmut Koester* (Minneapolis: Fortress Press, 1991), pp. 35-56; and M.M. Mitchell, 'New Testament Envoys in the Context of Greco–Roman Diplomatic and Epistolary Conventions: The Examples of Timothy and Titus', *JBL* 111 (1992), pp. 641-62.

Thus, it needs to be asked, when Paul starts the greeting of this letter with the appellation δέσμιος Χριστοῦ Ἰησοῦ, what is he trying to emphasize to Philemon, Apphia, Archippus and the others?

2. *Being 'Of Christ Jesus'*

The first readers of this letter could have understood the phrase δέσμιος Χριστοῦ Ἰησοῦ as having a variety of meanings. The genetive expression could be understood as a genitive of cause, a genitive of purpose or a genitive of possession.

If Χριστοῦ Ἰησοῦ is understood as a genitive of cause, Paul is seeing himself as a prisoner *because* of his dedication to Christ Jesus. G.H.P. Thompson, thus, sees Paul as emphasizing that 'his imprisonment has been the result of his loyalty to Jesus in preaching the Gospel'.[13]

The genitive of purpose is best translated 'for the sake of'. Thus, Paul could be emphasizing that his imprisonment was *for the sake of* Christ Jesus. P.T. O'Brien writes that 'the genitive Χριστοῦ Ἰησοῦ in the expression "prisoner *of* Christ Jesus" is best understood, with most commentators, to signify Paul has been imprisoned "for Christ's sake"'.[14] The genitive Χριστοῦ Ἰησοῦ would then be seen as modifying the word δέσμιος much as the genitive τοῦ εὐαγγελίου modifies ἐν τοῖς δεσμοῖς in v. 13. Thus, just as Paul was 'in chains *for the sake of* the gospel', so he was 'a prisoner *for the sake of* Christ Jesus'.

Or, if the most obvious meaning of the gentive is emphasized—that of simple possession—Paul could be asserting that he is a 'prisoner *of* Christ Jesus'. The genitive generally is used to denote simple possession. Thus, the appellation δέσμιος Χριστοῦ Ἰησοῦ could be rendered simply enough as 'prisoner of Christ Jesus'.

Although Paul was 'a prisoner', and—at the same time—although he was 'of Christ Jesus', most interpreters have wanted to see a direct relation between these two states. J.L. Houlden, aiming for a more pre-

13. G.H.P. Thompson, *The Letters of Paul to the Ephesians, to the Colossians and to Philemon* (Cambridge: University Press, 1967), p. 182, writes that Paul's 'imprisonment has been the result of his loyalty to Jesus in preaching the Gospel'. Also see M.R. Vincent, *A Critical and Exegetical Commentary on the Epistles to the Philippians and to Philemon* (Edinburgh: T. & T. Clark, 1945), p. 175; P. Stuhlmacher, *Der Brief an Philemon* (EKKNT; Zürich: Benzinger Verlag, 1981), p. 29; and H. Binder, *Der Brief des Paulus an Philemon* (THKNT, 11.2; Berlin: Evangelische Verlagsanstalt, 1990), p. 43.

14. O'Brien, *Colossians, Philemon*, p. 271.

cise translation, emphasizes that 'the more literal rendering is "Christ Jesus' prisoner"; he [Paul] thinks of his conversion as being made captive by Christ'.[15] G.B. Caird, like Houlden, stresses that this metaphorical meaning is linked closely to the literal one: 'The RSV translation obscures the double meaning of the Greek. Not only is Paul in a Roman prison for Christ's sake, he is also Christ's prisoner, and the metaphorical imprisonment is the cause of the literal.'[16]

Commentators seem to agree that the expression Χριστοῦ Ἰησοῦ can funcation as a genitive of purpose (cf. Phlm. 13). But what are the implications, if we also understand Χριστοῦ Ἰησοῦ as a genitive of possession? If Paul was emphasizing that he had been made captive by Christ, what would he have been seeking to express? In what context would this expression have best been understood?

In the greetings of almost all of his letters, Paul introduces himself with a title. Thus, Paul addressing himself in Phlm. 1 as a 'prisoner of Christ Jesus' is similar to his seeing himself in the salutations of other letters as an 'apostle of Christ Jesus'[17] or as a 'slave of Christ Jesus'.[18]

But what did it mean to be '*of* Christ Jesus'? In the vocabulary of Paul, the word Χριστοῦ almost seems to have a life of its own. Christians belong to Christ. Members of his communities (and this is something which Paul stresses repeatedly in his letters) are Χριστοῦ.[19] When Paul refers to himself with an appellation, followed by the expression Χριστοῦ Ἰησοῦ, such an expression reflects—at the very least—a basic religious truth for Paul: Paul is 'of' Christ Jesus. Christ Jesus is the source of his identity.

But does Paul intend for his readers to understand these appellations as having greater metaphorical implications? Paul—as apostle, slave and

15. J.L. Houlden, *Paul's Letters from Prison* (Baltimore: Penguin Books, 1970), p. 228.

16. G.B. Caird, *Paul's Letters from Prison* (London: Oxford University Press; 1976), p. 218. G.H.P. Thompson, *The Letters of Paul*, p. 182, writes that Paul's 'whole life has been captured by Jesus and by the need to serve him'. Here he points to Phil. 3.12 ('I was laid hold of by Christ Jesus') as a possible way of understanding what Paul meant here.

17. 1 Cor. 1.1 (κλητὸς ἀπόστολος Χριστοῦ Ἰησοῦ); 2 Cor. 1.1; Gal. 1.1 (ἀπόστολος...διὰ Ἰησοῦ Χριστοῦ); Eph. 1.1; Col. 1.1; 1 Tim. 1.1; and 2 Tim. 1.1. Cf. Rom. 1.1 and Titus 1.1.

18. Rom. 1.1 and Phil. 1.1 (where both he and Timothy are δοῦλοι Χριστοῦ Ἰησοῦ). Cf. Titus 1.1 (δοῦλος θεοῦ).

19. Cf. 1 Cor. 1.12; 3.23; 15.23; 2 Cor. 10.7; Gal. 3.29; 5.24.

prisoner—is 'of Christ Jesus' in a general spiritual sense, but are we also to understand the relationship between Paul and Christ Jesus in terms of typical Greco–Roman relationships? Is Christ Jesus, for example, to be understand as 'master' and Paul understood as 'slave'?[20] Is Christ Jesus to be seen as 'jailer' or 'captor' and Paul to be seen as 'prisoner'? Numerous commentators have answered this latter question in the affirmative. Two popular positions see Paul and Jesus' 'prisoner' or 'captor' relationship as existing within a fairly narrow metaphorical range of meaning.

A number of interpreters use 2 Cor. 2.14a ('Thanks be to God, who in Christ always leads us in triumph') as background material and then claim that Paul—in Philemon 1—seeks to evoke the metaphor of a triumphal march. Thus, when Paul refers to himself as δέσμιος Χριστοῦ Ἰησοῦ, he is referring to himself as one who was forced to march in such a triumph. Jesus had won the war, and Paul acknowledges that he is Jesus' prisoner.[21]

One of the difficulties of projecting the 'triumphal procession' metaphor in 2 Cor. 2.14 onto Paul's letter to Philemon has to do with how the processions ended: the prisoners were led to their execution.[22] In 2 Corinthians, maybe Paul did see his execution as inevitable.[23] However, within the context of Philemon, when Paul refers to himself as a δέσμιος Χριστοῦ Ἰησοῦ, he is not anticipating his death: in v. 22 he goes so far as to ask that lodging be prepared for him. Furthermore, it is

---

20. Cf. D.B. Martin, *Slavery as Salvation: The Metaphor of Slavery in Pauline Christianity* (New Haven: Yale University Press, 1990). Martin places the 'slave/master' metaphor within Greco–Roman society and emphasizes that 'in Paul's society it mattered less that one was a slave than whose slave one was' (p. 85). Paul's recognition of himself as a 'slave of Christ' is seen, in effect, as an acknowledgment of his own privileged position.

21. D. Stuhlmacher, *Der Brief an Philemon*, p. 29. Cf. E. Lohse, *Colossians and Philemon* (Hermenia; trans. W.R. Poehlmann and R.J. Karris; Philadelphia: Fortress Press, 1971), p. 189.

22. P.B. Duff, 'Metaphor, Motif, and Meaning: The Rhetorical Strategy behind the Image "Led in Triumph" in 2 Corinthians 2.14', *CBQ* 53 (1991), p. 92, acknowledges that such processions led to execution, but he suggests that 'the metaphor also leaves open the possibility that Paul is referring to something else, not a military parade like the Roman triumph but an epiphany procession, common throughout the Greco-Roman world'. See below for a discussion of epiphany processions.

23. Cf. S.J. Hafemann, *Suffering and the Spirit* (Tübingen: Mohr [Paul Siebeck], 1986), esp. pp. 18-39.

not entirely clear what aspect of the triumphal procession Paul wants to emphasize even in 2 Cor. 2.14.[24] Overall, it is impossible to know whether Paul's reference to himself as δέσμιος Χριστοῦ 'Ιησοῦ either would have inspired or was intended to inspire his readers to think of a triumphal march.

The other context often cited in trying to understand this appellation is that of the mystery religions. Before entering some mystery cults, the initiates allowed themselves to be 'imprisoned' in a courtyard, where they were then said to be prisoners of the god of that particular mystery.[25] This was seen as a preliminary step to the initiate's actual union with the god. Richard Reitzenstein believes that Paul may well have understood his incarceration as an imprisonment which then would unite him with the Lord.[26]

Although Reitzenstein's theory is intriguing, it is difficult to believe that Paul's use of this appellation would signal his readers to the comparison with the mystery cults. The literary context does not support Reitzenstein's theory. Furthermore, whereas the initiates into the mysteries saw their imprisonment as leading to union with the deity, Paul expects to be released from prison (v. 22).

Contemporary philosophy also offered a variety of categories and metaphors through which readers could have understood Paul as a 'prisoner of Christ Jesus'. Many ancient philosophical discussions saw humans as always surrounded by the walls of some prison: physical imprisonment was seen as only one type of incarceration.[27] Apollonius says that, 'We men are in a prison all the time which we choose to call life.'[28] Lucian refers to persons living a luxurious life as 'roaming at large in a great prison they cannot break out of'.[29] And, in general, God—for the philosophers—is seen as the only one who can either release or break humans out of this prison (a prison alternately referred to as 'body' or 'life').[30]

---

24. For a survey of the variety of interpretations on this passage, see V.P. Furnish, *II Corinthians* (AB, 32A; New York: Doubleday, 1984), pp. 174-75.

25. Cf. R. Reitzenstein, *Hellenistic Mystery-Religions: Their Basic Ideas and Significance* (trans. J.E. Steely; Pittsburgh: Pickwick Press, 1978), pp. 241-43.

26. Reitzenstein, *Hellenistic Mystery-Religions*, p. 258.

27. Cf. '"Prison" as Metaphor', pp. 75-79 of Chapter 1.

28. Philostratus, *VA* 7.26.

29. *VH* 1.39.

30. Cf. Philo, *Leg. All.* 3.14.42; *Rer. Div. Her.* 84–85; Epictetus, *Diss.* 1.9.16-17; Cicero, *Rep.* 6.15.15; *Tusc.* 1.30.74; Dio Chrysostom, *Or.* 30.10.

Sometimes humans are described as having taken their own freedom away, by openly submitting to metaphorical fetters and chains:

> But much more do I marvel at and pity you for the grievous and unlawful slavery under whose yoke you have placed your necks, for you have thrown about you not merely one set of fetters or two but thousands, fetters by which you are throttled and oppressed much more than are those who drag themselves along in chains and halters and shackles. For they have the chance of release or of breaking their bonds and fleeing, but you are always strengthening your bonds and making them more numerous and stronger...if I should wish to name all the prisons and the bonds of witless, wretched human beings by means of which you have made yourselves prisoners, possibly you would think me an exceedingly disagreeable and sorry poet for composing tragedies on your own misfortunes.[31]

Elsewhere, humans are seen as having given their freedom away, but they do so in order to pursue what they perceive as a greater good. Analyzing a painting, Lucian notes in the picture that Heracles 'drags after him a great crowd of men who are all tethered by the ears! His leashes are delicate chains fashioned of gold and amber.' Those who are chained, however, do not think of escaping, but 'they follow cheerfully and joyously, applauding their leader'.[32] According to Lucian's interpretation of the painting, the eloquence of Heracles was enough to make humans willingly submit to him. Similarly, in Ovid's *Heroides* and *Amores*, the author presents himself as a willing prisoner to the power of Cupid. In *Ep.* 20.85, he says, 'Bind me not with shackles nor with chains—I shall be kept in bonds by unyielding love for you.' In the *Amores* 1.2.20-30, the setting is that of a triumphal procession:

> Look, I confess! I am new prey of thine, O Cupid; I stretch forth my hands to be bound, submissive to thy laws. There is no need of war...In thy train shall be captive youths and captive maids; such a pomp will be for thee a stately triumph. Myself, a recent spoil, shall be there with wound all freshly dealt, and bear my new bonds with unresisting heart.

The notion of a willing imprisonment would not have been strange. Even Epictetus emphasized that God had brought him into prison in order to train him (cf. *Diss.* 3.24.112-14). Epictetus argues,

> I have been set free by God, I know His commands, no one has power any longer to make a slave of me, I have the right kind of emancipator and the right kind of judges...I regard God's will as better than my will. I shall

31. Dio Chrysostom, *Or.* 80.7-10.
32. *Heracles* 3.

attach myself to Him as a servant and follower, my choice is one with His, my desire one with His, in a word, my will is one with His will (*Diss.* 4.7.17-20).[33]

Life is imprisonment. All humans are imprisoned by different things in different ways. If bondage and imprisonment were seen as pervasive in antiquity, if Paul found himself actually incarcerated, this may well have been an appropriate time for him to emphasize the true nature of his imprisonment. He may well have been δέσμιος, but he was δέσμιος Χριστοῦ Ἰησοῦ.

Did Paul see himself as somehow imprisoned by Christ Jesus? Is Christ Jesus somehow to be understood as the jailer and Paul the prisoner? Did Paul willingly give himself over as a prisoner to Christ Jesus, just as others proudly gave themselves over to Cupid? It is possible that that is the case. It is possible that Paul and this community are communicating with terms and expressions which they alone share.

However, there are two significant difficulties with understanding this appellation in terms of triumphal processions, mystery cults and these particular metaphors. In each case, the method used involves positing a greater context in which the expression has its fundamental meaning. This context is not described in the letter, nor signalled by the rhetoric of the letter (through other exegetical cues), but is presumably known by the readers and expressed to them by the appellation alone.

Furthermore, regardless of how much sense it makes in English to translate δέσμιος Χριστοῦ Ἰησοῦ as 'prisoner of Christ Jesus', I have found no other instances in antiquity of the jailer or captor of a prisoner being described through this sort of genitive construction.[34] Therefore, we need to be cautious about constructing any sort of elaborate metaphorical meaning for an expression which does have a literal meaning: Paul is δέσμιος, and he is Χριστοῦ Ἰησοῦ.

Before seeking to understand how this expression can be illuminated through metaphors, it is helpful to focus on the literary context of δέσμιος Χριστοῦ Ἰησοῦ. A minimalistic approach that looks initially only at clues within the letter itself, keeps us from abandoning ourselves

33. Since 'slaves' and 'prisoners' both were subject to authorities (and since both often were bound), in Epictetus, as elsewhere, the terms sometimes appear together. One who was 'bound' could refer to himself or herself naturally as a slave (cf. Epictetus, *Gnom.* 32; Ignatius, *Rom.* 4.3; *Magn.* 12; Plato, *Ap.* 37C).

34. This may result merely from both the paucity of sources and the ways in which such sources discussed the relationship between the prison and the jailer or captor.

to all manner of speculation. In looking at Philemon, it is helpful to focus on the other appellations with which Paul refers to himself.

3. *Pauline Appellations in Philemon*

The epistle to Philemon is unique not only because of its length, as the shortest letter of Paul, but also because of the large number of self-appellations which Paul employs. He is not only a prisoner of Christ Jesus (δέσμιος Χριστοῦ 'Ιησοῦ) and an old man or ambassador (πρεσβύτης, v. 9), he not only refers to himself as a father to Onesimus[35] and a partner to the letter's addressee,[36] but by implication he is a brother,[37] a worker,[38] a soldier[39] and a prisoner of war.[40]

This epistle is saturated with relational language. Paul sees himself in a variety of ways. In understanding what Paul meant when he referred to himself as δέσμιος Χριστοῦ 'Ιησοῦ, the other appellations in this letter are illuminating. Here we will focus on three titles rarely used by Paul: πρεσβύτης, συστρατιώτης, and συναιχμάλωτος.

Verse 9: Ambassador or Old Man?
The rhetoric of v. 1 offers little context for determining what Paul was seeking to communicate, when he referred to himself as δέσμιος Χριστοῦ 'Ιησοῦ. His readers likely knew that he was a prisoner. They likely would not have been surprised to have seen him qualify this role with the genitive Χριστοῦ; after all, Paul always was 'of Christ'. Paul, however, does not free his readers from the responsibility of fully engaging this expression. A few verses later in vv. 8-9, he repeats this self-appellation:

> Διὸ πολλὴν ἐν Χριστῷ παρρησίαν ἔχων ἐπιτάσσειν σοι τὸ ἀνῆκον διὰ τὴν ἀγάπην μᾶλλον παρακαλῶ τοιοῦτος ὢν ὡς Παῦλος πρεσβύτης νυνὶ δὲ καὶ δέσμιος Χριστοῦ 'Ιησοῦ.

Unfortunately, whatever meaning may have been latent in the genitive construction in v. 1 is not made considerably more explicit in v. 9: the verse poses three significant exegetical difficulties. Not only can the

---

35. Phlm. 10.
36. Phlm. 17.
37. Timothy and Apphia are referred to as his brother and sister (vv. 1-2).
38. In v. 1 and v. 24, five persons are listed as fellow workers.
39. Archippus is a fellow soldier (v. 2).
40. Epaphras is presented as a fellow prisoner of war (v. 23).

participle ὤν in v. 9 function in two different ways, not only can the expression νυνὶ δὲ καὶ have two meanings, but, in addition, the appellation πρεσβύτης frequently is translated with two very different words. How these difficulties are addressed will go far in determining what Paul is trying to communicate. Initially it is important to sketch out the variety of interpretations.

The participle ὤν in v. 9 could function either in a concessive or in a causal manner. If concessive, Paul is appealing to Philemon, *although* Paul is πρεσβύτης νυνὶ δὲ καὶ δέσμιος Χριστοῦ 'Ιησοῦ. Conversely, if the participle is causal, Paul is appealing to Philemon, *because* he is πρεσβύτης νυνὶ δὲ καὶ δέσμιος Χριστοῦ 'Ιησοῦ. Is Paul appealing to his readers in spite of his present situation or because of it? The repeated use of the expression δέσμιος Χριστοῦ 'Ιησοῦ, at the very least, might signal that Paul sees this appellation—or wants Philemon to see it—in a positive light. Paul has nothing to be ashamed of: his appeal is based both on himself as πρεσβύτης and as δέσμιος Χριστοῦ 'Ιησοῦ. Although this explanation seems most plausible, although it seems most plausible that Paul is appealing to his readers *because* of his present situation, how one interprets the other exegetical issues in the passage does shape how one reads this participle.

Similarly, when Paul writes that he is πρεσβύτης νυνὶ δὲ καὶ δέσμιος Χριστοῦ 'Ιησοῦ, it is not clear whether the δέ in this sentence is adversative or conjunctive. Does Paul mean that he is a πρεσβύτης *but* now also a δέσμιος Χριστοῦ 'Ιησοῦ? Or does he mean that he is a πρεσβύτης *and* now even a δέσμιος Χριστοῦ 'Ιησοῦ?

How is νυνὶ δὲ καὶ to be understood? Norman R. Petersen has argued for the adversative sense of this expression. Verse 11, he writes, stands in 'a series of semantic contrasts between two terms, the second of which is contrasted with the first'.[41] Petersen sees ten such contrasts in vv. 8-16:

vv. 8-9a	bold enough to command	I prefer for love's sake to appeal
v. 9b	*presbutes*	a prisoner of Christ Jesus
v. 10	my son	whom I fathered
v. 11	formerly useless	now useful
vv. 12-13	whom I sent to you	whom I wanted to keep with me
v. 14	not by necessity	by free will

41. N.R. Petersen, *Rediscovering Paul: Philemon and the Sociology of Paul's Narrative World* (Philadelphia: Fortress Press, 1985), p. 126.

v. 15	he was parted from you for a while	that you might have him forever
v. 16a	not as a slave	as a beloved brother
v. 16b	especially to me	so much more to you
v. 16c	in the flesh	in the Lord[42]

According to Petersen's model, Paul's language and rhetoric within this pericope emphasize the disjuncture between his having been πρεσβύτης (or πρεσβύτης Χριστοῦ Ἰησοῦ) and his currently being a 'prisoner of Christ Jesus'. These two epithets are to be contrasted.

However, as Ronald F. Hock has noted, Petersen's analysis is 'weakened by the fact that at least three of the pairs are not contrasts— for example, "especially to me" and "so much more to you" (v. 16) is clearly an ascensive pair'.[43]

In seeking to understand how the phrase νυνὶ δὲ καὶ functions in v. 9, it is natural to look at the expression two verses later, in v. 11, where Paul writes that Onesimus 'formerly was useless to you but now is useful both to you and to me' (τόν ποτέ σοι ἄχρηστον νυνὶ δὲ καὶ σοὶ καὶ ἐμοὶ εὔχρηστον). In v. 11, there is clearly an adversative sense between the two parts of the sentence. However, this says nothing conclusive, since there is obviously a significant difference between the syntax in vv. 9 and 11. Paul's use of πότε in v. 11 makes clear that the word δέ here should be seen as functioning in an adversative manner; πότε clearly stands in contrast to νυνὶ. It needs to be asked, however, if the word πότε is used to clarify what might normally reflect either a more rhetorically ambiguous expression (νυνὶ δὲ καὶ), or an expression with a typically conjunctive function.

Although Peterson argues for the adversative use of νυνὶ δὲ καὶ, Hock offers a compelling argument that πρεσβύτης and δέσμιος Χριστοῦ Ἰησοῦ are not to be contrasted with each other, but are to be seen as an ascensive or conjunctive pair (which, as he notes 'is perfectly acceptable in the context of vv. 8-16').[44]

Because the participle ὢν and the expression νυνὶ δὲ καί can each

---

42. Petersen, *Rediscovering Paul*, p. 126. Although an adversative sense cannot be found in all of these pairs (e.g. v. 10), the numerous contrasts here lend support to the belief that the δέ in v. 9 is not simply conjunctive.

43. R.F. Hock, 'A Support for his Old Age: Paul's Plea on Behalf of Onesimus', in L.M. White and O.L. Yarbrough (eds.), *The Social World of the First Christians: Essays in Honor of Wayne A. Meeks* (Minneapolis, MN: Fortress Press, 1995), p. 74.

44. Hock, 'Paul's Plea on Behalf of Onesimus', p. 74.

have more than one meaning, an understanding of δέσμιος Χριστοῦ Ἰησοῦ hinges on the meaning and function of πρεσβύτης. What does Paul mean when he refers to himself as πρεσβύτης?

In its simplest form, the most important question in v. 9 may be whether Paul is referring to himself as an 'ambassador' or as an 'old man'. An increasing number of interpreters have seen πρεσβύτης as referring to Paul's role as 'ambassador'. Following Richard Bentley's emendation of the received text, J.B. Lightfoot claims that Paul refers to himself not as πρεσβύτης (an old man) but as πρεσβευτής (an ambassador).[45] Lightfoot continues by arguing that such an emendation was actually unnecessary; the word πρεσβύτης, he notes, occasionally can mean 'ambassador'.[46] On the basis of a limited number of texts in the Septuagint (with uncertain textual traditions),[47] many readers believe that Paul is seeking to emphasize his 'ambassadorial' role here in v. 9.[48]

One argument for translating this word as 'ambassador' is a rhetorical one. Houlden writes that

> 'Old man' and 'prisoner' hardly make a mounting pair of words to describe Paul's status; they are in different categories, the one relating to his person, the other to his role. Ambassador and prisoner fit together well.[49]

Furthermore, Paul obviously saw his role, at least in some respects, as that of an ambassador. In 2 Cor. 5.19b-20a, Paul emphasizes that God entrusted to Christians 'the ministry of reconciliation. So we are ambassadors for Christ (ὑπὲρ Χριστοῦ οὖν πρεσβεύομεν), God making his appeal through us.' Not only did Paul see himself as an ambassador on behalf of Christ, but that is also one way in which he was remembered. In Eph. 6.20, Paul is presented as saying: 'I am an ambassador in chains' (πρεσβεύω ἐν ἁλύσει).

If Paul did refer to himself as an ambassador elsewhere, and if that is how we are to understand the word πρεσβύτης in v. 9, why would he

45. J.B. Lightfoot, *Saint Paul's Epistles to the Colossians and to Philemon* (London: Macmillan and Co., 1904), p. 335.

46. Lightfoot, *Philemon*, pp. 336-37.

47. E.g., 2 Macc. 11.34; 2 Chron. 32.31 (Vaticanus); 1 Macc. 14.22 and 15.17 (Sinaiticus).

48. See Martin, *Colossians and Philemon*, p. 163; Stuhlmacher, *Der Brief an Philemon*, p. 37; Stöger, *The Epistle to Philemon* (trans. M. Dunne; New York: Herder and Herder, 1971), pp. 65-66; and O'Brien, *Colossians, Philemon*, p. 289.

49. J.L. Houlden, *Paul's Letters from Prison* (Baltimore: Penguin Books, 1970), p. 230.

have used this expression here? What purpose would that have served?

Paul may have been trying to emphasize that his role as ambassador led him to imprisonment: 'He is an ambassador of Jesus Christ and therefore imprisoned for the sake of his service.'[50] Furthermore, the contrast between 'ambassador' and 'prisoner' is a marked one. Paul was well-remembered in the church for being an 'ambassador' for Christ. He traveled far. He visited various congregations. He represented Christ in numerous ways.[51] Because 'the one who is sent should be treated according to the status of the one by whom he was sent, not the status which he individually holds',[52] the fact that the envoy of Christ was subsequently imprisoned amounted to a very sharp contrast in status. It was not just 'Paul' who was a prisoner. It was 'Paul, ambassador of Christ Jesus'.

Although a number of arguments have been made for translating πρεσβύτης as 'ambassador', there are also strong grounds for translating this term as 'old man'. Because Paul had just emphasized that he would not exploit his 'authority' (παρρησία) to give commands (v. 8), numerous commentators have wondered why Paul would then immediately emphasize that he is an 'ambassador', even an 'ambassador of Christ Jesus'.[53]

Furthermore, two of the most compelling arguments against the 'ambassador' translation are lexical ones. The grounds for claiming that πρεσβύτης is actually a corruption of πρεσβευτής are very weak; it is particularly unlikely that any sort of change would have resulted from phoneticconfusion.[54] Furthermore, although proponents of the 'ambassador' position occasionally claim that 'old man' and

---

50. Stuhlmacher, *Der Brief an Philemon*, p. 37. Translation here by Susan Wansink.

51. For a better understanding of ambassadors and envoys in antiquity, see Mitchell, 'New Testament Envoys', pp. 641-62. For a survey of the representative functions of envoys and ambassadors, see Diodorus Siculus, 18.66.3; 31.29-30; Dionysius of Halicarnassus, *Ant. Rom.* 5.52.5-5.53.3; 6.21.2; 6.32.1-2; Josephus, *Ant.* 17.145-46.

52. Mitchell, 'New Testament Envoys', p. 647.

53. See the discussions in Vincent, *Philemon*, p. 184; Lohse, *Colossians and Philemon*, p. 199; J. Gnilka, *Der Philemonbrief* (Freiburg: Herder, 1982), pp. 42-43; and G. Bornkamm, 'πρεσβύτης', *TDNT*, VI, p. 683.

54. For an extensive lexical analysis of the unlikely nature of such a corruption, see J.N. Birdsall, 'ΠΡΕΣΒΥΤΗΣ in Philemon 9: A Study in Conjectural Emendation', *NTS* 39 (1993), pp. 625-30.

'ambassador' are interchangeable possibilities in translating πρεσβύτης, R. Hock has convincingly argued that

> in Greek sources of the period there appears to be no such ambiguity in the meaning of πρεσβύτης...πρεσβύτης should virtually always be read as meaning 'old man'—and certainly in Philemon 9, where, after all, there is not even any confusion in the manuscripts.[55]

In the great majority of cases where πρεσβύτης is used, the meaning is clear: it simply means 'old man'.[56] This is what the term means in Lk. 1.18 and in Tit. 2.2. In Philemon also, Paul seems to be referring to his age. But why?

Joachim Gnilka emphasizes that Paul here is not just stating facts, he is trying to move his readers. Paul asks his readers to look at him, to recognize that he is not just an old man, but now even a prisoner:

> With inconspicuous gesture he points to himself, as if he wanted to say, 'Look at me—who I really am now—namely an old man and one who is in chains.' The word πρεσβύτης has been understood in the sense of 'ambassador of Christ Jesus'; be it with the help of conjecture, be it with the assertion of an alleged ambiguity of the term. Apart from the fact that this translation is uncertain, it overlooks the pathos with which Paul is speaking here. Age also necessarily implies authority (as Scripture emphasizes): 'You shall rise up before the hoary head, and honor the face of an old man' (Lev. 19.32).[57]

55. Hock, 'Paul's Plea on Behalf of Onesimus', p. 73.

56. This is seen most clearly in ancient definitions of the word. Pseudo-Hippocrates (cf. Philo, *Op. Mund.* 105) sees πρεσβύτης as the sixth of the seven ages which men experience. Those within this group are said to be between 49 and 56 years old; between the stages of 'mature man' (ἀνήρ) and 'old man' (γέρων). It appears that Hippocrates, himself, saw πρεσβύτης as the final stage in a person's life (*Aphorismi* 3.30-31) (cf. F. Boll, 'Die Lebensalter', *Neue Jahrbücher für das Klassische Altertum* 31 [1913], pp. 89-145, esp. pp. 114-18). Similarly, Aristoxenus, *Fr. Hist.* 35, sees πρεσβύτης as the last of five stages (cf. J. Gnilka, *Der Philemonbrief*, p. 43). Gnilka also points to a reference in the papyri to a 68 year old πρεσβύτης (*P. F. or.* 50, 62, 95), and Dio Chrysostom lists four stages of life, with the last being πρεσβύτης. Dio's list, however, is nothing like a scientific description. He writes, 'It would indeed be a blessing if, just as one becomes successively a lad (παῖς), a stripling (μειράκιον), a youth (νεανίσκος), and an old man (πρεσβύτης) by the passing of time, one might also in the same way become wise and just and trustworthy' (*Or.* 74.10).

57. Gnilka, *Der Philemonbrief*, p. 43 (translation by Susan Wansink). Similarly, Lohse, *Colossians and Philemon*, p. 199, writes that 'If Paul calls attention to his age and his imprisonment, he can expect that Philemon will pay due respect to his words.'

Paul is seeking empathy. He is old. Even moreso, he is also in a situation inappropriate for a person of his age: he is a prisoner of Christ Jesus.

There is reason to believe that an appeal to age would have created pathos. Ancient writers often refer to the tension and anxiety created when the elderly are forced to undergo public humiliation, torture or martyrdom. Thus, in *In Flacc.* 74, Philo describes the members of the Jewish Senate who were publicly humiliated in the theater. He stresses the disgrace of the occasion, when these old men were enchained (πρεσβύτας δεσμίους) and led through the market in a procession to their death. Eusebius also draws a sympathetic portrayal of Alexander, the bishop of the church of Jerusalem, who 'underwent the trial of imprisonment, crowned with the venerable hoary locks of ripe old age' (*Hist. eccl.* 6.39.2).

Perhaps one of the most inspirational anecdotes which appealed to age can be found in 4 Maccabees. This document makes frequent references to Eleazar's age and the incongruous punishment he underwent: 'When Antiochus saw him, he said, "Before I have the tortures begun on you, old man (ὦ πρεσβύτα), I would advise you to eat of the swine's flesh and save yourself. I respect your age and your gray hairs..." ' In a later panegyric, Eleazar is addressed by the author of 4 Maccabees as 'revered elder more vigorous than the flame' (7.10). The mother of the seven martyred brothers is also commended for her going through inordinate pain because of the death of her sons:

> She implored them and urged them on to death for the sake of religion. O mother, solider of God in the cause of religion, elder (πρεσβύτι) and woman. By steadfastness you have conquered even a tyrant, and in word and deed you have proved more powerful than a man. (16.13-14)

These examples are not unique. The ancients' concern for their elders can be seen throughout Greco–Roman literature, and the martyrdoms of the second and third centuries show us that the elderly who chose to die for their faith did inspire pathos.[58] Thus, Paul might have sought to inspire the same feelings. He was an old man and now, even more, he was a prisoner of Christ Jesus.

What is the logical connection between these two epithets? R. Hock, in discussing images of old age, points to several primary sources which illuminate how those who were older often were seen as vulnerable; they

---

58. E.g., *The Martyrdom of Polycarp* 9; *The Martyrs of Lyons* 28; Tacitus, *Ann.* 4.28. Cf. Epictetus, *Diss.* 1.4.24.

needed others to take care of them. Hock points to a *chreia* attributed to Diogenes Laertius. Asked whose life was truly miserable, Diogenes replied, 'An old man with no means of support' (6.51).[59] Just as an old man would depend on others for support, a prisoner even moreso would need the aid of others if he were to be provided with the basic needs of life; needs like food, drink, and rest. When Rabbi Joshua the grits-maker failed to bring the imprisoned Rabbi Akiba the water which he needed, Akiba said, 'Joshua, do you not know that I am an old man and my life depends on yours?' (*b. ʿErub.* 21b). Paul, like Akiba, was in need of support for at least two clear reaons. Paul, in v. 9, thus, is trying to appeal to his readers as an old man and even a prisoner of Christ Jesus.

The Military Imagery of Verses 2 and 23

Paul is fond of the Greek prefix συν-, which might be translated most colloquially into English as 'fellow'. Thus, Paul's συνεργός[60] would be his 'fellow worker', συστρατιώτης[61] would be his 'fellow soldier', and συναιχμάλωτος[62] would be his 'fellow prisoner of war'.[63] It is interesting to note that all three of these titles occur in Paul's brief epistle to Philemon. Whereas we have little reason to doubt that the first expression is a literal term, the latter two are distinctively metaphorical. Although Paul does not explicitly refer to himself as a 'soldier' or as a 'prisoner of war', by implication such appellations do refer not only to Archippus or to Epaphras, but also to the apostle himself.

This section will not seek to answer how Paul's 'fellow soldiers' or 'fellow prisoners of war' were different from his 'fellow workers'. Both a lack of context and very few clues from the early Christian communities make it difficult to know whether these titles were seen as apt characterizations of individuals' temperaments or circumstances, or whether they also referred to different functions or positions within the community.[64] In either case, it needs to be asked what Paul would have

59. Hock, 'Paul's Plea on Behalf of Onesimus', pp. 78-79.
60. Cf. Rom. 16.3, 9, 21; 1 Cor. 3.9; 2 Cor. 1.24; 8.23; Phil. 2.25; 4.3; Col. 4.11; 1 Thess. 3.2; Phlm. 1, 24.
61. Phil. 2.25; Phlm. 2.
62. Rom. 16.7; Col. 4.10; Phlm. 23.
63. The other use of 'συν-' in Pauline (or deutero-Pauline) construction of nouns is σύνδουλος (Col. 1.7; 4.7).
64. *Contra* A. Harnack, *Militia Christi: The Christian Religion and the Military in the First Three Centuries* (trans. D. McInnes Gracie; Philadelphia: Fortress Press, 1981), pp. 37-39, who wishes to see the 'soldiers' as occupying a specific position

been trying to communicate by using this military language.

It is not surprising that Paul would use words like συστρατιώτης or συναιχμάλωτος. Such imagery was a part of the thought world of the apostle; he uses similar language in other epistles.[65]

In his very first letter, Paul admonished those Christians who were preparing for the day of the Lord to 'be sober, and put on the breast-plate of faith and love, and for a helmet the hope of salvation' (1 Thess. 5.8). Elsewhere, Paul exhorts Christians to 'put on the armor of light' (Rom. 13.12) and to have 'the weapons of righteousness' (2 Cor. 6.7). Furthermore, Christians are referred to as being 'led in triumph' (2 Cor. 2.14) and the weapons of their warfare are said to be 'not worldly but have divine power to destroy strongholds' (2 Cor. 10.3-6). In another of his prison epistles, Paul uses military language to encourage the Philippians to 'stand firm in one spirit', to not break rank, 'with one mind striving side by side' (Phil. 1.27-30).[66]

In addition, in other epistles within the Pauline tradition, Timothy is exhorted to 'wage the good warfare' (1 Tim. 1.18). He is reminded that 'no soldier on service gets entangled in civilian pursuits, since his aim is to satisfy the one who enlisted him' (2 Tim. 2.3-4). In Col. 2.15, Paul says that Christ 'disarmed the principalities and powers...triumphing over them'. And finally, ch. 6 of Ephesians has Paul admonishing his readers to 'put on the whole armor of God, that you may be able to

within the church. The 'soldier', 'as a Christian missionary and teacher gets his living from others and does not involve himself in "civilian" pursuits. They are polar in their effect and therefore imply a whole class structure' (p. 39). John Knox, *Philemon among the Letters of Paul* (New York: Abingdon Press, rev. edn, 1959 [1935]), p. 68, acknowledges that the specific meaning of συστρατιώτης cannot be determined, but he sees the word as used 'to designate a helper in times of need, an ally, a befriender'. The texts which Harnack and Knox use are general in nature and allow a multiplicity of interpretations.

65. For more thorough discussions of the following texts, see A.J. Malherbe, 'Antisthenes and Odysseus, and Paul at War', *HTR* 76 (1983), pp. 143-73; R.A. Wild, 'The Warrior and the Prisoner: Some Reflections on Ephesians 6.10-20', *CBQ* 46 (1984), pp. 284-98; and R.G. Tanner, 'St Paul's View of Militia and Contemporary Social Values', *StudBib* 3 (1978), pp. 377-82. Also see Harnack, *Militia Christi*, esp. pp. 35-40.

66. For a discussion of military metaphors and their usage in Phil. 1.27-30, see E.M. Krentz, 'Military Language and Metaphors in Philippians', in B.H. McLean (ed.), *Origins and Method: Towards a New Understanding of Judaism and Christianity* (Festschrift J.C. Hurd; JSNTSup, 86; Sheffield: JSOT Press, 1993), pp. 105-127.

stand against the wiles of the devil' (6.11). Christians are to fasten the belt of truth around their waist, and have the breastplate of righteousness in position; feet are to be equipped with the gospel of peace, and the shield of faith is to be used as protection against the flaming darts of the evil one. The helmet of salvation and the sword of the Spirit (the word of God) complete the armor of God (6.13-17).

Not only did Paul himself employ martial imagery, but he also was remembered after his death both as one who used martial imagery and as a soldier for the faith. This latter point is best seen in the *The Martyrdom of Paul* (*The Acts of Paul* 11). Claiming that Christians 'are in the army of that king of the ages' (11.2), Paul stands before Caesar and says: 'Caesar, here I am—Paul, God's soldier. I am not dead, but alive in my God' (11.6).

It is interesting to note that earlier in *The Acts of Paul* 3.3, Paul is described as

> a man small in size, with a bald head and crooked legs; in good health; with eyebrows that met and a rather prominent nose; full of grace, for sometimes he looked like a man and sometimes he had the face of an angel.

Although the description may not sound flattering, Robert M. Grant has argued convincingly that this portrayal of Paul is essentially positive. Grant sees the author of this description as having been influenced by the transmission of a well-known description from Archilochus: 'I love not a tall general nor one long-shanked, nor with splendid curls or partly sheared. Let me have one who is short and bow-legged, firm on his feet, full of heart.'[67] Thus, Paul is portrayed as one who resembles a general. If Grant's thesis holds, not only was Paul remembered as a soldier, he also was treated as 'a general of God'.

Paul may have used military imagery, he may have been remembered as a 'soldier of God', but it still needs to be asked how the early Christians would have heard this language and what sort of images such language would have evoked. This can be seen best by examining the use of martial imagery in the Greco–Roman world.

Military metaphors were frequently employed in Greco–Roman philosophy and rhetoric, with such language often stressing the need for each

67. R.M. Grant, 'The Description of Paul in the Acts of Paul and Thecla', *VC* 36 (1982), p. 2. Also see A.J. Malherbe, 'A Physical Description of Paul', *HTR* 79 (1986), pp. 170-75.

person, as a 'soldier', to be totally obedient to his general.[68] Epictetus emphasizes 'the business of life being a campaign' (στρατεία τὸ χρῆμά ἐστιν):

> One man must mount guard, another go out on reconnaissance, and another out to fight. It is not possible for all to stay in the same place, nor is it better so. But you neglect to perform the duties assigned you by your commanding officer, and complain when some rather hard order is given you, and fail to understand to what a state you are bringing the army, as far as in you lies...[69]

Similarly, in a discussion of the virtuous man and the happy life, Seneca emphasizes the importance of 'the soldier' accepting his lot:

> That perfect man, who has attained virtue, never cursed his luck, and never received the results of chance with dejection; he believed that he was citizen and soldier of the universe, accepting his tasks as if they were his orders. Whatever happened, he did not spurn it as if it were evil and borne in upon him by hazard; he accepted it as if it were assigned to be his duty. 'Whatever this may be', he says, 'it is my lot; it is rough and it is hard, but I must work diligently at the task.'[70]

The perfect man does not complain, but, as a 'soldier of the universe', he accepts the task he is called to fulfill.

---

68. R.G. Tanner, 'St Paul's View of Militia and Contemporary Social Values', p. 377, sees this obedience as one of the two most distinctive values of this military system. Ovid presents an interesting example of the importance of obedience in the military. *Am.* 1.9 begins with the statement, 'Every lover is a soldier' (*Militat omnis amans*), and then focuses on the loyalty of both lovers and soldiers: 'The spirit that captains seek in the valiant soldier is the same the fair maid seeks in the man who mates with her. Both wake through the night; on the ground he takes his rest—the one guards his mistress's door, the other his captain's...' (1.9.5-8). For extended discussions on the role of military metaphors in Greco–Roman philosophy, also see Malherbe, 'Antisthenes and Odysseus', pp. 143-73; A. Harnack, *Militia Christi*; H. Emonds, 'Christlicher Kriegsdienst: Der Topos der militia spiritualis in der antiken Philosophie', reprinted in A. Harnack, *Militia Christi*, pp. 131-62; and E. Eidem, *Pauli bildvärld*. I. *Athletae et Milites Christi* (Lund: Gleerup, 1913).

69. Epictetus, *Diss.* 3.24.31-32. Cf. Epictetus, *Diss.* 3.2.34; Seneca, *Ep.* 96.5: 'Life is a battle' (*vivere militare est*).

70. *Ep.* 120.12. In *Ep.* 37, Seneca sees allegiance to virtue as a type of soldiering: 'You have promised to be a good man; you have enlisted under oath; that is the strongest chain which will hold you to a sound understanding. Any man will be but mocking you, if he declares that this is an effeminate and easy kind of soldiering' (37.1).

Seneca's depiction of the wise man as 'soldier' reflected a common-place in Greco–Roman philosophy. The metaphor extends back to Plato's portrayal of the most famous prisoner in the Mediterranean world: Socrates. Socrates saw loyalty to 'the god' (a loyalty which could lead even to death) as analogous to his previous loyalty to military commanders:

> Wherever a man stations himself, thinking it is best to be there, or is stationed by his commander, there he must, as it seems to me, remain and run his risks, considering neither death nor any other thing more than disgrace. So I should have done a terrible thing, if, when the commanders whom you chose to command me stationed me, both at Potidaea and at Amphipolis and at Delium, I remained where they stationed me, like any-body else, and ran the risk of death, but when the god gave me a station, as I believed and understood, with orders to spend my life in philosophy and in examining myself and others, then I were to desert my post through fear of death or anything else whatsoever.[71]

This example of Socrates can be seen throughout Greco–Roman philo-sophy. Resulting from a refusal to 'desert his post', Socrates' imprison-ment and death are often presented as ideals for those whom we might call prisoners of conscience. Seneca emphasizes that Socrates refused to flee and stayed in prison, 'in order to free mankind from the fear of two most grievous things, death and imprisonment' (*Ep.* 24.4-5). Epictetus also alludes to Socrates in his admonitions against suicide. Here again life is seen as warfare, and no one is to be a deserter: 'Men, wait upon God. When He shall give the signal and set you free from this service, then shall you depart to Him; but for the present endure to abide in this place, where He has stationed you' (1.9.16-17).[72]

---

71. *Ap.* 28 D–E. For a thorough discussion of this passage, see 'The Soldier of Apollo', in C.D.C. Reeve, *Socrates in the Apology* (Indianapolis: Hackett, 1989), pp. 108-114. Illuminating discussions of the portrayal of Socrates can be found in A.A. Long, 'Socrates in Hellenistic Philosophy', *Classical Quarterly* 38 (1988), pp. 150-71, and in E. Benz, 'Christus und Sokrates in der alten Kirche: Ein Beitrag zum altkirchlichen Verständnis des Märtyrers und des Martyriums', *ZNW* 43 (1950-51), pp. 195-224.

72. Not only does Epictetus often allude to Socrates' unwillingness to abandon his post, but in *Diss.* 1.9.23-24, he also presents a shortened version of Plato, *Ap.* 28 D-E. Here Socrates is lecturing his accusers: 'If you tell me now', says he, '"We will acquit you on these conditions, namely, that you will no longer engage in these discussions which you have conducted hitherto, nor trouble either the young or the old among us", I will answer, "You make yourselves ridiculous by thinking that, if

Thus, if there is one characteristic of soldiers which stands out above all others, it would be this characteristic which Socrates embodied: loyalty. Soldiers do not desert their post. They accept their fate. Just as soldiers swear allegiance to Caesar, Epictetus says that his readers should swear allegiance to God:

> Never to disobey under any circumstances, never to prefer charges, never to find fault with anything that God has given, never to let your will rebel when you have either to do or to suffer something that is inevitable. (*Diss.* 1.14.15-16)

This analogy is seen elsewhere in Epictetus. In life, 'you have to maintain the character of a soldier, and do each separate act at the bidding of the General, if possible divining what He wishes' (*Diss.* 3.24.34-35). Elsewhere, Epictetus discusses how great it is to say to oneself that Zeus wants to see what kind of soldier I am, so I am put in situations of poverty, sickness and prison. These situations do not show Zeus's neglect. Rather,

> He is training me, and making use of me as a witness to the rest of men. When I have been appointed to such a service, am I no longer to take thought as to where I am, or with whom, or what men say about me? Am I not wholly intent upon God, and His commands and ordinances. (*Diss.* 3.24.111-14)

Loyalty, perseverence and steadfastness are virtues which the ideal soldier was said to possess. Although other duties follow, 'the soldier's primary bond of union is his oath of allegiance and his love for the flag and a horror of desertion' (Seneca, *Ep.* 95.35).

The ideal soldier not only was loyal, but he also refused to desert his post, regardless of the consequences he might face. Thus, when soldiers died,[73] were imprisoned[74] or became prisoners of war, all of these fates

---

your general had stationed me at any post, I ought to hold and maintain it and choose rather to die ten thousand times than to desert it, but if God has stationed us in some place and in some manner of life we ought to desert that."'

73. E.g., Suetonius, *Iul.* 68, describes the steadfastness of individual soldiers like Cassius Scaeva and Gaius Acilius: 'Scaeva, with one eye gone, his thigh and shoulder wounded, and his shield bored through in a hundred and twenty places, continued to guard the gate of a fortress put in his charge. Acilius in the sea-fight at Massilia grasped the stern of one of the enemy's ships, and when his right hand was lopped off, rivalling the famous exploit of the Greek hero Cynegirus, boarded the ship and drove the enemy before him with the boss of his shield.' Tertullian, in *De Fuga* 10, emphasizes how Christians are not to abandon their faith during persecution: 'More

reflected their loyalty in the face of danger. Seneca the Elder writes that 'A Spartan, taken prisoner, said: "Kill me: I am no slave." He couldn't have been captured if he had been ready to retreat.'[75] The Greek term which Paul uses for 'fellow prisoner of war' (συναιχμάλωτος) is extremely rare and unfortunately is not illuminated by its use in other contexts.[76] Since few prisoners of war in antiquity had the opportunity or the facility to write, the rarity of the term is not entirely surprising. In any case, since the ancients repeatedly stressed the importance of not deserting one's post—regardless of the consequences—such words as συναιχμάλωτος and συστρατιώτης can be seen as reflecting similarly prized values. To be a prisoner of war means that one had held one's ground and had not retreated.

Regardless of how Paul may have used military imagery elsewhere, regardless of the source of this influence, it is not surprising to see a high concentration of this language in his letter to Philemon, an epistle written from prison. As described in Chapter 1 of this work, soldiers served in both policing cities and guarding the imprisoned. The prisons and the militia were linked in a number of ways: soldiers incarcerated criminals, guarded them, tortured them and executed them. If Paul had a propensity to use martial imagery, it would come as no surprise to see such language, particularly if he were writing from a place where soldiers surrounded him.[77]

glorious is the soldier pierced with a javelin in battle, than he who has a safe skin as a fugitive.'

74. Cf. Plato, *Ap.* 28E; Epictetus, *Diss.* 1.9.16; 3.24.111-14.

75. Seneca the Elder, *Suas.* 2.8.

76. In the New Testament this term can be found in Phlm. 23, in Rom. 16.7, and in Col. 4.10. In a letter as short as Philemon, the term does play a significant role in illuminating aspects of Paul's rhetoric which might go unnoticed in a much longer letter. The verbal form of this word can be seen in Rom. 7.23, 2 Cor. 10.5, and Lk. 21.24. Demades, *Orat.* 1.65 and Sextus Empiricus, *Math.* 1.295 refer to an aorist passive participle (συναιχμαλωτισθείς) and Pseudo-Lucian, *Asin.* 27, actually uses the same form as Paul, but in all three cases, the usages do not illuminate Paul's use of this noun.

77. Cf. Vincent, *Philemon,* 177. Similarly, the author of Ephesians could see the imprisoned Paul (Eph. 3.1; 4.1) as moved, in his circumstances, to employ the sorts of martial imagery found in Eph. 6.10-20.

4. *Self-Appellations within the Rhetoric of Philemon*

Paul presents himself in this letter as δέσμιος χριστοῦ Ἰησοῦ: he is 'a chained one'; he is 'a bound one'; he is 'a prisoner'.[78] Aside from the variety of possible metaphorical images which this appellation may have inspired in each reader's mind, one meaning should have been clear to all: Paul was in prison, and his imprisonment was somehow linked to his relationship with Christ Jesus. Paul was a 'prisoner of Christ Jesus'.

When Paul uses this appellation again in v. 9, he precedes it by referring to himself as an 'old man'. The Greek word πρεσβύτης carried with it connotations such as 'dependence' and 'lack of support'. Thus, when Paul refers to himself as an old man and now a prisoner, it is clear that he has found himself in a position where he was dependent on others' support.

However, in what respects was Paul a prisoner 'of Christ Jesus'? Verse 13 offers one answer. Just as Paul in v. 13 describes himself as 'in chains for the sake of the gospel' (ἐν τοῖς δεσμοῖς τοῦ εὐαγγελίου), so is he best understood as being 'chained for the sake of Christ Jesus (δέσμιος Χριστοῦ Ἰησοῦ)'.

Lest Paul's readers still not sense that his imprisonment was for Christ and the gospel, Paul uses military metaphors to make the point more explicit. We do not know how the first readers of this letter would have been struck when they heard Paul refer to Archippus as 'our fellow soldier' (τῷ συστρατιώτῃ ἡμῶν) in v. 2. Among all the appellations and titles, this reference may not have been all that striking; unusual, perhaps, but not entirely striking. However, a very odd appellation in v. 23 of this letter does make one reconsider Paul's words in vv. 1-2.

In the letter's final greetings, Paul writes, 'Epaphras, my fellow prisoner of war in Christ Jesus (ὁ συναιχμάλωτός μου ἐν Χριστῷ Ἰησοῦ), sends greetings to you.' Although many commentators do not focus on the epistle's closing greetings, although most translations of this verse translate συναιχμάλωτος only as 'fellow prisoner', the descrip-

---

78. H. Binder, *Philemon*, p. 43. Although the Greek word δέσμιος does mean 'prisoner', often it should be translated directly as 'chained one' or 'one in chains'. Cf. Diodorus Siculus, 34; 35.23; Dionysius of Halicarnassus, *Ant. Rom.* 6.21.2; 20.5.5; 20.16.1; Euripides, *Bacch.* 355; Herodian, 1.6.6; Josephus, *Ant.* 10.50; 13.203; 15.8, 104, 351; 17.145; 18.119, 192; 20.31; Nonnus, *Dion.* 1.192; 2.304; Philo, *In Flacc.* 74; Plutarch, *Ant.* 50.4; 72.3; *Phil.* 20.3; *Mor.* 305E; Polybius, 15.33.6; 24.7.8.

tion of Epaphras is a noteworthy one. Paul's reference to Epaphras as συναιχμάλωτος reminds readers not just that Paul is 'a chained one' (δέσμιος, vv. 1, 9), but also that he is to be understood as a 'prisoner of war'. Similarly, just as his chains come from his status as a 'prisoner of war',[79] so his condition as a 'prisoner of war' has resulted from his role as a 'soldier' (v. 2). A soldier becomes a prisoner of war, because—as a soldier—he 'could not have been captured if he had been ready to retreat'.[80]

The image of Socrates as a soldier was a popular one in the Greco–Roman philosophy of Paul's day: Epictetus and Seneca, as shown above, saw Socrates' loyalty as exemplary. Just as Socrates refused to desert the post to which his military commanders assigned him, so he refused to desert the post to which the god had assigned him. The loyalty of a soldier characterized both Socrates' military life and his philosophical life. Although Paul may have been hearkening to allusions to the pre-eminent imprisoned philosoher, he was not necessarily drawing on the image of Socrates. 'Soldiers' of Paul's day, in general, were characterized by their extreme loyalty. To be a soldier meant that you would be obedient to your general: you would be loyal; you would not abandon your post; you would be horrified by the idea of desertion.[81]

This metaphor was natural to use in describing one who reacted bravely to attacks on their faith. One example of faithfulness being described in military language can be found in 4 Maccabees. During the martyrdom of the seven brothers, their—and their mother's—endurance is seen as reflecting the virtues of a soldier. While the eldest brother was tortured on the wheel, he cried out, '"Imitate me, brothers", he said. "Do not leave your post in my struggle or renounce our courageous brother-hood. Fight the sacred and noble battle for religion"' (4 Macc. 9.23-24a). After all seven of the brothers faced their torturers and accepted death, the author of 4 Maccabees praises their mother:

79. The terms δέσμιος and αἰχμάλωτος frequently appear together in Greek literature. Cf. Diodorus Siculus, 34; 35.23; Herodian, 1.6.6; Josephus, *Ant.* 15.8.

80. Seneca the Elder, *Suas.* 2.8. J. Knox, 'Philemon', in *The Interpreter's Bible*, XI (New York: Abingdon Press, 1955), p. 561, refers to the constellation of these words and briefly notes that 'This hint that Paul is thinking of himself as engaged in a war for Christ's sake and as being now a battle casualty is confirmed by his reference to Archippus (v. 2) as "our fellow soldier".'

81. Seneca, *Ep.* 95.35.

O mother, soldier (στρατιωτί) of God in the cause of religion, elder (πρεσβύτι) and woman! By steadfastness you have conquered even a tyrant, and in word and deed you have proved more powerful than a man (16.14).

The mother's loyalty as a soldier (in a metaphorical sense) is heightened all the more since she is elderly (πρεσβύτι). This makes her worthy of praise and remembrance. The brothers' refusal to 'leave their posts' and their mother's 'steadfastness in the cause of religion' both point to a virtue seen as typical of soldiers. Whether this virtue be called obedience, loyalty or faithfulness, it was a concept seen throughout the Hellenistic thought world, and it is also to be seen in Philemon.

In his brief letter to Philemon, Paul has a request to make: he wants Onesimus to serve him during his imprisonment. Although Paul does not want to command Philemon 'to do what is required' (v. 8), he does appeal to Philemon's sense of goodness (v. 14) and to their relationship (vv. 17 and 19). He offers Philemon payment (vv. 18-19). He even expresses his confidence that Philemon 'will do even more' than what is requested (v. 21). One of Paul's appeals, however, is much more subtle. By referring to others as συστρατιώτης and συναιχμάλωτος, by referring to himself as both πρεσβύτης and δέσμιος χριστοῦ Ἰησοῦ,[82] Paul reminds Philemon that his imprisonment resulted from his dedication to Christ Jesus and that his imprisonment has resulted in a need for support. Paul presents himself as a prisoner, even a prisoner of war, who, in the battle for Christ Jesus and the gospel, is worthy of Philemon's attention and support.

5. *Conclusion*

Loyal soldiers refused to desert their post, regardless of the consequences. Thus, when Paul refers to himself, by implication, both as a soldier and as a prisoner of war, these military metaphors serve to explicate what he meant when he had referred to himself as δέσμιος Χριστοῦ Ἰησοῦ. Paul begins the letter to Philemon by acknowledging that he is in chains. However, through the genitive contruction Χριστοῦ Ἰησοῦ, through his emphasis on his status (in v. 9), and through the metaphorical use of military appellations, Paul implies that his imprisonment followed naturally

---

82. Paul's status as prisoner is the warrant of authority for his παρακαλῶ. Cf. Eph. 4.1, where the author presents Paul, who, as ὁ δέσμιος ἐν κυρίῳ, appeals (παρακαλῶ) to the Ephesians.

from his commitment to Christ Jesus and to the gospel. Like Socrates, that famous imprisoned philosopher, and like the ideal soldier of his day, the apostle Paul refused to desert his post, regardless if it would lead to imprisonment or death.

Thus, it is not surprising that a second-century work like the *The Acts of Paul* might remember the apostle as 'God's soldier'.[83] When Longus the prefect and Cestus the centurion offer to free Paul, if he stopped believing in Christ, the apostle is presented as saying that which is only implied in his letter to Philemon. Paul squares off to his prosecutors and states, 'I am no deserter from Christ, but a lawful soldier of the living God'.[84] Paul, the prisoner, was no deserter from Christ.

83. *The Acts of Paul* 11.6.
84. *The Acts of Paul* 11.4.

Chapter 5

ONESIMUS, EPAPHRODITUS AND BURRHUS:
MINISTERS TO THE IMPRISONED IN EARLY CHRISTIANITY

I have derived much joy and comfort from your love, my brother, because
the hearts of the saints have been refreshed through you.
—Philemon 20

1. *Introduction*

Because they are 'partners', Paul feels that the members of the
community which received his letter share something with him; perhaps
common concerns, common goals, maybe even common property. In
any case, when Paul returns a person to this community, a person who
had been with him in prison, the apostle feels justified in asking these
Christians to 'receive him in the Lord with all joy'. That is the scenario
in Paul's letter to the Philippians. Epaphroditus was messenger and
minister to the imprisoned apostle. He had been sent to Paul by the
Philippians, he had completed his service on their behalf, and then Paul
had sent him back to the community.

Of the seven epistles attributed to the imprisoned apostle,[1] Paul himself
generally is seen as having written only two: Philippians and Philemon. It
is interesting to note, however, that most interpretations of Philemon fail
to draw attention to similarities between the figures and roles of
Ephaphroditus and Onesimus.

A concern with the theological implications of Philemon appears to be
at least partially responsible for the lack of interest in the epistle's social
setting.[2] James Moffatt writes that this letter's

1.   The following epistles all claim to have been written by Paul in prison:
Ephesians, Philippians, Colossians, 2 Timothy, Philemon, *3 Corinthians*, and
Laodiceans.
2.   For an examination of how methodological presuppositions have shaped the

private character, its brevity, and its lack of dogmatic teaching threw it into positive disfavour with many Christians, especially throughout the Syrian church...Jerome, in his preface (AD 388), had to defend it against widespread depreciation (*a plerisque ueteribus repudiatam*).[3]

Philemon's place in the canon has been defended, however, through focus on the letter's wisdom and love.[4] Such wisdom and love is seen in Paul's munificence towards Onesimus, a slave who is often described by commentators as a thieving runaway. Ralph P. Martin offers a fairly standard position:

> For forgiveness to be shown to a criminal slave who had escaped was another matter. Paul's plea was a revolutionary thought in contrast with the contemporary treatment of runaway slaves whom the master could take steps to arrest and then brutally punish.[5]

Onesimus was a slave and he was with Paul in prison. At one time in his life he may also have been a thief and a runaway. Regardless if this actually were the case, Paul's letter to Philemon does not share this information with us. After briefly looking at Paul's relationship with Onesimus, and then examining the claim that Onesimus was a runaway, this chapter will show that Paul's incarceration was the occasion for Onesimus's presence in prison. By looking at messengers in antiquity, at attendants to the imprisoned, and at an early use of this epistle, we can see more clearly that Onesimus had not 'escaped *into* prison': he had been sent by his owner.[6]

interpretation of this letter, see S. Winter, 'Methodological Observations on a New Interpretation of Paul's Letter to Philemon', *USQR* 35 (1984), pp. 3-12.

3.   J. Moffatt, *An Introduction to the Literature of the New Testament* (New York: Charles Scribner's Sons, 1911), p. 164.

4.   In examining contemporary analyses of Philemon, J.G. Nordling, 'Onesimus Fugitivus: A Defense of the Runaway Slave Hypothesis in Philemon', *JSNT* 41 (1991), p. 119, writes, 'The ultimate danger of the "new" interpretation is that it could turn a letter which manifestly "breathes the great-hearted tenderness of the apostle" (Guthrie, *New Testament Introduction*, p. 638) into a rather dispassionate, non-theological financial transaction between Paul and Onesimus' owner. Yet I doubt that such a routine scrap of business correspondence would ever have become part of the canonical NT...Paul never ceased to be a theologian.'

5.   R.P. Martin, *Colossians and Philemon* (NCB; London: Oliphants, 1974), p. 146.

6.   J.L. Houlden, *Paul's Letters from Prison* (Baltimore: Penguin Books, 1970), p. 226, argues against the hypothesis which claims that Onesimus was a runaway: 'That he was a runaway slave and that this is why Paul is so delicate and charming in

2. *Paul's Relationship with Onesimus*

Regardless of how Paul and Onesimus first encountered each other, something unusual happened to this pagan slave: while with Paul in prison, the pagan Onesimus had converted to Christ. Now Paul is writing to Onesimus's owner, on behalf of the slave, but especially on behalf of himself.

Paul uses particularly intimate language to describe the conversion. Paul calls Onesimus his 'child' (τέκνον), having 'given birth to him in chains (ὅν ἐγέννησα ἐν τοῖς δεσμοῖς)'.[7] Paul has a fondness for familial language.[8] However, Paul refers to only a very limited number of individuals as his own 'children'.[9] In the Pauline and Deutero-Pauline literature, with the exception of Titus (Tit. 1.4) and Onesimus (Phlm. 10), only one other named individual is said to have been a 'child' of Paul. That person is Timothy.[10] Thus, the language which Paul uses to describe his relationship with Onesimus is strong.

Paul goes yet a step further in expressing his affection, referring to Onesimus as τὰ ἐμὰ σπλάγχνα (v. 12). Although this expression often is translated the same as it is in v. 7—that is, with the word 'heart'—it is also a synonym of the Greek word παῖς (child). Artemidorus is explicit in *Oneirocritica*: 'Children' (οἱ παῖδες), like the inward parts of the body, are also called σπλάγχνα (1.44).[11]

this letter aimed at assuaging his master's wrath is a legend without foundation. We just do not know how he came to be with Paul; probably he had been lent Paul to be of service to him over a difficult period. And the reason for Paul's delicacy is simply that he wishes to retain his services longer.' Houlden, whose interpretation is a minority position, stands in the tradition of J. Knox, *Philemon among the Letters of Paul: A New View of its Place and Importance* (Nashville: Abingdon Press, 1959). For a similar interpretation, see S. Winter, 'Paul's Letter to Philemon', *NTS* 33 (1987), pp. 1-15. The primary contribution of this chapter is to point to overlooked evidence and data which support this hypothesis.

7. Phlm. 10.

8. For a discussion of familial language in Philemon, see L.A. Lewis, 'An African American Appraisal of the Philemon-Paul-Onesimus Triangle', in C.H. Felder (ed.), *Stony the Road We Trod: African American Biblical Interpretation* (Minneapolis: Fortress Press, 1991), pp. 232-46.

9. In a hortatory context, Paul does refer to the Corinthians and the Galatians as his 'children' (1 Cor. 4.14; Gal. 4.19). Cf. 2 Cor. 6.13; 12.14; 1 Thess. 2.7, 11.

10. 1 Cor. 4.17; Phil. 2.22; 1 Tim. 1.2, 18; 2 Tim. 1.2; 2.1.

11. Artemidorus, *The Interpretation of Dreams* (trans. R.J. White; Torrance, CA:

Paul's relationship with this recent convert had become so strong that he wanted to retain him, so that Onesimus—on behalf of Philemon—could serve the apostle during his 'imprisonment for the gospel' (v. 13). Paul left no doubt that he was frustrated in having to return Onesimus to Philemon (vv. 12-14). Thus, in sending him back, Paul makes a request of Philemon: 'If you consider me your partner, receive him as you would receive me. If he has wronged you at all, or owes you anything, charge that to my account' (vv. 17-18). Paul does not ask that Philemon forgive Onesimus. He does ask Philemon to see Onesimus in a new light, to recognize him no longer as a slave, but as a beloved brother, perhaps even as a partner.

Then, following Paul's admonitions that Philemon view Onesimus in a new light, Paul is explicit about that which he desires:

> Yes, brother, I want some benefit from you (ἐγώ σου ὀναίμην) in the Lord. Refresh my heart (ἀνάπαυσόν μου τὰ σπλάγχνα) in Christ. Confident of your obedience, I write to you, knowing that you will do even more than I say. (vv. 20-21)

'Yes brother I want some benefit from you in the Lord.' The Greek word for 'benefit', the word used here, is etymologically related to Onesimus's name.[12] In other words, Paul is using word-plays much as he used them in v. 11. Similarly if we look at the way the Greek expression is used in v. 10, that verse is best translated 'I ask you for my child Onesimus'. In this letter, Paul sometimes is writing on behalf of Onesimus. Here, however, Paul is asking 'for' Onesimus; not on 'behalf

Original Books, 1975), p. 53. Cf. 5.57. This expression appears to have its origin in the phrase 'to come from the womb', which Pindar used to refer to children (*Ol.* 6.43; *Nem.* 1.35).

12. E. Lohse, *Colossians and Philemon* (Hermeneia; trans. W.R. Poehlmann and R.J. Karris; Philadelphia: Fortress Press, 1971), p. 205, writes that, 'In giving voice to this desire, Paul employs an expression that is almost a fixed formula. Consequently, a word-play on the name of Onesimus cannot be read out of ὀναίμην.'

Lohse's fundamental argument (cf. W.R. Schoedel, *Ignatius of Antioch* [Philadelphia: Fortress Press, 1985], pp. 45-46) is that this Greek expression is so common in epistolary situations that it should not be stressed here; that Paul here is not making a pun. Lohse's position is, at least in part, based on his reading of Onesimus as a runaway. However, since most puns do rely on clichés and familiar expressions, since Paul uses word-play in v. 11, and since there is a strong similarity between the sound of this verb and that of the slave's name, it seems both reasonable and likely that Paul is using word-play here.

of' him.[13] Paul wants Onesimus. Paul wants Onesimus to join him in his mission. As Knox writes,

> This is no merely generous appeal on behalf of a slave-boy in whom Paul had come to feel an interest. Paul's own affections and purposes are in the balance; he wants Onesimus to be returned to him.[14]

Paul desires that Onesimus be set free to return to work with him.

But is Paul also appealing on behalf of a runaway? Ralph P. Martin writes that 'the primary purpose of the letter is to act as a covering note to ensure that Philemon will receive back his delinquent slave'.[15] Paul is writing on behalf of a slave whom he hopes Philemon will accept 'no longer as a slave'. Paul is writing on behalf of himself, desiring that Onesimus might serve him during his imprisonment for the gospel. But the primary question remains: Is Paul also appealing on behalf of a slave who had run away from his master?

3. *Arguments against the 'Runaway' Hypotheses*

If the word 'runaway' is not used in this letter, if Paul writes nothing explicit about Onesimus having run away, what grounds are there to believe that this slave actually had escaped from his owner? Four main arguments have been employed by those who believe that this letter refers to a runaway slave or to a slave seeking assistance from a master's friend: 1) The rhetoric in Paul's letter is seen as similar to that of an ancient letter of mediation, Pliny's letter to Sabinianus; 2) when Paul refers to Onesimus as previously having been 'useless' (v. 11), this expression is understood as Paul's acknowledgment that Onesimus actually had been useless; 3) when Paul refers to Onesimus as having been 'parted' from Philemon (v. 15), this is seen as euphemistic language describing the slave's 'escape'; and 4) when Paul writes, 'If he has wronged you at all, or owes you anything, charge that to my account'

---

13. Cf. Knox, *Philemon among the Letters of Paul*, pp. 5-7. Also see Winter, 'Paul's Letter to Philemon', pp. 5-7. Winter writes, 'Although περί can have the meaning "on behalf of" (or a weak meaning of ὑπέρ), παρακαλῶ [τινὶ] περί τινος is a formula in which the noun following the preposition is the object of the request. Although in the Pauline corpus Phlm. 10 is the only occurrence of this formula, the formula can be found in the papyri' (p. 6). On p. 14 n. 45, Winter lists three illuminating examples from the papyri.

14. Knox, *Philemon among the Letters of Paul*, p. 8.

15. Martin, *Colossians and Philemon*, p. 145.

(v. 18), this is explained as acknowledgment that Onesimus indeed had wronged Philemon. When looked at individually, each of these arguments has serious difficulties.[16]

Friends often wrote each other, recommending or mediating on behalf of third parties. Pliny's letter to Sabinianus is an excellent example of a letter of mediation for a freedman who had angered his master:

> Your freedman with whom you said you were angry has been with me; he threw himself at my feet and clung to me with as much submission as he could have done at yours. He earnestly requested me with many tears, and even with all the eloquence of silent sorrow, to intercede for him; in short, he convinced me by his whole behavior, that he sincerely repents of his fault. And I am persuaded he is thoroughly reformed, because he knows that he was wrong...(*Ep.* 9.21)[17]

The situation described in Pliny's letter to Sabinianus often has been projected onto Paul's letter to Philemon.[18] Thus, just as Pliny serves as an intercessor between Sabinianus and his freedman, so it is said that Paul is interceding between Philemon and the 'runaway' Onesimus. Supporters of this position see the primary difference between the two in the fact that Pliny's admonitions to Sabinianus appeal to Stoic virtues, whereas Paul's admonitions to Philemon appeal to Christian love and faith.[19] Commentators often note the 'subtlety' of Paul, who avoids even mentioning Onesimus's 'flight'.[20]

Pliny's letter can be used only with caution. There are not enough concrete parallels between these two letters to presume that Onesimus, like the freedman, had run away. In addition, there are a number of other significant differences between these epistles. Pliny writes, 'Your freedman with whom you said you were angry has been with me; he threw himself at my feet and clung to me with as much submission as he could have done at yours' (*Ep.* 9.21). Sabinianus was clearly angry with his freedman, and his freedman was clearly repentant; he convinced

16. The following discussion builds on the arguments found in Winter, 'Paul's Letter to Philemon', pp. 4-5.

17. Cf. *Ep.* 9.24.

18. Lohse, *Colossians and Philemon*, pp. 196-97.

19. Lohse, *Colossians and Philemon*, p. 197.

20. F.F. Church, 'Rhetorical Structure and Design in Paul's Letter to Philemon', *HTR* 71 (1978), p. 32, implies that Paul, unlike Pliny, would not be so crass and explicit as to call Onesimus's owner to renewed love: 'The Christian case for love and real equality between persons, be they slave or free, would hardly be served by such an appeal, no matter how artful its advocate.'

Pliny 'by his whole behaviour, that he sincerely repents of his fault'. What is interesting, however, is that Philemon and Onesimus express neither of these emotions. If Philemon was angry, Paul does not acknowledge it in this letter. If Onesimus was repentant, Paul does not acknowledge it. Furthermore, Paul does not ask for pity or forgiveness on behalf of Onesimus.

Paul is appealing on behalf of Onesimus. But is he appealing on behalf of him as a runaway? If Onesimus were a runaway, Paul indeed might have sought to couch the delicate subject of his return in euphemistic language. Thus, he might have avoided discussing Onesimus's having run away. He might have stayed clear even of discussing the anger which Philemon might have felt. But it would have been odd to have avoided expressing, in any form, Onesimus's repentance.

In Paul's letter to Philemon, there is no appeal to pity or forgiveness; that is not an issue. There is absolutely no discussion of Onesimus's repenting in any way. Pliny's letter to Sabinianus, by itself, offers no compelling reason for us to assume that Onesimus was a runaway.

In v. 11, Paul writes to Philemon, that 'Formerly he (Onesimus) was useless to you, but now he is indeed useful to you and to me.' Paul's use of the Greek word ἄχρηστος (useless) raises some important questions: Why would Paul have called Onesimus 'useless'? What did he mean when he said this?

Initially, it is important to recognize that the name 'Onesimus' literally means 'useful'. In antiquity, naming a person after a favorable trait or an ideal was an accepted practice. Similarly, even in the twentieth century, names like 'Hope', 'Charity', 'Grace', and even 'Chastity' are not unusual. Thus, to the Greek ear, 'Onesimus' was not simply a collection of letters which constituted a name; it was an ideal.[21]

The reference in v. 11 to 'Onesimus' ('Ονήσιμος) as having been 'useless' (ἄχρηστος), would have sounded ironic to the original reader of this epistle. The rhetorical effect would be similar to our saying something like, 'Grace, who formerly was clumsy...', or 'Charity, who formerly was a penny-pincher...' The Greek word for 'useless' (ἄχρηστος) should not be understood exclusively in a literal sense; here Paul uses it rhetorically.

The wordplay is even more notable when we look at the Greek word

---

21. 'Onesimus' was the most common slave name in antiquity. Whether the name was given at birth or later in life, it points to an ideal of which the slave is called to be worthy.

ἄχρηστος in light of Philemon 10. Here Paul writes, 'I appeal to you for my child, Onesimus, whose father I have become in my imprisonment.' The Greek in v. 10 literally says that Paul bore Onesimus (ὃν ἐγέννησα); Paul gave birth to him. In other words, Onesimus became a Christian while with Paul.[22] Paul's pun, then, is easier to understand. Before Onesimus met Paul he was not a Christian. He was α-Χρίστος (without Christ).

Because 'eta' (η) and 'iota' (ι) were often pronounced the same (and often interchanged in inscriptions), Paul here exploits the homonymous side of α-Χρίστος and ἄχρηστος.[23] Thus Paul is saying: Before Onesimus was a Christian, he was named Onesimus (or 'useful'). At that time, however, he was not truly useful (εὔχρηστος), because he was ἄχρηστος (that is α-Χρίστος). Now that he is in Christ, however, he is truly 'useful'.[24]

Paul exploits the Greek language in vv. 10-11 to make a point. The irony and the word-plays actually highlight something which needs to be seen as amazing in itself: the conversion of Onesimus.

In v. 15 Paul writes to Philemon, 'Perhaps this is why he (Onesimus) was parted from you for a while, that you might have him back forever, no longer as a slave but more than a slave, as a beloved brother...' Most commentators, working under the assumption that Onesimus was a runaway, simply read that assumption into this verse. Thus, Alois Stöger writes, 'When Onesimus ran away, it was by God's providential design.'[25] Similarly, Eduard Lohse says

---

22. Cf. Gal. 4.19.

23. From the earliest church, Christian writers exploited the similarities between the Greek words 'Χρίστος' and 'χρήστος'. Cf. 1 Pet. 2.3; *1 Clem.* 14.3; Justin Martyr, *1 Apol.* 4.1.1 and 46.4; and Theophilus, *Autol.* 1.1. Clement of Alexandria, *Str.* 2.5, writes, 'Those who believe in Christ both are and are called 'χρήστοι.' In Acts 11.26; 26.28; and 1 Pet. 4.16—in every instance of the word 'Christian' in the New Testament—the uncorrected Codex Sinaiticus has the variant ΧΡΗΣΤΙΑΝΟΙ where ΧΡΙΣΤΙΑΝΟΙ stands in the majority of the manuscript traditions. Christians' puns may have started with the natural confusion encountered with these homophones.

24. Winter, 'Paul's Letter to Philemon', p. 4, notes that 'Paul's use of ἄχρηστον is justified simply by the word play on Onesimus' name; and just as in 1 Cor 15.33 Paul uses a literary reference with a play on χρηστά/Χριστός that cannot be related in a one-to-one fashion to the matter of that particular passage, ἄχρηστον need not function literally outside the word play'.

25. A. Stöger, *The Epistle to Philemon* (trans. Michael Dunne; New York: Herder and Herder, 1971), p. 85.

> In reviewing Onesimus' flight, Paul chooses his words very carefully...
> The passive verb 'he was separated from' (ἐχωρίσθη) plainly intimates
> that God's hidden purpose may have been behind this incident which has
> caused Philemon so much annoyance.[26]

Since the letter offers no indication that Philemon was bothered, let
alone annoyed, it is interesting to note the assumption that ἐχωρίσθη is
a tactful euphemism.

In itself, the verb indicates only that Onesimus was 'separated' from
the household in which he served. That does not necessarily mean that
he ran away. It just means that for some reason he was not there. Slaves
were often separated from their owners, conducting business for them
elsewhere, delivering letters, administering projects, or simply working
where labor was needed.[27] Regardless, any explanation of this verse, any
explanation of this letter, does need to explain why Onesimus was
separated from the household he served.

But was Onesimus a thief? Commentators often answer this in the
affirmative, turning to Philemon 18. Here Paul writes, 'If he (Onesimus)
has wronged you at all, or owes you anything, charge that to my
account.' G.B. Caird says, 'The sentence is hypothetical only in form.
Paul knows very well that Onesimus has *wronged* his master and owes
him a considerable sum of money.'[28] Eduard Lohse writes that Paul

> does not necessarily imply that the slave, in running away, had pilfered
> something from his master. For he had already caused injury to Philemon's
> property solely by running away, even if he did not steal anything.[29]

Just as there is no need to assume that Onesimus ran away, so there is
no need to assume that Onesimus had stolen anything. Paul simply
writes, '*if* Onesimus has wronged you at all, or owes you anything,

---

26. Lohse, *Colossians and Philemon*, pp. 202-203.

27. Cf. D.B. Martin, *Slavery as Salvation: The Metaphor of Slavery in Pauline
Christianity* (New Haven: Yale University Press, 1990), p. 2, 11-22; S.S. Bartchy,
*MALLON CRHSAI: First-Century Slavery and the Interpretation of 1 Corinthians
7:21* (SBLDS, 11; Missoula: SBL, 1973), pp. 38-39; G.E.M. de Ste. Croix, *The
Class Struggle in the Ancient Greek World from the Archaic Age to the Arab
Conquests* (Ithaca, NY: Cornell University Press, 1981), esp. pp. 179, 186 and 200-
202.

28. G.B. Caird, *Paul's Letters from Prison* (New York: Oxford University Press,
1976), pp. 222-23. Emphasis his.

29. E. Lohse, *Colossians and Philemon*, p. 204.

charge that to my account'.[30] Two questions need to be asked: 1) Are there reasons, other than theft, which could account for Onesimus's being in debt to Philemon? and 2) Is there any reason to assume that Onesimus actually was in debt to Philemon?

Slavery in first-century Greco–Roman society was much different from slavery in the nineteenth century in the United States.[31] Slaves who were forced to come to the United States had no choice of whether or not they wanted to be slaves. Slaves in the Greco–Roman world often did. Slavery in Roman times was often the result of personal bankruptcy or need; people sold themselves or their children into slavery for a set amount of time in order to pay off their personal debts or to receive money.[32] In *1 Clem.* 55.2, for instance, we are told that even Christians sold themselves into slavery, so as to use that money to buy food for others. Clement writes: 'We know that many among ourselves have given themselves to bondage that they might ransom others. Many have delivered themselves to slavery and provided food for others with the price they received for themselves.' It was not unusual if one sold one's self or one's children into slavery. The buyers who put up the cash to retire those debts were then entitled to that slave's services for a fixed time period. Onesimus, a pagan, could have become a slave under those circumstances.[33]

Even if Onesimus had not sold himself into slavery, even if others had not sold him into slavery, his 'being accepted as a brother'—which Paul expects here—very well may have resulted in debts. Philemon would have been seen as justified in expecting return on his investment.[34] If Paul now expects Philemon to 'receive' Onesimus as he would receive Paul (v. 17), if Philemon now is to see Onesimus 'no longer as a slave but more than a slave...both in the flesh and in the Lord' (v. 17),

---

30. Emphasis mine.

31. For an extended discussion on a number of such differences, see R. Jewett, *Paul the Apostle to America: Cultural Trends and Pauline Scholarship* (Louisville, KY: Westminster Press/John Knox, 1994), esp. pp. 60-63.

32. Cf. Plutarch, *Mor.* 829E. See G.E.M. de Ste. Croix, *The Class Struggle in the Ancient Greek World from the Archaic Age to the Arab Conquests*, pp. 163-70. Cf. Mt. 18.23-27.

33. Since 'Onesimus' was a common name for a slave, the name may suggest that Onesimus was either born a slave or sold into slavery at an early age. If this was the case, his having sold *himself* into slavery, for debt repayment, is less plausible.

34. Cf. Martin, *Slavery as Salvation*, p. 8, and T. Wiedemann, *Greek and Roman Slavery* (London: Routledge & Kegan Paul, 1981), pp. 54-56, 118-19.

dramatic changes will occur. Paul realizes that Philemon, as Onesimus' owner, had an investment in the slave. Such an investment would be lost if Onesimus were no longer to be seen as a slave.

Are there reasons, other than theft, which could account for Onesimus' being in debt to Philemon? Definitely. However, an even more fundamental question needs to be posed. Is there any reason to assume that Onesimus actually was in debt to Philemon?

In vv. 18-19, Paul emphasizes to Philemon that if Onesimus had wronged him at all or owed him anything (εἰ δέ τι ἠδόκησέν σε ἤ ὀφείλει), this was to be charged to Paul's account. Paul continues, 'I will repay it—to say nothing of your owing me even your own self'. Verse 18 is a simple conditional sentence: 'εἰ' means 'if', not 'because'. A.T. Robinson and W. Hersey Davis cite a classic example of a simple conditional sentence in looking at Mt. 12.27: 'In Mt. 12.27 εἰ ἐγὼ ἐν Βεελζεβοὺλ ἐκβάλλω τὰ δαιμόνια *if I by Beelzeboul cast out the demons*, Jesus *assumes* as true the charge of the Pharisees against him, but merely for the sake of argument.'[35]

Paul, similarly, does not emphasize either the reality or the probability of this condition in v. 18. As Clarice J. Martin writes, 'it is plausible that v. 18 may exhibit a fully rhetorical intent, that is, Paul's commercial allusions are merely for the sake of argument'.[36] By employing the rhetorical device of anticipation and by anticipating possible objections and concerns of Philemon, Paul uses commercial language to persuade Philemon of the depth of his convictions:

> Paul's willingness to place his economic resources fully at Philemon's disposal on behalf of Onesimus represents a powerful and moving 'appeal to pity' and an example of the true nature of sacrificial Christian love on behalf of others.[37]

---

35. *A New Short Grammar of the Greek Testament* (Grand Rapids: Baker, 10th edn, 1979), pp. 350-51 (emphasis theirs), quoted in C.J. Martin, 'The Rhetorical Function of Commercial Language in Paul's Letter to Philemon (Verse 18)', in D.F. Watson (ed.), *Persuasive Artistry: Studies in New Testament Rhetoric in Honor of George A. Kennedy* (JSNTSup, 50; Sheffield: JSOT Press), p. 334.

36. Martin, 'The Rhetorical Function of Commercial Language', p. 334. 'One cannot deduce from the commercial terminology in the conditional protasis alone that a crime has occurred' (p. 332). Cf. A.D. Callahan, 'Paul's Epistle to Philemon: Toward an Alternative *Argumentum*', *HTR* 86 (1993), pp. 374-75.

37. Martin, 'The Rhetorical Function of Commercial Language', p. 335.

Had Onesimus wronged Philemon? Was he in debt to him? We simply do not know. Even if we could prove that Onesimus was in debt to Philemon, that should not surprise us. Slaves were often in debt to their masters (that is why many of them were slaves). Furthermore, if a slave was to be freed, or sold to a third-party, the slave's owner would expect recompense: he would be reluctant to give away what he considered to be an investment.

Was Onesimus a runaway? S. Scott Bartchy notes that Onesimus does not engage in the sort of behavior in which runaway fugitives engaged. Onesimus does not seek asylum, go underground in a large city, or join an outlaw band. Rather, he is to be found with Paul; a person whom his owner respects.[38] Bartchy goes on to argue that Onesimus was not a runaway in the traditional sense. In some aspects of Roman law, an estranged slave could appeal to an owner's friend (*amicus domini*), asking that person to help resolve difficulties between the slave and owner. In fleeing to such an intercessor, a slave was not seen as a fugitive (*fugitivus*) liable to punishment.

Thus, according to this interpretation, Onesimus was not a fugitive but, rather, a slave who had wronged his master and then, seeking to have better relationships with Philemon, deliberately sought out Paul to intercede on his behalf. Bartchy's argument builds on the hypothesis developed by Peter Lampe[39] and elaborated by B.M. Rapske.[40] Rapske states the position succinctly: 'Onesimus, in a bid to be happily restored to his estranged master, *runs to Paul* who is his master's *friend*.'[41]

Overall, this hypothesis is possible, but it is not the most plausible explanation. There are four main difficulties with this hypothesis. First, it seems clear from the beginning of the letter (especially the thanksgiving)[42] that Philemon knew that Onesimus was with Paul in prison. However, if Onesimus had run away from his master (legally or illegally), there is no reason to assume that Philemon knew where he was going.

38. S.S Bartchy, 'Philemon, Paul's Letter to', in D.N. Freedman (ed.), *The Anchor Bible Dictionary*, V (New York: Doubleday, 1992), pp. 307.

39. Cf. P. Lampe, 'Keine "Sklavenflucht" des Onesimus', *ZNW* 76 (1985), pp. 135-37.

40. B.M. Rapske, 'The Prisoner Paul in the Eyes of Onesimus', *NTS* 37 (1991), pp. 187-203. Rapske sketches out six hypotheses describing how Paul and Onesimus came to be together in prison.

41. Rapske, 'The Prisoner Paul', p. 187 (Rapske's emphasis).

42. See the discussion below from S. Winter, 'Paul's Letter to Philemon', p. 3.

Secondly, it is difficult to imagine Onesimus running away from his master to, in effect, escape *into* prison, where he would confer with an *imprisoned amicus domini*. Such a hypothesis seems to ignore the social location from which Paul is writing: Paul is in prison. How would Onesimus have found Paul?[43] As C.H. Cosgrove writes, 'It strains credulity to think this is sheer coincidence.'[44] Did his status as a 'runaway' eventually lead to his arrest and coincidental confinement with Paul?[45] Did Onesimus escape from his owner with the intention of hunting down Paul, who happened to be in prison?[46] Was Onesimus familiar with the place of Paul's incarceration, having visited the apostle with his owner? Paul's imprisonment adds an odd dimension to this discussion. If Onesimus were a slave who ran to Paul, could the imprisoned apostle simply have sent him back to his owner? Even if Paul was only under a loose form of house arrest, could a slave have simply approached him?

Thirdly, if Onesimus was estranged from Philemon and in need of reconciliation, is Philemon supposed to believe that Onesimus's conversion to Christianity is a genuine one? Regardless of Onesimus's legal status—regardless if Onesimus were a *fugitivus*—would Philemon have had confidence that Paul clearly understood Onesimus's character and motives? If Onesimus were estranged, his conversion to the Christian faith could well appear hollow and feigned, artificial, opportunistic; anything to get him in good with his angry master.

43. G.B. Caird, *Paul's Letters from Prison*, p. 214, is one of many interpreters who avoids the issue of how Onesimus might have come to encounter Paul: 'Rome might seem a long way from Colossae, yet its cosmopolitan populace offered better cover for the fugitive than anywhere else in the world. Half the population of the capital were slaves...We need not attempt to conjecture by what chance Onesimus in Rome fell in with Paul.'
    Also see E. Lohmeyer, *Die Briefe an die Philipper, an die Kolosser und an Philemon* (Göttingen: Vandenhoeck & Ruprecht, 1930), pp. 171-72; and J. Ernst, *Die Briefe an die Philipper, an Philemon, an die Kolosser, an die Epheser* (Regensburg: Verlag Friedrich Pustet, 1974), p. 123.
44. C.H. Cosgrove, 'Philemon', in W.E. Mills and R.F. Wilson (eds.), *Mercer Commentary on the Bible* (Macon, GA: Mercer University Press, 1995), p. 1263.
45. Cf. C.J. Roetzel, *The Letters of Paul: Conversations in Context* (Atlanta: John Knox, 2nd edn, 1982), pp. 79-80.
46. E. Lohse, *Colossians and Philemon*, p. 187, writes of Onesimus that 'Perhaps he had heard the Apostle's name mentioned in the house of his Christian master and had now hastened to him for help in his perplexity.' See also J. Gnilka, *Der Philemonbrief* (Freiburg: Herder, 1982), pp. 1-3; and P. Stuhlmacher, *Der Brief an Philemon* (EKKNT; Köln: Neukirchener Verlag, 2nd edn, 1981), p. 23.

Fourthly, it needs to be noted that Paul does not make excuses for Onesimus's behavior, Onesimus is not presented as being the least bit remorseful or sorry, and Philemon is not asked to exercise mercy. If Paul is interceding on Onesimus's behalf, his subtlety is overwhelming. There are very good reasons to assume that Paul was not interceding for a thieving runaway. But still, one question remains: why was Onesimus separated from his owner? A look into prisons is illuminating.

4. *Messenger and Minister to Paul's Needs*

Why was Onesimus separated from his owner? That which was obvious to Paul, Onesimus and Philemon is not stated explicitly in this epistle. The letter's thanksgiving (vv. 4-7), however, is an illuminating place to begin to answer this question.

Paul Schubert, in studying the role of 'thanksgiving' sections in the Pauline epistles, has shown that these sections function to establish the epistles' major themes. They anticipate the discussions which arise in the body of the letters.[47] If Onesimus had done something wrong, if that had been the occasion for the letter, Paul likely would have dealt with it in the epistle's thanksgiving, going to the point immediately, as he does in his other letters.

However, as Sara Winter emphasizes, Paul says nothing directly about Onesimus in the thanksgiving:

> From the thanksgiving's apparent failure to mention Onesimus' arrival with Paul, given that the main body of the letter is a request concerning Onesimus, one must either posit a previous letter (or communication) or conclude that the recipient knew that Onesimus was with Paul.[48]

In the thanksgiving, Paul does not discuss Onesimus directly. If Onesimus were a runaway, that likely would have been mentioned here. Although we will need to return to the epistle's thanksgiving, initially it is important to see that Philemon apparently knew, or could have assumed, that Onesimus was with Paul.

Why was Onesimus separated from his owner? One way of answering this question would be to turn to Paul's letter to the Philippians. This epistle offers a concrete example of the church's ministry to the imprisoned Paul. Paul thanks the Philippians for their κοινωνία, their

---

47. P. Schubert, *The Form and Function of the Pauline Thanksgiving* (Berlin: Töpelmann, 1939), esp. pp.166-81.

48. Winter, 'Paul's Letter to Philemon', p. 3.

partnership in the gospel (1.5). In v. 7, Paul uses a variant of the same word, to say that all of the Philippians are co-partners (συγκοινωνοί) with him in his imprisonment. What this means is made more clear in 2.25-30, where it is said that Epaphroditus had ministered to Paul's need. Finally, in 4.18, Paul acknowledges the gifts which were sent from the Philippians through Epaphroditus. Epaphroditus, Paul's 'brother, fellow worker, and fellow soldier', stands out as an example of a person, sent by a Christian community, to be 'messenger and minister' to Paul's need.[49]

If Epaphroditus was a messenger and minister to the needs of the imprisoned Paul, are we justified in believing that the slave Onesimus, similarly, might have been sent either as a messenger or as an attendant to the imprisoned Paul (or to other imprisoned Christians)? Or, conversely, is a comparison between Epaphroditus and Onesimus little more than an exercise in harmonization of the Pauline corpus?

Before answering these questions, it is helpful to look at how both messengers and 'attendants' to the imprisoned functioned. A distinction between the two is somewhat artificial: persons such as Epaphroditus often served as both. In any case, in the following discussion the term 'messengers' will be used to refer to persons who were primarily on the road, engaged in the process of delivering messages, letters, gifts or themselves. 'Attendants' or 'ministers' will refer to those—either pagan or Christian—who served and cared for the imprisoned.

In antiquity, there was nothing like a mail delivery service run by the state. Slaves, travelers, freedmen and friends generally were the ones responsible for delivery of letters, messages or gifts.[50] As can be imagined, communication in antiquity could involve numerous complexities: difficulties often centered on the availability of messengers.

Cicero explains to Atticus that he had not promptly replied to his letter, for want of a reliable messenger: 'There are very few who can carry a letter of weight without lightening it by a perusal.'[51] In other

---

49. Cf. Phil. 2.25.

50. E.J. Epp, 'New Testament Papyrus Manuscripts and Letter Carrying in Greco-Roman Times', in B.A. Pearson (ed.), *The Future of Early Christianity: Essays in Honor of Helmut Koester* (Minneapolis: Fortress Press, 1991), pp. 43-55. Cf. M.M. Mitchell, 'New Testament Envoys in the Context of Greco–Roman Diplomatic and Epistolary Conventions', *JBL* 111 (1992), pp. 641-62.

51. *Att*.1.13. Cf. Pliny, *Ep*. 8.3, 'I will send it to you as soon as I can meet with a trustworthy post-carrier'.

situations, messengers—in general—were not available.[52] Sometimes, persons did not have access to messengers and, if it was more important for them to share news with others, they might request the use of other persons' letter carriers.[53] To get messages or news to Atticus, Cicero asks him to send letter carriers (whom Cicero himself might use).[54] Even if one generally had access to messengers, if those messengers had been sent out and not promptly returned (or if they did not return promptly on their own), a backlog of correspondence might result.[55]

When servants, envoys, or letter carriers were sent to a person (regardless of whether that person was imprisoned), this recipient apparently had some discretion in determining how long the messenger was to stay. Cicero, thus, could write to Atticus, 'I have been rather slow in sending back your letter-carrier, because there was no opportunity of sending him'.[56] To ensure that the messengers were returned promptly, some writers were explicit about how long messengers were to remain with the recipients of the correspondence. When Cicero writes to Dolabella, he concludes, 'You too, on your part, honourable and courteous as you are, will see that the letter-carrier I have sent to you may be enabled to return to me, and that he brings me back a letter from you.'[57] Similarly, when the Roman Christians write to the Corinthians (*1 Clem.* 65.1), Clement concludes the letter with the following instructions:

> Send back quickly (ἐν τάχει ἀναπέμψατε) to us our messengers Claudius Ephebus and Valerius Vito and Fortunatus, in peace with gladness, in order that they may report the sooner the peace and concord which we pray for and desire, that we also may the more speedily rejoice in your good order.

The verb which Clement uses in referring to the return of the messengers is the same verb which Paul employs in Philemon 12, when

52. Pliny, *Ep.* 3.17.

53. To use a contemporary example, reporters at a news conference might need messengers to relay information to their newspaper, while they remain at the conference. There would, however, be little need for the newspaper to use these messengers to send information back to the reporters.

54. *Att.* 5.18, 6.1.

55. Cicero writes, 'I have had a letter on my hands for many days on account of delay on the part of the letter-carriers' (*QFr.* 3.1.23). Cf. *Att.* 13.21, 16.14.

56. *Att.* 11.2. Cf. 11.3, where Cicero acknowledges, 'I have kept him longer than I should'.

57. *Fam.* 9.9.

he writes, 'I am sending (ἀνέπεμψα) him (Onesimus) back to you...'
Writers could use this verb to refer to the actions both of simply
returning something, or of sending a messenger, a letter, or any sort of
representative.[58] Thus, when Claudius wanted to 'inform the senate
of his sentiments', he 'sent (ἀναπέμπει) Agrippa off as his envoy
(πρεσβευτής)'.[59] When Cestius was having difficulties in Jerusalem, he
sent (ἀνέπεμψεν) Saul and his companions to inform Nero of the
problems.[60]

If Onesimus had been sent by Philemon—to bring the imprisoned
Paul either a message, or some sort of material or financial support—
Paul would have used a verb like ἀναπέμπω in referring to the return
of Onesimus. And, in v. 12, that is what Paul does. Onesimus might
have been sent to deliver something, perhaps a letter or gift, to Paul or
to other Christians in prison. Or he might have been sent to serve them.

Comforting and aiding the imprisoned was a common practice among
the ancients. Because prisoners often faced death through starvation,
malnutrition or weakness, they depended on friends, family and
attendants—outside the prison—to bring them food or sustenance.[61] The
philosopher Epicurus mentioned the importance of friends who would
help those who were in prison or in want,[62] and numerous examples
of such help have been preserved. When Agrippa was imprisoned,
his friend, Silas and two of his freedmen brought his favorite food and
did whatever they could for him, even fashioning a bed for him out of
some garments.[63] Cleomenes had his own slaves and attendants with
him.[64] And although Musonius discouraged Apollonius from visiting
him in prison, Apollonius declared his willingness to do so (referring
to the prison as Musonius's 'lodgings'): 'I would fain come unto you,
to share (κοινωνῆσαι) your conversation and your lodgings (στέγη),

---

58. Cf. Josephus, *War* 1.3, 359, 666; 3.398; 6.379.; Polybius 5.28.4; Plutarch,
Galba 8.4; *Mor.* 361C; *Mor.* 556F; etc.
59. *War* 2.207. Both *Ant.* 6.293 and *War* 2.450 also use this verb to refer to the
return of envoys or ambassadors.
60. *War* 2.558.
61. See Chapter 1, esp. 'Visitors and Bribery'. Also of interest is B.M. Rapske,
'The Importance of Helpers to the Imprisoned Paul in the Book of Acts', *TynBul*
42.1 (1991), pp. 3-30.
62. Seneca, *Ep.* 9.8.
63. Josephus, *Ant.* 18.204.
64. Polybius, 5.39.1-2.

in the hope of being of some use to you.'[65]

In general, attendants or ministers to the imprisoned—whether they be friends, relatives, or slaves—sought to make the experience of imprisonment as tolerable and comfortable as was possible. Among the horrors of Gallus's imprisonment, Dio Cassius writes, was that he 'had no companion or servant with him'.[66] In crowded, loud, disease-infested prisons, any comfort which others could provide would be appreciated. Prison was not a relaxing experience: sleep would have been difficult. Philopoemen is described as not being able to sleep, 'overwhelmed with trouble and grief'.[67] Once Demetrius entered prison, to be at his friend Antiphilus's side, he 'took care that Antiphilus should sleep as well as possible and should suffer less distress'.[68] Similarly, Christians—as described in Lucian's *Peregr.* 12—bribed the guards where Peregrinus was imprisoned, so they might sleep inside the prison with him.[69]

Christians also brought food, money and moral support to the imprisoned Peregrinus. At least from Lucian's account, the church in Asia had gained notoriety in the second century for its enthusiasm in this practice. The satirist Lucian incredulously describes the zeal of those Christians who had visited Peregrinus:

> From the very break of day aged widows and orphan children could be seen waiting near the prison, while their officials even slept inside with him after bribing the guards. Then elaborate meals were brought in, and sacred books of theirs were read aloud...Indeed, people came even from the cities in Asia,[70] sent by Christians at their common expense to help, defend and encourage the man. They show incredible speed whenever any such public action is taken; for in no time they lavish their all (12–13)

Lucian had heard of Christian communities in Asia, who sent support to the imprisoned. This tradition had deep roots: Paul himself appears to have received support from Colossae. An entourage serving the imprisoned apostle is discussed in Col. 4.7-14, with one person—

65. Philostratus, *VA* 4.46.

66. Dio, 58.5.

67. Plutarch, *Phil.* 20.2. Cf. Philostratus, *VA* 7.30.

68. Lucian, *Tox.* 32.

69. Cf. *The Martyrdom of Perpetua and Felicitas* 3.7, where the deacons Tertius and Pomponius 'bribed the soldiers to allow us to go to a better part of the prison to refresh ourselves for a few hours'.

70. It is difficult to appreciate what Lucian is emphasizing here, since the text does not clearly state where Peregrinus was imprisoned. Lucian seems to be implying that the incarceration was in the eastern part of the Empire; perhaps Palestine (cf. 11).

Epaphras—having come from Colossae itself (4.12).

Just as churches in Asia are remembered as having sent support to Peregrinus and Paul, just as the Philippians sent Epaphroditus to minister to the imprisoned apostle, so the possibility needs to be considered that Philemon sent Onesimus as a messenger or minister to Paul's need: Onesimus was with Paul in prison because he had been sent there. This is illuminated, at least in part, by the the actions of other churches in ancient Asia; churches in Ephesus and in Smyrna. Before looking at how these churches served prisoners, it is important to return for a moment to Paul's letter to Philemon.

As mentioned earlier, the focus in this letter's thanksgiving (vv. 4-7) is on Paul's thankfulness for the love and faith of Onesimus's owner.[71] Paul has 'derived much joy and comfort', because, through Philemon, 'the hearts of the saints have been refreshed (τὰ σπλάγχνα τῶν ἁγίων ἀναπέπαυται)'.

After completing the epistle, however, it becomes evident that these words play a role more significant than they initially might be seen to play. Paul not only refers to Onesimus as τὰ ἐμὰ σπλάγχνα in v. 12, but also exhorts Philemon in v. 20, writing, ἀνάπαυσόν μου τὰ σπλάγχνα ἐν χριστῷ. What did Paul mean by τὰ σπλάγχνα τῶν ἁγίων ἀναπέπαυται (v. 7)? What did it mean to 'refresh the hearts of the saints'?

The Pauline epistles are not at all explicit about what the apostle meant, when he used the verb ἀναπαύω. In 1 Cor. 16.18, Paul writes that Stephanas, Fortunatus, and Achaicus 'refreshed' his spirit (ἀνέπαυσαν γὰρ τὸ ἐμὸν πνεῦμα), but he does not say how they did so. Similarly, when Paul writes to the Romans, he hopes to be 'refreshed' in their company (συναναπαύσωμαι ὑμῖν, Rom. 15.32). Apparently, Paul desires to stay with them and hopes that they will support him in his journey, but again Paul is not explicit.

Though this verb, in pagan literature, can refer either to rest and relaxation[72] or to sleep,[73] it is interesting to note that Epictetus uses a

71. Winter, 'Paul's Letter to Philemon', p. 3.

72. Cf. Plutarch, *Lyc.* 28.2; *Aem.* 15.9; *Cat. Mai.* 24.11; *Brut.* 40.1; *Oth.* 17.2; *Mor.* 60D; Lucian, *Tim.* 58; *Merc. Cond.* 13; *D. Mar.* 3.1.

73. Cf. Lucian, *Tox.* 31; Epictetus, *Diss.*, 3.13.2; Plutarch, *Dion* 48.2; *Mor.* 728C. The term also has a derived meaning: 'to sleep' can mean 'to sleep with' (or 'to have sex'). Cf. Plutarch, *Pomp.* 36.3; *Dion* 3.4; *Mor.* 259F.; 273A.

194 Chained in Christ

variant of it to refer to an action taken on behalf of a person unable to support himself:

> And shall it be necessary for our philosopher, forsooth, when he goes abroad, to depend upon others for his assurance and his refreshment (ἐπαναπαυόμενον), instead of taking care of himself, and to be more vile and craven than the irrational animals, every one of which is sufficient to himself, and lacks neither its own proper food nor that way of life which is appropriate to it and in harmony with nature? (*Diss.* 1.9.9)

If persons are not self-sufficient, others are called on to refresh them. Similarly, Epictetus presents imaginary interlocutors—dualists—who are tired of having to take care of their 'dependent' bodies: 'We can no longer endure to be imprisoned (δεδεμένοι) with this paltry body, giving it food and drink, and resting (ἀναπαύοντες) and cleansing it.'[74]

If someone is not self-sufficient, others are called on to refresh that person. This meaning of the verb is illuminated well by Ignatius of Antioch. Ignatius, a bishop in the early second century, was taken under guard, from Antioch to Rome, in order to be executed. En route, this prisoner was supported by a number of churches, who sent representatives to support and serve him. Thus, in writing to the Trallians, Ignatius greets them 'from Smyrna together with the Churches of God that are present with me, men who in all things have given me rest in the flesh and in the spirit (οἳ κατὰ πάντα με ἀνέπαυσαν σαρκί τε καὶ πνεύωματι).'[75] Similarly, in his letter to the Ephesians, Ignatius names a number of persons from their church who had stayed with him and supported him while he had been in chains:

> Now concerning my fellow servant, Burrhus, your deacon by the will of God, who is blessed in all things, I beg that he may stay longer, for your honour and for that of the bishop. And Crocus also, who is worthy of God and of you, whom I received as an example of your love, has relieved me in every way (κατὰ πάντα με ἀνέπαυσεν, 2.1).

In the letter to the Smyrnaeans, written from Troas, Burrhus is still with Ignatius, serving as his scribe (or letter-carrier):

---

74. *Diss.* 1.9.12. 'Rest', thus, is sometimes presented as a type of maintenance. In *Diss.* 1.6.14, Epictetus says that for animals, 'it is sufficient to eat and drink and rest (ἀναπαύεσθαι) and procreate'.
75. *Trall.* 12.1. Cf. *Magn.* 15.1, where Ignatius writes the same.

I am writing to you by Burrhus, whom you together with the Ephesians your brothers sent with me, and he has in every way refreshed me (με ἀνέπαυσεν). Would that all imitated him, for he is a pattern of the ministry of God (12.1).[76]

In writing to the Trallians and to the Magnesians, Ignatius lets them know that persons had been sent to 'refresh him'. In writing to the Ephesians and to the Smyrnaeans, he uses the same term to let them know that Burrhus had 'refreshed' him. Ignatius writes that he had been given rest both in the flesh and in the spirit. Since prisoners were not treated well by jailers or the state, it would not be surprising if persons visited Ignatius with food, clothing, letters of support or words of encouragement and comfort.

The terminology in Ignatius's epistles helps illuminate Philemon 7. Paul is in prison. When Paul refers to Philemon's having refreshed the hearts of the saints, we need to consider that Philemon may have accomplished this through a messenger, an envoy or a servant; someone who aided the imprisoned—Paul included—on behalf of Philemon or his church. If persons are not self-sufficient, others are called on to refresh them.

But is this a likely scenario? If Philemon had sent Onesimus either as a messenger or as an attendant to the imprisoned Paul, is it plausible that Paul would have felt a need to write an appeal to retain the services of Onesimus? The appeal of another prisoner, for the services of another 'slave', might bring us closer to answering this question in the affirmative.

In his epistle to the Ephesians, Ignatius exploits the fact that an important reader of his epistle to them would have been the community's bishop, a man by the name of Onesimus. Regardless whether this was the same man who was with Paul in prison, Ignatius shapes the appeals of this letter as if this community, or this bishop, would have been familiar with echoes of Paul's letter to Philemon.

John Knox writes, 'The striking character of this use of Philemon by Ignatius is impossible to exaggerate.'[77] Although Knox's enthusiasm needs to be tempered,[78] Ignatius's discussion in *Eph.* 2.1-2, to take one

---

76. *Phld.* 11.2 also mentions that Burrhus had been sent with Ignatius 'by the Ephesians and Smyrnaeans as a mark of honour'.

77. Knox, *Philemon among the Letters of Paul*, p. 53.

78. W.R. Schoedel, *Ignatius of Antioch*, pp. 9-10, following A.E. Barnett, *Paul Becomes a Literary Influence* (Chicago: University of Chicago Press, 1941), is much more cautious about seeing Philemon as a conscious influence on Ignatius. Cf. J. Moffatt, *An Introduction to the Literature of the New Testament*, p. 164.

example, has a number of striking similarities to the situation found in Paul's letter to Philemon:[79]

> Now concerning my fellow servant (σύνδουλος), Burrhus, your deacon (διάκονος) by the will of God, who is blessed in all things, I beg that he may stay longer, for your honour and for that of the bishop. And Crocus also, who is worthy of God and of you, whom I received as an example of your love (ἀγάπη), has relieved me (με ἀνέπαυσεν) in every way—may the Father of Jesus Christ refresh him in like manner—together with Onesimus and Burrhus and Euplus and Fronto, in whose persons I have seen you all in love. May I ever have joy of you (ὀναίμην ὑμῶν), if I be but worthy.

The echoes from Paul's letter to Philemon are clear. Just as Onesimus is a slave (δοῦλος, Phlm. 16), Burrhus is referred to as a fellow slave (σύνδουλος). Just as Paul hoped that Onesimus might remain in prison and serve (διακονέω) him (v. 13), so Ignatius hoped that Burrhus (as a διάκονος) might stay longer with him. Just as Onesimus would have been seen as ministering to Paul on behalf of Philemon, so Burrhus would have been seen as ministering to Ignatius on behalf of the Ephesians.[80] By referring to Burrhus as σύνδουλος and as διάκονος, Ignatius begins to create links between this epistle and Paul's letter to Philemon.

The links, however, become more striking. In Paul's letter to Philemon, the imprisoned apostle emphasizes that it is because of Philemon's love (ἀγάπη), that the hearts of the saints have been refreshed (τὰ σπλάγχνα τῶν ἁγίων ἀναπέπαυται διὰ σοῦ). Ignatius also writes that it is because of the love of the Ephesians that he was refreshed. Their love (ἀγάπη) was exemplified through Crocus and others whom they sent to be with him when he was a prisoner: Crocus refreshed (ἀνέπαυσεν) him in every way.

Ignatius's letter to the Ephesians uses language similar to that of Paul's letter to Philemon, in hearkening to a significant event from the past. By appealing to the apostle with whom the Ephesian community

J.W. Martens, 'Ignatius and Onesimus: John Knox Reconsidered', *SecCent* 9 (1992), pp. 73-86, is reluctant to recognize any allusions to Philemon in Ignatius. Although Martens unrealistically expects absolute verbal parallels from Ignatius (as if this prisoner would have either memorized or had immediate access to Paul's letter to Philemon), some of his reservations about Knox's method are insightful.

79. For a more general discussion of the relationship between these two epistles, see John Knox, *Philemon among the Letters of Paul*, pp. 50-56.

80. Cf. *Eph.* 2.1, *Trall.* 1.1, and *Magn.* 2.1, where individuals who were sent to Ignatius are seen as representing the communities from which they were sent.

traditionally had had a close relationship,[81] by appealing to Bishop Onesimus' past (or to the past of his namesake), Ignatius reminds these Christians of what Paul had desired and expected from Philemon.

Just as Paul hoped to be benefitted by Philemon (σου ὀναίμην, v. 20), so Ignatius hoped to be benefitted by the Ephesians (ὀναίμην ὑμῶν). The Greek word ὀναίμην is not necessarily a technical term. Ignatius uses the word a number of times.[82] Regardless if he is making a pun on the bishop's name ('Ονήσιμος), just as Paul did on the slave's (Phlm. 20), regardless if he is recalling Paul's letter to Philemon, and regardless of how Ignatius employs the term elsewhere, it is clear in this letter what Ignatius expects. Here, he writes, the Ephesians can 'benefit' him or 'be of use' to him by allowing Burrhus to stay longer with him.

We do not know why Ignatius wanted Burrhus to stay longer, nor do we know why he felt compelled to ask the Ephesians. Perhaps Burrhus was sent for only a short period of time. Perhaps he was just to deliver a message or gift and then return to the Ephesians. In any case, then—as now—churches had limited resources; Ignatius felt the need to ask if Burrhus could remain longer. He asks, however, apparently framing his request within language and images from Paul's letter to Philemon.

Regardless, even if Ignatius had never even read Paul's letter to Philemon, the similarites between these epistles, in situation, word choice and rhetoric, is remarkable. Each prisoner responds to a church's having refreshed them. Each prisoner asks for the services of a 'slave'. Each prisoner sees the 'slave' as a representative of a particular church community.

Why would Philemon have initially sent Onesimus, a non-Christian slave, to the imprisoned apostle? Because he was available? Because he had a particular skill? Because he was a non-Christian and would not be under suspicion?[83] Regardless, once Onesimus had completed his service, it would have been appropriate for Paul to return him to his owner. As Clement explicitly reminded the Corinthians, 'Send back quickly (ἐν

81. Cf. Ignatius, *Eph.* 13.2.

82. Ignatius also uses this expression in *Magn.* 2.1; 12.1; *Pol.* 1.1; 6.2 (cf. *Rom.* 5.2).

83. Guilt by association carried with it the harshest of penalties (e.g. Dio, 58.3.7, 58.11.5-6; Tacitus, *Ann.* 6.5.9; Plutarch, *Dion* 57.5. In Philostratus, *VA* 4.46, we are told that Apollonius did not visit the imprisoned Musonius, lest both of their lives be endangered. However, the two of them did send messages to each other through 'Menippus and Damis, who went to and fro the prison'.

τάχει ἀναπέμψατε) to us our messengers.'[84] Paul returns Onesimus, but makes clear why he does so: 'I preferred to do nothing without your consent in order that your goodness might not be by compulsion but of your own free will' (Phlm. 14). Paul knew that he was to return Onesimus, and he did so. However, at the same time, conditions had changed. Paul makes it clear that he now wants Onesimus to serve him, on Philemon's behalf, during the 'imprisonment for the gospel'.

5. *Conclusion*

Perhaps Onesimus was a runaway slave. Perhaps his conversion to the Christian faith was hollow, opportunistic and manipulative. We do know that Onesimus was separated from his owner; he even may have been in debt to him. However, these are far from being adequate reasons to believe that this slave either was a fugitive or that he ran away from his master in hopes of finding Paul as an intercessor.

Paul's letter gives us no reason to believe that Onesimus was sorry, regretful, or repentant of anything he may have done. This letter does not mention any anger or disappointment on the part of Philemon. This letter gives us no reason to believe that Philemon was ignorant of Onesimus's presence with Paul.

Onesimus's separation from his owner can best be understood within the context of Paul's incarceration. In prison, Paul—like other prisoners in antiquity—would havedepended upon the support of outsiders. Through food, clothes, letters, and even moral support, outsiders 'refreshed' the imprisoned. We know that churches in Philippi and Colossae sent persons to minister to Paul's need; churches in Asia sent support to Ignatius and Peregrinus. Any hypothesis which explains how Onesimus and Paul came to be together needs to take Paul's imprisonment into account. It seems most reasonable that Philemon sent Onesimus either to deliver support or to serve the imprisoned apostle.

Paul appreciated such support. Just as he rejoices in the Philippians' concern for him during his incarceration (Phil. 4.10-20), so he 'derives much joy and comfort' from Philemon's love, 'because the hearts of the saints have been refreshed through you' (Phlm. 7). Paul praises not only the sources of the support, but also the bearers. Serving the imprisoned was a task filled with stress. Epaphroditus and Onesimus understandably returned home as changed persons: Epaphroditus nearly died, risking his

84. *1 Clem.* 65.1.

life to complete the Philippians' service to Paul (Phil. 2.26-27, 30); Onesimus returned 'more useful', as a Christian (Phlm. 11). Thus, Paul hopes both that the Philippians receive Epaphroditus 'in the Lord with all joy, and hold such persons as honorable' (Phil. 2.29), and that Philemon receive Onesimus 'as you would receive me' (Phlm. 17).

Like the aged (cf. Phlm. 9), the incarcerated were not self-sufficent; they depended on those outside the prison for 'refreshment'. If the pagan slave Onesimus was sent by his owner to 'refresh' the imprisoned, if he was no runaway looking for quick redemption and forgiveness, generations of Christian interpreters have cheated Onesimus out of the integrity of his faith. Onesimus deserves better.

Epilogue

'SEVEN TIMES HE WAS IN BONDS':
MEMORIES OF THE IMPRISONED APOSTLE

Through jealousy and strife Paul showed the way to the prize of endurance; seven times he was in bonds, he was exiled, he was stoned, he was a herald both in the East and in the West, he gained the noble fame of his faith.

—*1 Clem.* 5.5-6

1. *Introduction*

For Paul, a person who is reported to have previously imprisoned Christians,[1] his own incarceration ironically came to constitute one of the distinctive ways in which his mission was understood and remembered. Paul was in chains not just once or twice: the author of *1 Clement* writes that this apostle was 'in bonds seven times' (5.6); and Paul himself claims that he had experienced 'far more imprisonments' than his opponents (2 Cor. 11.23). In Luke's second volume, Paul is remembered as having been imprisoned in Philippi (16.19-40), Caesarea (23.23–24.27) and Rome (28.16-31). And in *The Acts of Paul*, he is seen incarcerated in Iconium (3.17-20), Ephesus (6), Philippi (8), and Rome (11). It is not surprising that Paul, throughout the Christian world, would have been remembered as a prisoner.

But what did it mean that Paul had been 'chained in Christ'? Depending on what they sought to accomplish, early Christians remembered Paul's imprisonment in different ways. Some saw it as a time of trial, character-building and literary activity and, thus, they wrote letters in Paul's name. Some remembered it through narratives, which highlighted their own theological perspectives. And some referred back to it as a time which exemplified appropriate behavior and beliefs.

---

1.   Cf. Acts 8.3; 22.4; and 26.10. See A.J. Hultgren, 'Paul's Pre-Christian Persecutions of the Church: Their Purpose, Locale, and Nature', *JBL* 95 (1976), pp. 97-111.

What happened to the image of Paul as a prisoner? This epilogue will point to a number of ways in which Paul's imprisonment—in the wake of his authentic letters—became a stock motif for early Christian leadership and martyrdom. As the imprisoned apostle, Paul was remembered as an author, as a dramatic exemplary character and as a source.[2]

2. *The Imprisoned Paul as Author*

Letters attributed to the apostle Paul are addressed to such places as Laodicea, Corinth, Ephesus, Colossae and Philippi, to a faithful sidekick named Timothy and to a community affiliated with Philemon. So far, this book has focused on Paul's letters to the Philippians and to Philemon.

But what about the others? Did Paul write *3 Corinthians*? The epistle to the *Laodiceans*? Ephesians? Colossians? 2 Timothy? Although each of these letters claims to have been written by the apostle Paul, most scholars argue that they were not. Stylistic differences, unique vocabulary and distinct theological perspectives all have been cited in arguments claiming that these epistles are actually pseudepigraphical; attributed to Paul, but not written by him. What scholars have overlooked, however, is the function of the social location from which each of these

---

2. For more general discussions of how Paul was remembered in the early church, see M.C. de Boer, 'Images of Paul in the Post-Apostolic Period', *CBQ* 42 (1980), pp. 359-80; L. Keck, 'Images of Paul in the New Testament', *Interpretation* 43 (1989), pp. 341-51; H.-M. Schenke, 'Das Weiterwirken des Paulus und die Pflege seines Erbes durch die Paulus-Schule', *NTS* 21 (1975), pp. 505-518; W.S. Babcock (ed.), *Paul and the Legacies of Paul* (Dallas: Southern Methodist University Press, 1990); E. Dassmann, *Der Stachel im Fleisch: Paulus in der frühchristlichen Literatur bis Irenaeus* (Münster: Aschendorff, 1979); D.K. Rensberger, 'As the Apostle Teaches: The Development of the Use of Paul's Letters in Second-Century Christianity' (PhD dissertation, Yale University, 1981); J. Jervell, 'Paulus in der Apostelgeschichte und die Geschichte des Urchristentums', *NTS* 32 (1986), pp. 378-92; J.C. Beker, *Heirs of Paul: Paul's Legacy in the New Testament and in the Church Today* (Minneapolis: Fortress Press, 1991); K. Kertelge (ed.), *Paulus in den neutestamentlichen Spätschriften: Zur Paulusrezeption im Neuen Testament* (Quaestiones Disputatae, 89; Freiburg, Basel and Vienna, 1981); A. Lindemann, *Paulus im ältesten Christentum: Das Bild des Apostels und die Rezeption der paulinischen Theologie in der frühchristlichen Literatur bis Marcion* (Beiträge zur historischen Theologie, 58; Tübingen: Mohr, 1979); and G. Schille, *Das älteste Paulus-Bild: Beobachtungen zur lukanischen und zur deuteropaulinischen Paulus-Darstellung* (Berlin: Evangelische Verlagsanstalt, 1979).

epistles is said to have been written: each claims to have been written from prison.

If these letters were not written by Paul, significant questions need to be posed: Why do so many pseudepigraphical epistles claim to have been written from prison? How did imprisonment give 'Paul' or his imitators credibility? How did this creative fiction function in pseudepigraphy?

Although these five epistles—2 Timothy, Colossians, Ephesians, *Laodiceans* and *3 Corinthians*—are difficult to date, they are generally seen as having been written between 50 and 150 CE. Most refer to Paul's imprisonment in general ways, doing little more than claiming it as the social context from which they were written. In 2 Timothy, however, there is a sustained discussion of what prisoners like Paul actually would have experienced.

The link between shame and imprisonment is central here. In the pastoral epistles, the word 'ashamed' occurs three times, with all three instances found in the first chapter of 2 Timothy. In addition to these specific terms, other references to shame fill the letter's first two chapters. In the thanksgiving, for instance, the author (hereafter referred to as 'Paul') claims that he is serving God 'with a clear conscience' (1.3); and goes on to emphasize that 'God did not give us a spirit of timidity, but a spirit of power...'(1.7) Therefore, Timothy is exhorted: 'Do not be ashamed then of testifying to our Lord, nor of me his prisoner, but share in suffering for the gospel in the power of God...(1.8) Paul knows why he is suffering (1.11-12), but he is 'not ashamed' (1.12).

Paul then contrasts Phygelus and Hermogenes, who 'turned away' from him (1.15), with Onesiphorus and his household, who were 'not ashamed' of Paul's chains (1.16). Indeed, as Paul says, although he is suffering for the gospel, and 'wearing fetters like a criminal, the word of God is not fettered' (2.9). Timothy is encouraged to 'share in suffering as a good soldier of Christ Jesus' (2.3), and to 'do your best to present yourself to God as one approved, a workman who has no need to be ashamed' (2.15).

There were obvious reasons why and how persons were either shamed or ashamed as prisoners, but the author here tries to transform what must have been a natural reaction both to Paul's imprisonment and to the imprisonment of other Christians.

'Shame' is closely linked with the exhortation to 'testify' in 2 Tim. 1.8: 'Do not be ashamed then of testifying to our Lord, nor of me his prisoner.' The reader is immediately within the realm of ancient Roman legal activity. Whatever universal meaning the word μαρτύριον may have had, in its context here the legal implications are striking. Thus, the letter presents a concrete reason for Paul's wanting Timothy to visit (4.9, 21): he requests Timothy's support in the courtroom.[3] When, at the end of the letter, Paul says, 'At my first defense no one took my part; all deserted me' (4.16), he seems to be using shame to reiterate the admonition of 1.8. Although the Lord rescued and will rescue Paul, Paul wants Timothy to join him. Overall, in 2 Timothy, the message is straightforward. The author encourages the reader not to be ashamed of those who are imprisoned, but even to go so far as to testify on their behalf.[4]

In other epistles presumed to be pseudepigraphical, there is less focus on the world of prison than on an abstract concept of imprisonment itself.[5] The epistle to the Colossians, for instance, concludes with only vague references to Paul's circumstances: the author refers to Aristarchus as a 'fellow prisoner' (4.10), claims that he is in prison 'on account of declaring the mystery of Christ' (4.3), and appeals to his readers to 'remember my fetters' (4.18). He unabashedly sees his imprisonment as related to Christ and, in the last verse of the letter, sees his fetters as a sort of claim he can make on the Colossians. Paul's sufferings, mentioned earlier in the letter, are even seen as having a redemptive function for others: 'Now I rejoice in my sufferings for your sake, and in my flesh I complete what is lacking in Christ's afflictions for the sake of his body, that is, the church' (1.24).

In the letter to the Ephesians, allusions to imprisonment are also few. However, three explicit references stand out. In Eph. 3.1, the author refers to himself as 'I, Paul, a prisoner for Christ Jesus on behalf of you Gentiles...' In 4.1, he writes, 'I therefore, a prisoner for the Lord, beg you to lead a life worthy of the calling to which you have been called.' In 6.19-20, he encourages the Ephesians to 'keep alert with all perseverance, making supplication for all the saints, and also for me', since he is

3. Cf. M. Prior, *Paul the Letter-Writer and the Second Letter to Timothy* (JSNTSup, 23; Sheffield: JSOT Press, 1989), p. 146.

4. Cf. Keck, 'Images of Paul', p. 347, who writes that '*This* Paul comes through as a real person, a bit irked because he wears fetters "like a criminal"... If the pastorals were genuine, the Paul of the New Testament would leave us as a somewhat lonely prisoner, slightly jaded if not embittered, having a decidely negative view of the world' (Keck's emphasis).

5. In a discussion of Ephesians, for example, Keck, 'Images of Paul', p. 346, writes, 'This "Paul" presents himself as a prisoner (3.1, 13; 4.1), but apart from 6.18-20 discloses no personal response to the situation.'

'an ambassador in chains' for the proclamation of the mystery of the gospel.

In Ephesians, there is no indication that shame might result from imprisonment. Conversely, the author boldly refers to himself as a 'prisoner for Christ Jesus'. The author is not apologetic in any sense. Imprisonment is a badge not of shame, but of honor. Furthermore, the author's imprisonment for the Lord (or for Christ Jesus) is what gives him both credibility and authority.

The epistle to the *Laodiceans* may be a prison epistle, but it clearly seems to have been written in response to Col. 4.16: 'And when this letter has been read among you, have it read also in the church of the Laodiceans; and see that you read also the letter from Laodicea.' The epistle itself is an awkward collection of Pauline verses, mostly from Paul's letter to the Philippians.[6] The one explicit reference to imprisonment is found in v. 6: 'And now my bonds are manifest, which I suffer in Christ, on account of which I am glad and rejoice.'[7] Because this verse clearly is a convolution of verses from an authentic prison epistle (Phil. 1.13 and 1.18), and because Colossians was said to have been written from prison, a reference to 'bonds' in *Laodiceans* is not unexpected. In this case, it does not function in a distinctively theological manner but, as part of the entire epistle, helps fill a natural gap in the Pauline epistle corpus. The verse reiterates Pauline thought, but does not develop it.

Finally, *3 Corinthians*, as part of the narrative of *The Acts of Paul*, is said to have been written from a prison in Philippi (*The Acts of Paul* 8.2). In responding to correspondence from Corinth, Paul begins the letter by addressing himself as 'Paul, the prisoner of Jesus Christ' (8.3.1).[8] In a discussion of theology, Paul refers to chains in a metaphorical sense, where he writes that the unrighteous prince who 'wished himself to be God...fettered all flesh of men to the passions' (8.3.11), but that 'by his own body, Jesus Christ saved all flesh' (8.3.16). Finally, near the letter's conclusion, Paul writes,

6.　See P. Sellew, 'Laodiceans and the Philippians Fragments Hypothesis', *HTR* 87 (1994), pp. 17-28.

7.　All quotations from *Laodiceans* come from W. Schneemelcher, 'The Epistle to the Laodiceans', in E. Hennecke and W. Schneemelcher (eds.), *New Testament Apocrypha*, II (trans. R.McL. Wilson; Philadelphia: Westminster Press, 1965), pp. 131-32.

8.　All quotations from *3 Corinthians* and the *The Acts of Paul* come from W. Schneemelcher, 'The Acts of Paul', in E. Hennecke and W. Schneemelcher (eds.), *New Testament Apocrypha*, II, pp. 352-90.

> But if you receive anything else, do not cause me trouble; for I have these
> fetters on my hands that I may gain Christ, and his marks in my body that
> I may attain to the resurrection of the dead (8.3.34-35).

Here, in *3 Corinthians*, an epistle from prison fits in well with the overall narrative of the story. Paul's fetters prompt an apt metaphor in arguing against teachers of dualism (or gnosticism). And, finally, Paul's concluding statements (8.3.34f.)—a mixture of words and ideas from Galatians and Philippians—show that imprisonment gave the author the expectation that he would be treated in a worthy manner.

With the exception of 2 Timothy, the pseudepigraphical epistles do not seem interested or concerned with Paul's imprisonment *per se*. Imprisonment is significant in these letters only insofar as it is the alleged social context from which these epistles came. If 2 Timothy, Colossians, Ephesians, *Laodiceans*, and *3 Corinthians* were not written by Paul, if they are pseudepigraphical epistles, the social location from which each of these epistles is said to have been written is not insignificant. As the church faced increased persecution, Paul's words from prison had greater credibility. Paul's imprisonment for Christ and for the sake of others is what makes the message and admonitions of these epistles particularly authoritative. Paul's status as prisoner is presented as the warrant for his authority.

3. *The Imprisoned Paul as Dramatic Exemplary Character*

Since Paul's prison epistles did not fully describe either why he was in prison or what he experienced while there, some writings served to fill these blanks in the historical memory of early Christianity. Thus, scenes of Paul in prison can be found in writings such as the Acts of the Apostles and *The Acts of Paul* . These writings are not as interested in what Paul said from prison. They are interested in why he was imprisoned and what he experienced while there. Paul's actions in prison, as shaped by the author's theological interests, become the lens through which his imprisonment is understood.

Three main passages in Acts stand out. In Acts 16.19-40, Paul is found in the inner prison in Philippi. With his feet in stocks, he prays and sings hymns, while others listen. When the force of an earthquake unfastens his fetters and throws open the prison doors, Paul does not escape. Rather, he uses the opportunity to comfort the jailer and then convert both him and his family. In this pericope, Paul clearly is unencumbered by his imprisonment. This circumstance, rather, creates the opportunity for mission work.

In Acts 24.22-27, the governor Felix is holding Paul in custody. Here Luke's portrayal of Paul points both to a truism about prisons and to a truism about Paul: the first is that persons often were imprisoned despite logical reasons; the second is that, even on legal grounds, Paul's imprisonment seems unjustified. With Felix wanting money from Paul (24.26), the apostle remained imprisoned.

Paul's time in Rome—as described in Acts 28.16 and 28.30-31—has received much attention. The main focus of these verses seems to rest on the last words of Acts: Paul is left under house arrest 'preaching the kingdom of God and teaching about the Lord Jesus Christ quite openly and unhindered (μετὰ πάσης παρρησίας ἀκωλύτως)' (28.31c). Against all theexamples in antiquity which show that παρρησία[9] (often translated as 'boldness') is what led to imprisonment or exile,[10] against all evidence which shows that imprisonment resulted in the loss of παρρησία, Luke presents an ironic picture of Paul as imprisoned but unhindered, faithfully preaching the kingdom of God 'with all boldness'.[11]

In numerous respects, Acts functions apologetically.[12] Paul's status as prisoner is one condition which needed to be defended. In a 1994

9. S.B. Marrow, '*Parrhesia* and the New Testament', *CBQ* 44 (1982), pp. 431-36, offers a helpful study of the use of this term in both pagan and sacred Greek literature. Also see E. Peterson, 'Zur Bedeutungsgeschichte von *Parrhesia*', in W. Koepp (ed.), *Reinhold Seeberg Festschrift*. I. *Zur Theorie des Christentums* (Leipzig: D. Werner Scholl, 1929), pp. 283-97; and W.C. van Unnik, 'The Christian's Freedom of Speech in the New Testament', *BJRL* 44 (1961–62), pp. 466-88.

10. Examples can be found in R. MacMullen, *Enemies of the Roman Order: Treason, Unrest, and Alienation in the Empire* (Cambridge, MA: Harvard University Press, 1966), pp. 15, 61-62, 64-67, 83-84, 88-89, 133, 299, 311 and 319.

11. R.A. Wild, 'The Warrior and the Prisoner: Some Reflections on Ephesians 6.10-20', *CBQ* 46 (1984), p. 291, articulates well the irony of Paul's preaching 'with all boldness': 'Parrhesia most properly refers to the mode of speech which befits a free human being. It is, therefore, first and foremost associated with freedom, whether this freedom be conceived of in the political, moral, or even cosmic order.'

12. Cf. B.S. Easton, *The Purpose of Acts* (London: Society for Promoting Christian Knowledge, 1936); P.W. Walaskay *'And So We Came to Rome': The Political Perspective of St Luke* (SNTSMS, 49; New York: Cambridge University Press, 1983); G.E. Sterling, *Historiography and Self-Definition: Josephus, Luke–Acts, and Apologetic Historiography* (SNT, 64; New York: Brill, 1992); and K.L. Cukrowski, *Pagan Polemic and Lukan Apologetic: The Function of Acts 20.17-38* (Yale University, unpublished PhD dissertation, 1994).

monograph, Brian Rapske emphasizes that the author of Acts defends the prisoner Paul in three main ways: 1) Luke shows that Paul continued to be an effective missionary despite being imprisoned; 2) he shows that others were not ashamed of Paul's imprisonment, but that they helped and served him; and 3) he emphasizes that Paul, as both missionary and prisoner, was divinely approved.[13] In the book of Acts, regardless of where or when Paul is imprisoned, Luke makes clear that such imprisonments do not stifle the Christian message.[14]

Similarly, the second-century document known as *The Acts of Paul* (*AP*) also presents the imprisoned apostle as one whose mission remains active, who is supported by others, and whose imprisonment is validated by God.

In *AP*3.17-20, Paul finds himself imprisoned first in Iconium. Although the antagonists in this narrative have claimed that Paul is a sorceror, the author makes clear that the apostle's chains resulted from his having preached the gospel. In prison, we are told, Paul was visited by Thecla. Furthermore, he both taught and 'feared nothing, but comported himself with full confidence in God' (3.18).

Later, imprisoned in Ephesus, Paul was visited by Artemilla and Eubula, he dined, his bonds were loosened by a 'youth very comely in grace', and he even baptized and apparently engaged in the Lord's Supper with a recent convert (*AP* 7). This incident is followed by Paul's imprisonment in Philippi (*AP* 8). Because *AP* 8 is fragmentary, other than presenting *3 Corinthians*, it tells us little about Paul in prison.

Although Paul faces a variety of types of imprisonment in the *The Acts of Paul*, although he is supported by others, vindicated by God and

13. B. Rapske, *The Book of Acts and Paul in Roman Custody* (Grand Rapids, MI: Eerdmans, 1994), esp. pp. 423-36. For broader discussions on Luke's portrayal of Paul, see both V. Stolle, *Der Zeuge als Angeklagter: Untersuchungen zum Paulusbild des Lukas* (Berlin: Verlag W. Kohlhammer, 1973), and R. Maddox, 'The Picture of Paul in Acts', in *The Purpose of Luke–Acts* (Göttingen: Vandenhoeck & Ruprecht, 1982), pp. 66-90.

14. Cf. D.R. Schwartz, 'The Accusation and the Accusers at Philippi (Acts 16,20-21)', *Biblica* 65 (1984), pp. 357-63; B.J. Koet, 'Paul in Rome (Acts 28.16-31): A Farewell to Judaism?', *Bijdragen: Tijdschrift voor Philosophie en Theologie* 48 (1987), pp. 397-415; C.B. Puskas, 'The Conclusion of Luke–Acts: An Investigation of the Literary Function and Theological Significance of Acts 28.16-31' (PhD dissertation, St Louis University, 1980); and H.J. Hauser, *Strukturen der Abschlusserzählung der Apostelgeschichte (Apg 28,16-31)* (Analecta Biblica, 86; Rome: Biblical Institute Press, 1979).

active in his missionary work, the primary impression conveyed by this document is that of Paul as an imprisoned soldier. At the end of *The Acts of Paul*, when Nero is described as imprisoning Christians, he

> issued a decree to this effect, that all who were found to be Christians and soldiers of Christ should be put to death. And among the many Paul also was brought bound; to him all his fellow-prisoners gave heed, so that Caesar observed that he was the man in command. And he said to him: 'Man of the great king, but (now) my prisoner, why did it seem good to thee to come secretly into the empire of the Romans and enlist soldiers from my province?' But Paul, filled with the Holy Spirit, said before them all: 'Caesar, not only from thy province do we enlist soldiers, but from the whole world' (11.2-3).

The nearness of death in prison seems to have inspired military metaphors. Paul continues, telling Nero that 'I am no deserter from Christ, but a lawful soldier of the living God' (11.4). This leads to Paul's execution. However, after Paul is beheaded, he returns, stands before Caesar, and exclaims: 'Caesar, here I am—Paul, God's soldier. I am not dead, but alive in my God' (11.6).

Because Paul is described as a soldier earlier in *The Acts of Paul*,[15] this description, in *AP* 11, is not entirely surprising. Paul, as a soldier, is loyal, he will not retreat, and—through the strength of God—he will overcome.

The success of the portrayals of Paul in these two narratives is evident. As a result of *The Acts of Paul*, collective Christian memory identifies this apostle as having been beheaded in prison. As a result of one description in Acts, Luke's second volume, many historians and readers picture Paul's incarceration only in terms of a loose house arrest. The pictures left by these narratives are some of the most vivid in Christian consciousness.

4. *The Imprisoned Paul as Source*

Paul's imprisonment and martyrdom became increasingly significant in the second century. Ignatius (*Eph.* 12.1-2), Clement (*1 Clem.* 5.5-7), and Polycarp (*Phil.* 9.1) appeal to Paul's authority as prisoner. Furthermore, these Christians also begin to quote and allude to words which the incarcerated apostle had penned.

---

15. R.M. Grant, 'The Description of Paul in the Acts of Paul and Thecla', *VC* 36 (1982), pp. 1-4, shows how Paul, in *AP* 3.3, is described in a manner consistent with how ancient military generals were described.

Because Ignatius was writing as a prisoner, allusions to chains run throughout his epistles.[16] It is not surprising that Ignatius would have been in a particularly appropriate position to use both the language and the model of early Christianity's most famous prisoner.

Although Ignatius rarely quotes Paul directly, he frequently alludes to Pauline passages. As Helmut Koester states, 'the many allusions to the Pauline correspondence demonstrate that Ignatius repeatedly returned to those letters to find guidance and instruction'.[17] As shown above, in Chapter 5 of this work, one of the more subtle uses of Paul's prison epistles can be seen in *Ephesians* 2. Here, Ignatius—a prisoner en route to Rome—uses echoes of Paul's letter to Philemon, in appealing for support from the church at Ephesus. Ignatius's understanding of his bondage and death are clearly informed and shaped by his reading of Paul.[18]

Ignatius's theology and actions are shaped not only by the legacy of Paul's writings, but also by the model of Paul's own sacrifice. Ignatius writes in *Eph.* 12.1-2,

> I know who I am and to whom I am writing. I am a convict; you have been pardoned; I risk danger; you are secure. You are the way for those who are being slain for God—fellow initiates with Paul, the sanctified, the approved, worthy of blessing (may I be found in his footsteps when I reach God!), who in a whole letter makes mention of you in Christ Jesus [see Eph. 1.1].[19]

16. Examples can be seen in *Eph.* 2.1-2; 3.1-2; 11.2; 21.2; *Magn.* 12; *Trall.* 10; 12.2; *Rom.* 1.1; 4.3; *Smyrn.* 4.2; 10.2; *Polycarp* 2.3.

17. H. Koester, *History and Literature of Early Christianity* (Philadelphia: Fortress Press; 1982), p.284.

18. See H. Rathke, *Ignatius von Antiochien und die Paulusbriefe* (Texte und Untersuchungen zur Geschichte der altchristlichen Literatur, 99; Berlin: Akademie-Verlag, 1967). Rathke points to Ignatius's literary imitation of the Pauline letters, and argues that Ignatius was consciously adopting Paul as a model, 'the prototypical martyr', in his own letters. R.J. Stoops also discusses Ignatius's dependence on and reaction to Paul in 'If I Suffer: Epistolary Authority in Ignatius of Antioch', *HTR* 80 (1987), pp. 161-78. See also W. Rebell, 'Das Leidenverständnis bei Paulus und Ignatius von Antiochien', *NTS* 32 (1986), pp. 457-65. For somewhat different perspectives, note A.T. Hanson, 'The Theology of Suffering in the Pastoral Epistles and Ignatius of Antioch', in E. Livingstone (ed.), *Studia Patristica*, XVII.2 (Oxford: Pergamum Press, 1982), pp. 694-96; and R.G. Tanner, 'Martyrdom in Saint Ignatius and the Stoic View of Suicide', in E. Livingstone (ed.), *Studia Patristica*, XVI.2 (Oxford: Pergamum Press, 1985), pp. 201-205.

19. R.M. Grant (trans.), 'The Letter of Ignatius of Antioch, Ephesians', in J.N. Sparks (ed.), *The Apostolic Fathers* (New York: Thomas Nelson, 1978), p. 81.

Ignatius's epistles reflect an important bridge between Paul's reflections in prison and what became the church's later understanding of the role of martyrdom.

In *1 Clement* 5.5-7, the author emphasizes that Paul, like Peter, experienced much because of jealousy and envy:

> Because of jealousy and strife, Paul showed how to win the prize of patient endurance [cf. 2 Cor. 11.23ff.]: seven times he was in bonds, he was banished, he was stoned, he became a messenger (of the gospel) in both East and West, and earned well-merited fame for his faith; for he taught righteousness to the whole world, having traveled to the limits of the West [cf. Rom. 15.24-28]; and when he had borne his witness before the rulers, he departed from the world an outstanding example of patient endurance.[20]

Clement seeks to show both the dangers of jealousy and the appropriate responses to it. The discussion of Paul's imprisonment, then, occurs within a series of difficulties which Paul is seen as having overcome. The imprisonment is not a cause of glory. It is merely yet another example of that which Paul patiently endured in accomplishing his mission.

The letter of Polycarp to the *Philippians* mentions Paul as authoritative for, and supportive of, the Philippians (3.2 and 11.2-3). The touchstone of the epistle seems to be in Polycarp's discussion of the martyrs:

> I exhort all of you, then, to obey the word of righteousness and to exercise all endurance, which you also saw before your eyes not only in the blessed Ignatius and Zosimus and Rufus, but also in others from among you and in Paul himself and the rest of the apostles; being persuaded that all these 'did not run in vain', but in faith and righteousness, and that they are 'in their due place' beside the Lord with whom they also suffered. For they did not 'love the present world' but him who died for us and was raised by God because of us.[21]

Not only is Paul cited as an example of one who was willing to die for the faith but, even moreso, words attributed to him are quoted in support of the act of martyrdom. In a discussion of martyrdom, it is not surprising that Polycarp would appeal to quotations which come from a prison epistle. What is ironic, however, is that the epistle which he most frequently quotes is not Paul's letter to the Philippians, but 2 Timothy. Both Paul's actions and the words attributed to him are formative when

20. H.H. Graham (trans.), 'The Letter of Clement of Rome to Corinth', in Sparks (ed.), *The Apostolic Fathers*, p. 21.

21. W.R. Schoedel, 'The Letter of Polycarp to the Philippians', in Sparks (ed.), *The Apostolic Fathers*, pp. 133-34.

Polycarp develops his theological position on martyrdom.

In reflecting on Paul's incarceration and sacrifice, Ignatius, Clement and Polycarp use Paul's endurance and his willingness to be in chains as examples for Christians of their own day. Both Paul's actions and his words from prison were authoritative.

5. *Conclusion*

Paul is sometimes referred to as the first Christian theologian or as the apostle to the Gentiles. However, it is important to remember that Paul's social circumstances—his imprisonment, in particular—significantly shaped how he was remembered. Paul's message of grace and his invitation to the Gentiles greatly shaped Christianity, but the memory of his imprisonment served to sustain the nascent church in ways that the message alone did not. Paul's presence in prison took on a normative role.

Whatever difficulties Paul's incarceration might have caused the earliest Christians, the image of Paul the prisoner came to function in a number of significant ways in the nascent church. The early Christians struggled with, adapted and exploited what could have been a potentially controversial image, 'reducing' the offensive nature of Paul's imprisonment and, in the process, using Paul's incarceration as a bridge, enabling them to deal with situations of persecution in the early church. Potential shame became a source of glory.

BIBLIOGRAPHY

Alexander, L., 'Hellenistic Letter-Forms and the Structure of Philippians', *JSNT* 37 (1989), pp. 87-101.

Arbandt, S., and W. Macheiner, 'Gefangenschaft', in T. Klauser (ed.), *Reallexikon für Antike und Christentum*, IX (Stuttgart: Anton Hiersemann, 1976), pp. 318-45.

Artemidori D., *Onirocriticon*, V (ed. R.A. Pack; Leipzig: Teubner, 1963).

Artemidorus, *The Interpretation of Dreams (Oneirocritica)* (trans. R.J. White; Torrance, CA: Original Books, 1975).

Aune, D.E., 'Revelation', in J.L. Mays (ed.), *Harper's Bible Commentary* (San Francisco: Harper & Row, 1988), pp. 1300-319.

Babcock, W.S. (ed.), *Paul and the Legacies of Paul* (Dallas: Southern Methodist University Press, 1990).

Bahr, C.J., 'The Subscriptions in the Pauline Letters', *JBL* 87 (1968), pp. 27-41.

Balch, D.L., *Let Wives Be Submissive: The Domestic Code in I Peter* (SBLDS, 26; Atlanta: Scholars Press, 1981).

Balsdon, J.P.V.D., *Romans and Aliens* (London: Gerald Duckworth, 1979).

Barclay, J.M.G., 'Paul, Philemon and the Dilemma of Christian Slave-Ownership', *NTS* 37 (1991), pp. 161-86.

Barnett, A.E., *Paul Becomes a Literary Influence* (Chicago: University of Chicago Press, 1941).

Bartchy, S.S., *MALLON CRHSAI : First-Century Slavery and the Interpretation of I Corinthians 7.21* (SBLDS, 11; Missoula: SBL, 1973).

—'Philemon, Epistle to', in D.N. Freedman (ed.), *The Anchor Bible Dictionary*, V (New York: Doubleday, 1992), pp. 305-310.

Beker, J.C., *Heirs of Paul: Paul's Legacy in the New Testament and in the Church Today* (Minneapolis: Fortress Press, 1991).

Benz, E., 'Christus und Sokrates in der alten Kirche: Ein Beitrag zum altkirchlichen Verständnis des Märtyrers und des Martyriums', *ZNW* 43 (1950–51), pp. 195-224.

Berger, A., 'Prison', in N.G.L. Hammond and H. H. Scullard (eds.), *The Oxford Classical Dictionary* (Oxford: Clarendon Press, 2nd edn, 1970), p. 879.

Berkeley, C., *Some Roman Monuments in the Light of History* (Banbury: F. Gough, 1931).

Betz, H.D. (ed.), *The Greek Magical Papyri in Translation* (Chicago: University of Chicago Press, 1986).

Binder, H., *Der Brief des Paulus an Philemon* (THKNT, 11.2; Berlin: Evangelische Verlagsanstalt, 1990).

Birdsall, J.N., 'ΠΡΕΣΒΥΤΗΣ in Philemon 9: A Study in Conjectural Emendation', *NTS* 39 (1993), pp. 625-30.

Black, D.A., 'The Discourse Structure of Philippians: A Study in Textlinguistics', *NovT* 37 (1995), pp. 16-49.

Boer, M.C. de, 'Images of Paul in the Post-Apostolic Period', *CBQ* 42 (1980), pp. 359-80.

Boll, F., 'Die Lebensalter', *Neue Jahrbücher für das Klassische Altertum* 31 (1913), pp. 89-145.

Bornkamm, G., 'πρεσβύτης', in *TDNT*, VI, p. 683.

Bram, J.R. (trans.), *Julius Firmicus Maternus, Ancient Astrology: Theory and Practice* (Park Ridge, NJ: Noyes Press, 1975).

Braudel, F., 'History and the Social Sciences: The Longue Durée', in *idem, On History* (trans. S. Matthews; Chicago: University of Chicago Press, 1980), pp. 28-54.

Brettler, M.Z., and M. Poliakoff, 'Rabbi Simeon ben Lakish at the Gladiator's Banquet: Rabbinic Observations on the Roman Arena', *HTR* 83 (1990), pp. 93-98.

Brock, S.P., and S.A. Harvey, *Holy Women of the Syrian Orient* (Berkeley: University of California Press, 1987).

Buchanan, C.O., 'Epaphroditus' Sickness and the Letter to the Philippians', *EvQ* 36 (1964), pp. 157-66.

Buchanan, G.W., *To the Hebrews* (AB, 36; Garden City, New York: Doubleday, 1972).

Byrne, B., 'The Letter to the Philippians', in R.E. Brown *et al.* (eds.), *The New Jerome Biblical Commentary* (Englewood Cliffs, NJ: Prentice–Hall, 1990), pp. 791-97.

Caird, G.B., *Paul's Letters from Prison* (Oxford: Oxford University Press, 1976).

Callahan, A.D., 'Paul's Epistle to Philemon: Toward an Alternative Argumentum', *HTR* 86 (1993), pp. 357-76.

Calvin, J., *Calvin's Commentaries: The Epistles of Paul the Apostle to the Galatians, Ephesians, Philippians and Colossians* (eds. D.W. and T.F. Torrance; trans. T.H.L. Parker; Grand Rapids, MI: Eerdmans, 1965 [1548]).

Capper, B.J., 'Paul's Dispute with Philippi: Understanding Paul's Argument in Phil. 1–2 from his Thanks in 4.10-20', *TZ* 49 (1993), pp. 193-214.

Cartlidge, D.R., and D.L. Dungan, *Documents for the Study of the Gospels* (Philadelphia: Fortress Press, 1980).

Chadwick, O., *Western Asceticism* (Philadelphia: Westminster Press, 1958).

Church, F. F., 'Rhetorical Structure and Design in Paul's Letter to Philemon', *HTR* 71 (1978), pp. 17-33.

Coleman, T.R., 'Paul's Prison Life' (PhD dissertation, Southern Baptist Theological Seminary, Louisville, 1939).

Collange, J.-F., *The Epistle of Saint Paul to the Philippians* (trans. A.W. Heathcote; London: Epworth Press, 1979).

Cosgrove, C.H., 'Philemon', in W.E. Mills and R.F. Wilson (eds.), *Mercer Commentary on the Bible* (Macon, GA: Mercer University Press, 1995), pp. 1263-66.

Craddock, F.B., *Philippians* (Interpretation; Atlanta: John Knox, 1985).

Cukrowski, K.L., *Pagan Polemic and Lukan Apologetic: The Function of Acts 20:17-38* (PhD dissertation, Yale University, 1994).

Dahl, N.A., 'Euodia and Syntyche and Paul's Letter to the Philippians', in L.M. White and O.L. Yarbrough (eds.), *The Social World of the First Christians: Essays in Honor of Wayne A. Meeks* (Minneapolis: Fortress Press, 1995), pp. 3-15.

—'The Origin of the Earliest Prologues to the Pauline Letters', *Semeia* 12 (1978), pp. 233-77.

Dalton, W.J. 'The Integrity of Philippians', *Bib* 60 (1979), pp. 97-102.

Dassmann, E., 'Archaeological Traces of Early Christian Veneration of Paul', in W.S. Babcock (ed.), *Paul and the Legacies of Paul* (Dallas: Southern Methodist University Press, 1990), pp. 281-306.

—*Der Stachel im Fleisch: Paulus in der frühchristlichen Literatur bis Irenaeus* (Münster: Aschendorff, 1979).

Deissmann, A., 'Zur ephesinischen Gefangenschaft des Apostels Paulus', in W.H. Buckler and W.M. Calder (eds.), *Anatolian Studies Presented to Sir W.M. Ramsay* (Manchester: Manchester University Press, 1923), pp. 121-27.

Derrett, J.D.M., 'The Functions of the Epistle to Philemon', *ZNW* 79 (1988). pp. 63-91.

Dionisotti, A.C., 'From Ausonius' Schooldays? A Schoolbook and its Relatives', *JRS* 72 (1982), pp. 83-125.

Dodd, C.H. *New Testament Studies* (Manchester: University of Manchester Press, 1953).

Droge, A.J., 'Did Paul Commit Suicide?', *BibRev* (Dec. 1989), pp. 14-21.

—'Mori Lucrum: Paul and Ancient Theories of Suicide', *NovT* 30 (1988), pp. 263-86.

Droge, A.J. and J.D. Tabor, *A Noble Death: Suicide & Martyrdom Among Christians and Jews in Antiquity* (San Francisco: Harper & Row, 1992).

—'Suicide', in D.N. Freedman (ed.), *The Anchor Bible Dictionary*, VI (New York: Doubleday, 1992), pp. 225-31.

Duff, P.B., 'Metaphor, Motif, and Meaning: The Rhetorical Strategy behind the Image "Led in Triumph" in 2 Corinthians 2.14', *CBQ* 53 (1991), pp. 79-92.

Duncan, G.S. 'Important Hypotheses Reconsidered: VI. Were Paul's Imprisonment Epistles Written from Ephesus?', *ExpTim* 67 (1955), pp. 163-66.

—*St Paul's Ephesian Ministry: A Reconstruction* (London: Hodder and Stoughton, 1929).

Eadie, J., *A Commentary on the Greek Text of the Epistle of Paul to the Philippians* (Edinburgh: T. & T. Clark, 1896).

Easton, B.S., *The Purpose of Acts* (London: Society for Promoting Christian Knowledge, 1936).

Echols, E., 'The Roman City Police', *Classical Journal* 53 (1958), pp. 377-85.

Eidem, E, *Pauli bildvärld*. I. *Athletae et Milites Christi* (Lund: Gleerup, 1913).

Eisenhut, W., 'Die römische Gefängnisstrafe', in H. Temporini (ed.), *ANRW*.I.2. *Geschichte und Kultur Roms im Spiegel der neueren Forschung* (New York: de Gruyter, 1972), pp. 268-82.

Emonds, H., 'Christlicher Kriegsdienst. Der Topos der militia spiritualis in der antiken Philosophie', reprinted in A. Harnack, *Militia Christi: Die christliche Religion und der Soldatenstand in den ersten drei Jahrhunderten* (Darmstadt: Wissenschaftliche Buchgesellschaft, 1963 [1905]), pp. 131-62.

Epp, E.J. 'New Testament Papyrus Manuscripts and Letter Carrying in Greco–Roman Times', in B.A. Pearson (ed.), *The Future of Early Christianity: Essays in Honor of Helmut Koester* (Minneapolis: Fortress Press, 1991), pp. 35-56.

Epstein, I. (ed.), *The Babylonian Talmud* (London: Soncino Press, 1938).

Ernst, J., *Die Briefe an die Philipper, an Philemon, an die Kolosser, an die Epheser* (Regensburg: Verlag Friedrich Pustet, 1974).

Ewald, D.P., *Der Brief des Paulus an die Philipper* (Lepizig: A. Deichert [Georg Böhme], 1908).

Finegan, J., *The Archaeology of the New Testament: The Mediterranean World of the Early Christian Apostles* (Boulder, CO: Westview Press, 1981).

Fiore, B., S.J., *The Function of Personal Example in the Socratic and Pastoral Epistles* (Analecta Biblica, 105; Rome: Biblical Institute Press, 1986).

Fitzgerald, J.T. *Cracks in an Earthen Vessel: An Examination of the Catalogues of Hardships in the Corinthian Correspondence* (SBLDS, 99; Atlanta: Scholars Press, 1988).

—'Philippians, Epistle to the', in D.N. Freedman (ed.), *The Anchor Bible Dictionary*, V (New York: Doubleday, 1992), pp. 318-26.

Fortna, R.T., 'Philippians: Paul's Most Egocentric Letter', in R.T. Fortna and B.R. Gaventa (eds.), *The Conversation Continues: Studies in Paul and John in Honor of J. Louis Martyn* (Nashville: Abingdon Press, 1990), pp. 220-34.

Foucault, M., *Discipline and Punishment: The Birth of the Prison* (trans. A. Sheridan; New York: Vintage Books, 1979).

Fox, R.L., *Pagans and Christians* (San Francisco: Harper & Row, 1986).

Furnish, V.P., *II Corinthians* (AB, 32A; Garden City, NY: Doubleday, 1984).

Gallonio, A., *De sanctorum martyrum cruciatibus* (Paris, 1660; English edition, *Tortures and Torments of the Christian Martyrs* [trans. A.R. Allinson; Paris, 1903; repr., Los Angeles: Feral House, 1989]).

Gardner, J.F., *Women in Roman Law and Society* (Bloomington: Indiana University Press, 1986).

Garland, D.E., 'The Composition and Unity of Philippians: Some Neglected Literary Factors', *NovT* 27 (1985), pp. 141-73.

—'Philippians 1.21-26 The Defense and Confirmation of the Gospel', *RevExp* 77 (1980), pp. 327-36.

Garnsey, P., *Social Status and Legal Privilege in the Roman Empire* (Oxford: Oxford University Press, 1970).

Garrett, S.R., The Demise of the Devil: Magic and the Demonic in Luke's Writings (Minneapolis: Fortress Press, 1989).

Getty, M.A., *Philippians and Philemon* (NTM, 14; Wilmington, DE: Michael Glazier, 1980).

Gilchrist, J.M., 'On What Charge was St Paul Brought to Rome?', *ExpTim* 78 (1966–67), pp. 264-66.

Gnilka, J., *The Epistle to the Philippians* (trans. R.A. Wilson; New York: Herder & Herder, 1971).

—*Der Philemonbrief* (Freiburg: Herder, 1982).

Goodenough, E.R., 'Paul and Onesimus', *HTR* 22 (1929), pp. 181-83.

Graham, H.H. (trans.), 'The Letter of Clement of Rome to Corinth', in J.N. Sparks (ed.), *The Apostolic Fathers* (New York: Nelson, 1978), pp. 18-54.

Grant, R.M., 'The Description of Paul in the Acts of Paul and Thecla', *VC* 36 (1982), pp. 1-4.

Grant R.M. (trans.), 'The Letters of Ignatius of Antioch, Ephesians', in J.N. Sparks (ed.), *The Apostolic Fathers* (New York: Nelson, 1978), pp. 77-84.

Greenidge, A.H.J., *The Legal Procedure of Cicero's Time* (Oxford: Clarendon Press, 1901).

Grenfell, B.P., and A.S. Hunt (eds.), *The Oxyrhynchus Papyri*, II–III (London: Egypt Exploration Fund, 1899–1903).

Gunther, J.J., *Paul: Messenger and Exile* (Valley Forge, PA: Judson, 1972).

Hafemann, S.J., *Suffering and the Spirit* (Tübingen: Mohr [Paul Siebeck], 1986).

Hanson, A.T., 'The Theology of Suffering in the Pastoral Epistles and Ignatius of

Antioch', in E. Livingstone (ed.), *Studia Patristica*, XVII.2 (Oxford: Pergamum Press, 1982), pp. 694-96.

Harnack, A., *Militia Christi: The Christian Religion and the Military in the First Three Centuries* (trans. D.M. Gracie; Philadelphia: Fortress Press, 1981).

Haupt, E., *Die Gefangenschaftsbrief* (Göttingen: Vandenhoeck & Ruprecht, 1897).

Hauser, H.J., *Strukturen der Abschlusserzählung der Apostelgeschichte (Apg 28,16-31)* (Analecta Biblica, 86; Rome: Biblical Institute Press, 1979).

Hawthorne, G.F., *Philippians* (WBC, 43; Waco, Texas: Word Books, 1983).

—'Philippians, Letter to the', in G.F. Hawthorne and R.P. Martin (eds.), *Dictionary of Paul and His Letters* (Downers Grove, IL: Inter-Varsity Press, 1993), pp. 707-713.

Haykin, M.A.G., 'Praying Together: A Note on Philemon 22', *EvQ* 66 (1994), pp. 331-35.

Hays, R.B., *Echoes of Scripture in the Letters of Paul* (New Haven: Yale University Press, 1989).

Hendriksen, W., *Exposition of Philippians* (Grand Rapids: Baker Book House, 1962).

Hennecke, E., and W. Schneemelcher (eds.), *New Testament Apocrypha* (trans. R.M. Wilson; Philadelphia: Westminster Press, 1965).

Hitchcock, F.R.M., 'The Pastorals and a Second Trial for Paul', *ExpTim* 41 (1929–30), pp. 20-23.

Hitzig, H., 'Carcer', in G. Wissowa (ed.), *Pauly's Realencyclopädie der classischen Altertumswissenschaft*, III.2 (Stuttgart: J. B. Metzlersche Verlagsbuchhandlung, 1899), pp. 1576-81.

Hock, R.F., 'Philippians', in J.L. Mays (ed.), *Harper's Bible Commentary* (New York: Harper & Row, 1988), pp. 1220-25.

—'A Support for his Old Age: Paul's Plea on Behalf of Onesimus', in L.M. White and O.L. Yarbrough (eds.), *The Social World of the First Christians: Essays in Honor of Wayne A. Meeks* (Minneapolis: Fortress Press, 1995), pp. 67-81.

Hooff, A.J.L. van, *From Autothanasia to Suicide: Self-Killing in Classical Antiquity* (New York: Routledge & Kegan Paul, 1990).

Houlden, J.L., *Paul's Letters from Prison* (Baltimore: Penguin Books, 1970).

Hülsen, C., *Das Forum Romanum Seine Geschichte und seine Denkmäler* (Rom: Verlag von Loescher, 1905).

—*Forum und Palatin* (München: Drei Masken Verlag, 1926).

Hultgren, A.J., 'Paul's Pre-Christian Persecutions of the Church: Their Purpose, Locale, and Nature', *JBL* 95 (1976), pp. 97-111.

Hunt, A.S., and J.G. Smyly, (eds.), *The Tebtunis Papyri*, III.1 (London: Oxford University Press, 1933).

Hunter, W.A., *Roman Law* (London: William Maxwell & Son, 2nd edn, 1885).

Jay, E.G., *New Testament Greek: An Introductory Grammar* (London: SPCK, 1958).

Jennison, G., *Animals for Show and Pleasure in Ancient Rome* (Manchester: Manchester University Press, 1937).

Jervell, J., 'Paulus in der Apostelgeschichte und die Geschichte des Urchristentums', *NTS* 32 (1986), pp. 378-92.

Jewett, R., 'Conflicting Movements in the Early Church as Reflected in Philippians', *NovT* 12 (1970), pp. 362-90.

—'The Epistolary Thanksgiving and the Integrity of Philippians', *NovT* 12 (1970), pp. 40-53.

—*Paul the Apostle to America: Cultural Trends and Pauline Scholarship* (Louisville, KY: Westminster Press/John Knox, 1994).

Johnson, L.T., *The Writings of the New Testament: An Interpretation* (Philadelphia: Fortress Press, 1986).

Jones, A.H.M., *The Criminal Courts of the Roman Republic and Principate* (Totowa, NJ: Rowman and Littlefield, 1972).

—*The Greek City from Alexander to Justinian* (Oxford: Clarendon Press, 1940).

Jones, M., *The Epistle to the Philippians* (London: Methuen, 1918).

Keck, L., 'Images of Paul in the New Testament', *Interpretation* 43 (1989), pp. 341-51.

Kelly, J.M., *Roman Litigation* (Oxford: Oxford University Press, 1966).

Kelly, J.N.D., *A Commentary on the Pastoral Epistles* (Grand Rapids: Baker, 1981).

Kertelge, K. (ed.), *Paulus in den neutestamentlichen Spätschriften: Zur Paulusrezeption im Neuen Testament* (Quaestiones Disputatae, 89; Freiburg, Basel, and Vienna, 1981).

Kittel, G., 'δεσμός, δέσμιος', *TDNT*, II (1964), p. 43.

Klijn, A.F.J., *De Brief van Paulus aan de Filippenzen* (Nijkerk: Uitgeverij G.F. Callenbach N. V., 1969).

Knox, J., 'Philemon', in G.A. Buttrick (ed.), *The Interpreter's Bible*, XI (New York: Abingdon Press, 1955), pp. 555-73.

—*Philemon among the Letters of Paul: A New View of its Place and Importance* (Nashville: Abingdon Press, rev. edn, 1959 [1935]).

Koester, H., *History and Literature of Early Christianity* (Philadelphia: Fortress Press, 1983).

Koet, B.J., 'Paul in Rome (Acts 28.16-31): A Farewell to Judaism?', *Bijdragen: Tijdschrift voor Philosophie en Theologie* 48 (1987), pp. 397-415.

Kraftchick, S.J., 'A Necessary Detour: Paul's Metaphorical Understanding of the Philippian Hymn', *HBT* 15 (1993), pp. 1-37.

Kratz, R., *Rettungswunder: Motiv-, traditions- und formkritische Aufarbeitung einer biblischen Gattung* (Las Vegas: Peter Lang, 1979).

Krauss, F.A.K., *Im Kerker vor und nach Christus* (Tübingen: Mohr [Paul Siebeck], 1895).

Lampe, P., 'Keine "Sklavenflucht" des Onesimus', *ZNW* 76 (1985), pp. 135-37.

Levick, B., *The Government of the Roman Empire: A Sourcebook* (Totowa, NJ: Barnes & Noble Books, 1985).

Lewis, L.A., 'An African American Appraisal of the Philemon–Paul–Onesimus Triangle', in C.H. Felder (ed.), *Stony the Road We Trod: African American Biblical Interpretation* (Minneapolis: Fortress Press, 1991), pp. 232-46.

Lightfoot, J.B., *Saint Paul's Epistles to the Colossians and to Philemon* (London: Macmillan and Co., 1904).

Lindemann, A., *Paulus im ältesten Christentum: Das Bild des Apostels und die Rezeption der paulinischen Theologie in der frühchristlichen Literatur bis Marcion* (Beiträge zur historischen Theologie, 58; Tübingen: Mohr, 1979).

Lisco, H., *Vincula Sanctorum: Ein Beitrag zur Erklärung der Gefangenschaftsbriefe des Apostels Paulus* (Berlin: F. Schneider & Co. [H. Klinsmann], 1900).

Lohmeyer, E., *Die Briefe an die Philipper, und die Kolosser und an Philemon* (Göttingen: Vandenhoeck & Ruprecht, 1930).

—*Kyrios Jesus, Eine Untersuchungen zu Phil 2, 5-11* (Heidelberg: C. Winter, 2nd edn, 1961).

Lohse, E., *Colossians and Philemon* (trans. W.R. Poehlmann and R.J. Karris; Hermeneia; Philadelphia: Fortress Press, 1971).

Long, A.A., 'Socrates in Hellenistic Philosophy', *Classical Quarterly* 38 (1988), pp. 150-71.

MacDonald, D.R., *The Acts of Andrew and The Acts of Andrew and Matthias in the City of the Cannibals* (Atlanta: Scholars Press, 1990).

MacMullen, R., *Corruption and the Decline of Rome* (New Haven: Yale University Press, 1988).

—'Judicial Savagery in the Roman Empire', in *idem, Changes in the Roman Empire: Essays in the Ordinary* (Princeton: Princeton University Press, 1990), pp. 204-217.

—'Personal Power in the Roman Empire', in *idem, Changes in the Roman Empire: Essays in the Ordinary* (Princeton: Princeton University Press, 1990), pp. 190-97.

—*Soldier and Civilian in the Later Roman Empire* (Cambridge, MA: Harvard University Press, 1963).

Maddox, R., *The Purpose of Luke–Acts* (Göttingen: Vandenhoeck & Ruprecht, 1982).

Malherbe, A.J., trans., *Ancient Epistolary Theorists* (SBLSBS, 19; Atlanta: Scholars Press, 1988).

—'Antisthenes and Odysseus, and Paul at War', *HTR* 76 (1983), pp. 143-73.

—*The Cynic Epistles: A Study Edition* (SBLSBS, 12; Missoula, MT: Scholars Press, 1977).

—'A Physical Description of Paul', *HTR* 79 (1986), pp. 170-75.

—*Social Aspects of Early Christianity* (Philadelphia: Fortress Press, 2nd edn, 1983).

Manson, T.W., 'St Paul in Ephesus: The Date of the Epistle to the Philippians', *BJRL* 23 (1939), pp. 182-200.

Marrow, S.B., '*Parrhesia* and the New Testament', *CBQ* 44 (1982), pp. 431-36.

Martens, J.W., 'Ignatius and Onesimus: John Knox Reconsidered', *SecCent* 9 (1992), pp. 73-86.

Martin, C.J., 'The Rhetorical Function of Commercial Language in Paul's Letter to Philemon (Verse 18)', in D.F. Watson (ed.), *Persuasive Artistry: Studies in New Testament Rhetoric in Honor of George A. Kennedy* (JSNT, 50; Sheffield: JSOT Press), pp. 321-37.

Martin, D.B., *Slavery as Salvation: The Metaphor of Slavery in Pauline Christianity* (New Haven: Yale University Press, 1990).

Martin, R.P., *Carmen Christi: Philippians ii.5-11 in Recent Interpretation and in the Setting of Early Christian Worship* (Cambridge: Cambridge University Press, 1967).

—*Colossians and Philemon* (NCB; London: Oliphants, 1974).

—*Philippians* (NCB; Grand Rapids: Eerdmans, 1980).

Meeks, W.A., 'The Man from Heaven in Paul's Letter to the Philippians', in B.A. Pearson (ed.), *The Future of Early Christianity: Essays in Honor of Helmut Koester* (Minneapolis: Fortress Press, 1991).

Mitchell, M.M., 'The Archetypal Image: John Chrysostom's Portraits of Paul', *Journal of Religion* 75 (1995), pp. 15-43.

—'New Testament Envoys in the Context of Greco–Roman Diplomatic and Epistolary Conventions: The Examples of Timothy and Titus', *JBL* 111 (1992), pp. 641-62.

Moda, A., 'La Lettera a Filippesi e gli ultimi anni di Paolo prigioniero', *BeO* 27 (1985), pp. 17-30.

Moffatt, J., *An Introduction to the Literature of the New Testament* (New York: Charles Scribner's Sons, 1911).

Mommsen, T., Kreuger, P., and Watson, A. (eds.), *The Digest of Justinian*, I–IV (Philadelphia: University of Pennsylvania Press, 1985)

—*Römisches Strafrecht* (Leipzig: Verlag von Duncker & Humbolt, 1899).

Moule, H.C.G., *Philippians* (Cambridge: Cambridge University Press, 1903).

Musurillo, H., trans., *The Acts of the Christian Martyrs* (Oxford: Clarendon Press, 1972).

—*The Acts of the Pagan Martyrs: Acta Alexandrinorum* (Oxford: Clarendon Press, 1954).

Neusner, J., *The Mishnah: A New Translation* (New Haven: Yale University Press, 1988).

Nippel, W., 'Policing Rome', *JRS* 74 (1984), pp. 20-29.

Nock, A.D., *St Paul* (New York: Oxford University Press, 1953).

Nordling, J.G., 'Onesimus Fugitivus: A Defense of the Runaway Slave Hypothesis in Philemon', *JSNT* 41 (1991), pp. 97-119.

O'Brien, P.T., *Colossians, Philemon* (WBC, 44; Waco, TX: Word Books, 1982).

—*The Epistle to the Philippians: A Commentary on the Greek Text* (Grand Rapids, MI: Eerdmans, 1991).

—'The Importance of the Gospel in Philippians', in *idem* (ed.), *God who is Rich in Mercy: Essays Presented to Dr D.B. Knox* (Homebush West, NSW: Lancer Books, 1986), pp. 213-33.

Osiek, C., 'The Ransom of Captives: Evolution of a Tradition', *HTR* 74 (1981), pp. 365-86.

Pack, R.A., *Studies in Libanius and Antiochene Society under Theodosius* (1935).

Parks, E.P., *The Roman Rhetorical Schools as a Preparation of the Courts under the Early Empire* (Baltimore: The Johns Hopkins University Press, 1945).

Patzia, A., 'Philemon, Letter to', in G.F. Hawthorne and R.P. Martin (eds.), *Dictionary of Paul and his Letters* (Downers Grove, IL: Inter-Varsity Press, 1993), pp. 703-707.

Perkins, P., 'Philippians' and 'Philemon', in C.A. Newsom and S.H. Ringe (eds.), *The Women's Bible Commentary* (Louisville, KY: Westminster Press/John Knox), pp. 343-45, 362-63.

Peterman, G.W., '"Thankless Thanks": The Epistolary Social Conventions in Philippians 4.10-20', *TynBul* 42.2 (1991), pp. 261-70.

Petersen, N.R., 'Philemon', in J.L. Mays (ed.), *Harper's Bible Commentary* (New York: Harper & Row, 1988), pp. 1245-48.

—*Rediscovering Paul: Philemon and the Sociology of Paul's Narrative World* (Philadelphia: Fortress Press, 1985).

Peterson, E., 'Zur Bedeutungsgeschichte von Parrhesia', in W. Koepp (ed.), *Reinhold Seeberg Festschrift*. I. *Zur Theorie des Christentums* (Leipzig: D. Werner Scholl, 1929), pp. 283-97.

Phillips, C.R., 'The Sociology of Religious Knowledge in the Roman Empire to AD 284', in W. Haase (ed.), *Aufstieg und Niedergang der römischen Welt. Part II: Principat*, XVI.3 (New York: de Gruyter; 1986), pp. 2677-773.

Pobee, J.S., *Persecution and Martyrdom in the Theology of Paul* (JSNT, 6; Sheffield: JSOT Press, 1985).

Porter, S.E., 'Word Order and Clause Structure in New Testament Greek: An Unexplored Area of Greek Linguistics Using Philippians as a Test Case', *FN* 6 (1993), pp. 177-205.

Preisendanz, K., ed. and trans., *Papyri Graecae Magicae: Die griechischen Zauberpapyri* (Stuttgart: Teubner, 2nd edn, 1973–1974).

Price, S.R.F., 'The Future of Dreams: From Freud to Artemidorus', *Past and Present* 113 (1986), pp. 3-37.

Prior, M., *Paul the Letter-Writer and the Second Letter to Timothy* (JSNTSup, 23; Sheffield: Sheffield Academic Press, 1989).

Puskas, C.B., 'The Conclusion of Luke–Acts: An Investigation of the Literary Function and Theological Significance of Acts 28.16-31' (Unpublished PhD dissertation, St Louis University, 1980).

Quinn, J.D., '"Seven Times He Wore Chains" (I Clem. 5.6)', *JBL* 97 (1978), pp. 574-76.

Rahtjen, B.D., 'The Three Letters of Paul to the Philippian', *NTS* 6 (1959–60), pp. 167-73.

Rapske, B.M., *The Book of Acts and Paul in Roman Custody* (Grand Rapids, MI: Eerdmans, 1994).

—'The Importance of Helpers to the Imprisoned Paul in the Book of Acts', *TynBul* 42 (1991), pp. 3-30.

—'The Prisoner Paul in the Eyes of Onesimus', *NTS* 37 (1991), pp. 187-203.

Rathke, H., *Ignatius von Antiochien und die Paulusbriefe* (Texte und Untersuchungen zur Geschichte der altchristlichen Literatur, 99; Berlin: Akademie–Verlag, 1967).

Rea, J.R. (ed.), *The Oxyrhynchus Papyri*, XLIII (London: Egypt Exploration Society, 1975).

Reardon, B.P., 'Aspects of the Greek Novel', *Greece and Rome* 23 (1976), pp. 118-31.

Rebell, W., 'Das Leidenverständnis bei Paulus und Ignatius von Antiochien', *NTS* 32 (1986), pp. 457-65.

Reeve, C.D.C., *Socrates in the Apology* (Indianapolis: Hackett, 1989).

Reid, D.G., 'Prison, Prisoner', in G.F. Hawthorne and R.P. Martin (eds.), *Dictionary of Paul and his Letters* (Downers Grove, IL: Inter-Varsity Press, 1993), pp. 752-54.

Rein, W., *Das Criminalrecht der Römer von Romulus bis auf Justinianus* (Lepizig: K.F. Köhler Verlag, 1884).

Reitzenstein, R., *Hellenistic Mystery-Religions: Their Basic Ideas and Significance* (trans. J.E. Steely; Pittsburgh: Pickwick Press, 1978).

Rensberger, D.K., 'As the Apostle Teaches: The Development of the Use of Paul's Letters in Second-Century Christianity' (Unpublished PhD dissertation, Yale University Press, 1981).

Reumann, J., 'Contributions of the Philippian Community to Paul and to Earliest Christianity', *NTS* 39 (1993), pp. 438-57.

Richardson, L., Jr., *Pompeii: An Architectural History* (Baltimore: The Johns Hopkins University Press, 1988).

Roberts, A., and Donaldson, J. (eds.), *Ante-Nicene Christian Library: Translations of the Writings of the Fathers Down to AD 325* (Edinburgh: T. & T. Clark, 1867).

Robinson, A.T., and W.H. Davis, *A New Short Grammar of the Greek Testament* (Grand Rapids: Baker, 10th edn, 1979).

Robinson, O.F., *Ancient Rome: City Planning and Administration* (New York: Routledge & Kegan Paul, 1992).

Roetzel, C.J., *The Letters of Paul: Conversations in Context* (Atlanta: John Knox, 3nd edn, 1982).

Rowlingson, D.T., 'Paul's Ephesian Imprisonment: An Evaluation of the Evidence', *ATR* 32 (1950), pp. 1-7.

Ryle, G., 'The Thinking of Thoughts', in *Collected Papers*. II. *Collected Essays 1929–1968* (New York: Barnes & Noble, 1971), pp. 480-96.

Ste. Croix, G.E.M. de, *The Class Struggle in the Ancient Greek World from the Archaic Age to the Arab Conquests* (Ithaca, New York: Cornell University Press, 1981).

Ste. Croix, G.E.M. de, and A.N. Sherwin-White, 'Why Were the Early Christians Persecuted?—An Amendment', *Past and Present* 27 (1964), pp. 23-33.

Sampley, J.P., *Pauline Partnership in Christ: Christian Community and Commitment in Light of Roman Law* (Philadelphia: Fortress Press, 1980).

—*Walking between the Times: Paul's Moral Reasoning* (Minneapolis: Fortress Press, 1991).

Sandnes, K.O., 'Paul and Socrates: The Aim of Paul's Areopagus Speech', *JSNT* 50 (1993), pp. 13-26.

Schenk, W., *Die Philipperbriefe des Paulus* (Stuttgart: Kohlmanner, 1984).

Schenke, H.-M., 'Das Weiterwirken des Paulus und die Pflege seines Erbes durch die Paulus-Schule', *NTS* 21 (1975), pp. 505-518.

Schille, G., *Das älteste Paulus-Bild: Beobachtungen zur lukanischen und zur deutero-paulinischen Paulus-Darstellung* (Berlin: Evangelische Verlagsanstalt, 1979).

Schmid, J., *Zeit und Ort der paulinischen Gefangenschaftsbreife* (Freiburg: Herder, 1931).

Schneemelcher, W., 'The Epistle to the Laodiceans' and 'The Acts of Paul', in E. Hennecke, *New Testament Apocrypha*, II (ed. W. Schneemelcher; trans. R.M. Wilson; Philadelphia: Westminster Press, 1965), pp. 128-32, 322-90.

Schoedel, W.R., *Ignatius of Antioch* (Hermeneia; Philadelphia: Fortress Press, 1985).

—trans., 'The Letter of Polycarp to the Philippians', in J.N. Sparks (ed.), *The Apostolic Fathers* (New York: Nelson, 1978), pp. 126-37.

Schubert, P., *The Form and Function of the Pauline Thanksgiving* (Berlin: Töpelmann, 1939).

Schwartz, D.R., 'The Accusation and the Accusers at Philippi (Acts 16,20-21)', *Bib* 65 (1984), pp. 357-63.

Seaford, R., 'The Imprisonment of Women in Greek Tragedy', *JHS* 110 (1990), pp. 76-90.

Sellew, P., 'Laodiceans and the Philippians Fragments Hypothesis', *HTR* 87 (1994), pp. 17-28.

Shelton, J., *As the Romans Did: A Source Book in Roman Social History* (Oxford: Oxford University Press, 1988).

Shippee, A.B., and P.L. Culbertson (eds.), *The Pastor: Readings from the Patristic Period* (Minneapolis: Fortress Press, 1990).

Silva, M., *Philippians* (WEC; Chicago: Moody Press, 1988).

Skeat, T.C., 'Did Paul Write to "Bishops and Deacons" at Philippi? A Note on Philippians 1.1', *Nov Test* 37 (1995), pp. 12-15.

Staden, H. von (ed. and trans.), *The Art of Medicine in Early Alexandria (Herophilus)* (New York: Cambridge University Press, 1989).

Stambaugh, J.E., *The Ancient Roman City* (Baltimore: The Johns Hopkins University Press, 1988).

Sterling, G., *Historiography and Self-Definition: Josephus, Luke–Acts, and Apologetic Historiography* (SNTSMS, 64; New York: Brill, 1992).

Stöger, A., *The Epistle to Philemon* (ed. J.L. McKenzie; trans. M. Dunne; New York: Herder and Herder, 1971).

Stolle, V. *Der Zeuge als Angeklagter: Untersuchungen zum Paulusbild des Lukas* (Berlin: Verlag W. Kohlhammer, 1973).

Stoops, R.J., 'If I Suffer: Epistolary Authority in Ignatius of Antioch', *HTR* 80 (1987), pp. 161-78.

Stowers, S.K., 'Friends and Enemies in the Politics of Heaven', in J.M. Bassler (ed.), *Pauline Theology. I. Thessalonians, Philippians, Galatians, Philemon* (Minneapolis: Fortress Press, 1991), pp. 105-121.

—*Letter-Writing in Greco–Roman Antiquity* (LEC, 5; Philadelphia: Westminster Press, 1986).

Stuhlmacher, P., *Der Brief an Philemon* (EKKNT; Zürich: Benziger Verlag, 1981).

Talbert, C.H., 'Philippians', in W.E. Mills and R.F. Wilson (eds.), *Mercer Commentary on the Bible* (Macon, GA: Mercer University Press, 1995), pp. 1227-34.

Tanner, R.G., 'Martyrdom in Saint Ignatius and the Stoic View of Suicide', in E. Livingstone (ed.), *Studia Patristica*, XVI.2 (Oxford: Pergamum Press, 1985), pp. 201-205.

—'St Paul's View of Militia and Contemporary Social Values', *StudBib* 3 (1978), pp. 377-82.

Thompson, G.H.P., *The Letters of Paul to the Ephesians, to the Colossians and to Philemon* (Cambridge: Cambridge University Press, 1967).

Unnik, W.C. van, 'The Christian's Freedom of Speech in the New Testament', *BJRL* 44 (1961–62), pp. 466-88.

Vincent, M.R., *A Critical and Exegetical Commentary on the Epistles to the Philippians and to Philemon* (Edinburgh: T. & T. Clark, 1945).

Vos, C.S. de, 'The Significance of the Change from ΟΙΚΟΣ to ΟΙΚΙΑ in Luke's Account of the Philippian Gaoler (Acts 16.30-34)', *NTS* 41 (1995), pp. 292-96.

Walaskay, P.W., *'And So We Came to Rome': The Political Perspective of St Luke* (SNTSMS, 49; New York: Cambridge University Press, 1983).

Watson, D.F., 'A Rhetorical Analysis of Philippians and its Implications for the Unity Question', *NovT* 30 (1988), pp. 57-88.

Watson, G.R., *The Roman Soldier* (Ithaca, NY: Cornell University Press, 1969).

Wenham, J.W., *The Elements of New Testament Greek* (New York: Cambridge University Press, 1965).

White, J., *Light from Ancient Letters* (Philadelphia: Fortress Press, 1986).

White, L.M., 'Morality Between Two Worlds: A Paradigm of Friendship in Philippians', in D.L. Balch *et al.* (eds.), *Greeks, Romans, and Christians: Essays in Honor of Abraham J. Malherbe* (Minneapolis: Fortress Press, 1990), pp. 201-215.

Wiedemann, T., *Greek and Roman Slavery* (London: Routledge & Kegan Paul, 1981).

Wild, R.A., 'The Warrior and the Prisoner: Some Reflections on Ephesians 6.10-20', *CBQ* 46 (1984), pp. 284-98.

Wilhelm-Hooijbergh, A.E., 'In 2 Tim. 1.17 the Greek and Latin Texts May Have a Different Meaning', *StudBib* 3 (1978), pp. 435-38.

Williams, C.B., 'The Caesarean Imprisonment of Paul', *The Biblical World* 34 (1909), pp. 271-80.

Willis, W.L., *Idol Meat in Corinth: The Pauline Argument in 1 Corinthians 8 and 10* (SBLDS, 68; Chico, CA: Scholars Press, 1985).

Wilson, A., 'The Pragmatics of Politeness and Pauline Epistolography: A Case Study of the Letter to Philemon', *JSNT* 48 (1992), pp. 107-119.

Winreich, O., 'Türöffnung im Wunder-, Prodigien- und Zauberglauben der Antike, des Judentums und Christentums', in *idem et al.* (eds.), *Genethliakon W. Schmid zum 70: Geburtstag* (Tübinger Beiträge zur Altertumswissenschaft, 5; Stuttgart: W. Kohlhammer, 1929), pp. 200-264.

Winter, P., *On the Trial of Jesus* (New York: de Gruyter, 1974).

Winter, S., 'Methodological Observations on a New Interpretation of Paul's Letter to Philemon', *USQR* 35 (1984), pp. 3-12.

—'Paul's Letter to Philemon', *NTS* 33 (1987), pp. 1-15.

Witherington, B., III, *Friendship and Finances in Philippi* (The New Testament in Context; Valley Forge, PA: Trinity Press International, 1994).

Zwicky, H., *Zur Verwendung des Militärs in der Verwaltung der römischen Kaiserzeit* (Zurich: Buchdruckerei Winterthur AG, 1944).

INDEXES

INDEX OF REFERENCES

OLD TESTAMENT

NEW TESTAMENT

CHRISTIAN AUTHORS

CLASSICAL

INDEX OF AUTHORS

JOURNAL FOR THE STUDY OF THE NEW TESTAMENT
SUPPLEMENT SERIES